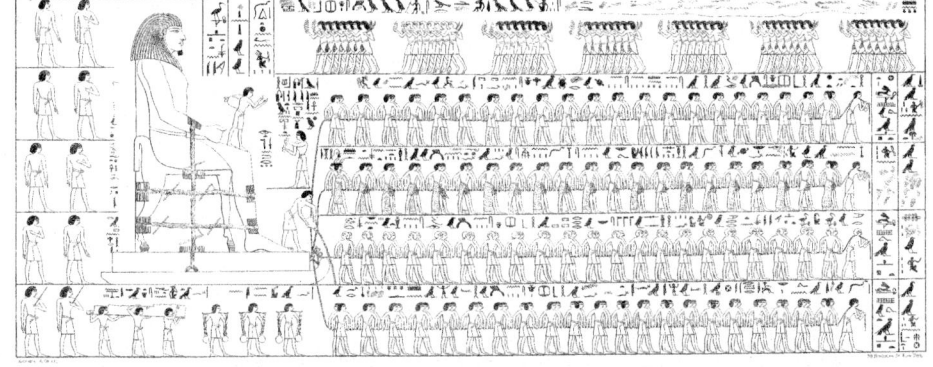

THE [SCHOOL EDITION.]

FOUNDATIONS OF HISTORY,

A SERIES OF

FIRST THINGS.

BY

SAMUEL B. SCHIEFFELIN.

"BUILT UPON THE FOUNDATION OF THE APOSTLES AND PROPHETS, JESUS CHRIST HIM-
SELF BEING THE CHIEF CORNER STONE."   EPH. II. 20.

THIRD EDITION.

NEW YORK:
ANSON D. F. RANDOLPH,
No. 683 BROADWAY.
1864.

Entered according to Act of Congress, in the year 1863, by
SAMUEL B. SCHIEFFELIN,
In the Clerk's Office of the District Court of the United States, for the Southern District of
New York.

EDWARD O. JENKINS,
STEREOTYPER & PRINTER,
No. 20 North William Street.

PREFACE.

THE Board of Publication of the Reformed Dutch Church have recently commenced publishing a series of Christian School Books, designed to restore Christianity to its proper place in Education. The first books of that series, the Primer and Readers, expressly prepared by able men whose hearts were interested in the subject, have already been issued. The plan of the series embraced, among other works, a History of the World, on Christian Principles. Not finding a suitable person willing to prepare such a History as was needed, the writer was led to commit to paper some foundation thoughts, which he wished to be brought out prominently in it. His desire was that the student of history might learn, that the Creator had a purpose in view when he created the world: that the history of the world, in connection with divine revelation, is a development of that purpose: that everything that happens, from the minutest providence to the overthrow of empires, is subservient to that purpose, and is part of it: and that all inventions, and all knowledge imparted to man, are for the same end: and that is, *the revelation of Himself in the Lord Jesus Christ; and the manifestation of His glory through His church.*

These foundation thoughts, connecting the first facts in History with all the subsequent history of the world, and with the world to come, have necessarily been extended.

PREFACE.

The work was commenced as a History of the World, in chronological order, from the creation to the deluge. During its progress the plan was changed, so as to make it a Series of First Things in History to the Christian era.

In what he has written, the thoughts and writings of others have been freely culled from and used. "The Universal History on Scriptural Principles," by Bagster & Sons, has rendered aid. Bagster's Comprehensive Bible, with the authorized various readings, marginal notes, parallel passages, etc., etc., he has found not only useful for this work, but also for many years an invaluable assistant in studying the Holy Scriptures. In the preparation of some of the later chapters he was assisted by Bishop Meade's learned and interesting work, entitled "The Bible and the Classics." Other acknowledgments will be found in the body of the work.

His hope is yet, that some sanctified heart and able head may furnish a history of the world, in small form, for schools and for general reading, which may benefit the reader by giving glory to God the Father, the Son, and the Holy Ghost.

New York, May, 1863. S. B. S.

CONTENTS.

CHAPTER I.
INTRODUCTORY, ... 1

CHAPTER II.
FIRST HISTORIES OF THE WORLD — FIRST HISTORIANS — FIRST POPULAR LECTURERS, ... 5

CHAPTER III.
FIRST WRITING—FIRST WRITING MATERIALS, ... 8

CHAPTER IV.
THE CREATOR OF THE WORLD—APPEARANCES AND MANIFESTATIONS OF THE CREATOR, ... 13

CHAPTER V.
WHY THE WORLD WAS CREATED, ... 17

CHAPTER VI.
CREATION—THE AGE OF THE WORLD, ... 19

CHAPTER VII.
ANGELS, ... 21

CHAPTER VIII.
THE GARDEN OF EDEN, OR THE FIRST ABODE, ... 25

CHAPTER IX.
THE FIRST MAN—THE FIRST WOMAN, ... 27

CHAPTER X.
THE FIRST MARRIAGE, ... 32

CONTENTS.

CHAPTER XI.
THE FIRST LANGUAGE, ... 36

CHAPTER XII.
FIRST WORK—FIRST SABBATH—FIRST FOOD, ... 39

CHAPTER XIII.
THE DEVIL—DEMONS—FAMILIAR SPIRITS, ... 44

CHAPTER XIV.
THE FIRST SIN—THE FALL—THE FIRST EFFECTS OF SIN—THE FIRST GOSPEL CALL, ... 50

CHAPTER XV.
THE FIRST PROMISE OF A SAVIOUR—FIRST EFFECTS OF THE CURSE—FIRST CLOTHING—EXPULSION FROM EDEN, ... 53

CHAPTER XVI.
THE FIRST CHILD—FIRST SACRIFICE—FIRST DEATH, ... 57

CHAPTER XVII.
FIRST PERSECUTION—FIRST MARTYR—FIRST MURDER—BURIALS—FIRST DEATH PENALTY, ... 62

CHAPTER XVIII.
CAIN—FIRST CITY—POWER OF THE SEED OF THE SERPENT—FIRST POLYGAMY, ... 65

CHAPTER XIX.
FIRST INVENTIONS—FIRST MUSICIANS—FIRST ARTIFICERS—EARLY KNOWLEDGE OF THE ARTS, ... 68

CHAPTER XX.
THE CHURCH—ITS PRESERVATION A CONSTANT MIRACLE, ... 76

CHAPTER XXI.
FIRST GATHERING OF THE CHURCH—VISIBLE CHURCH, CHILDREN AND SLAVES, MEMBERS—FIRST PUBLIC WORSHIP—FIRST REVIVAL OF RELIGION—FIRST PRAYER MEETING, ... 81

CONTENTS.

CHAPTER XXII.

FIRST CONSECRATION OF PROPERTY—FIRST PROPHETS—FIRST TRANSLATION OF THE BODY—FIRST PREACHERS, ... 85

CHAPTER XXIII.

FIRST LENGTH OF HUMAN LIFE—INCREASE OF POPULATION AND DECREASE OF THE CHURCH—MIXED MARRIAGES—FIRST GIANTS—GIGANTIC ANIMALS, 89

CHAPTER XXIV.

THE FIRST VESSEL—FIRST DESTRUCTION OF THE WORLD—THE DELUGE—THE CRADLE OF THE WORLD AND OF THE CHURCH, . . . 94

CHAPTER XXV.

CHRONOLOGICAL TABLE, BEFORE THE FLOOD, ... 98

CHAPTER XXVI.

FIRST THING DONE AFTER THE FLOOD—FLESH FIRST GIVEN FOR FOOD—FIRST OCCUPATION—FIRST DRUNKENNESS, ... 100

CHAPTER XXVII.

FIRST GOVERNMENT—FIRST DESPOTISM—FIRST SLAVERY—FIRST SLAVE-HOLDER—DIVINE INJUNCTIONS TO MASTERS, SLAVES AND SUBJECTS—THE FOUNDATIONS OF FREEDOM, ... 103

CHAPTER XXVIII.

DESCENDANTS OF HAM—FIRST KINGDOMS—NIMROD—FIRST CITY AND FIRST BUILDING AFTER THE FLOOD—BABEL OR BABYLON—FIRST ASTRONOMICAL OBSERVATIONS, ... 113

CHAPTER XXIX.

NINEVEH—THE ASSYRIANS—SEMIRAMIS, ... 120

CHAPTER XXX.

EGYPT—ITS EARLY PROSPERITY—ITS ABASEMENT—HIEROGLYPHICS—SESOSTRIS, ... 127

CHAPTER XXXI.

OTHER DESCENDANTS OF HAM—THE CANAANITES—SIDON AND TYRE—THE PHILISTINES—AMALEKITES—AFRICANS, ... 135

CONTENTS.

PAGE

CHAPTER XXXII.
JAPHET AND HIS DESCENDANTS, ... 140

CHAPTER XXXIII.
SHEM AND HIS DESCENDANTS, ... 143

CHAPTER XXXIV.
THE CALL OF ABRAHAM—SEPARATION OF THE CHURCH—FIRST PROCLAMATION OF THE GOSPEL—THE JEWS—ISHMAELITES—ESAU, . . . 145

CHAPTER XXXV.
FAITH—FIRST FALSE RELIGIONS—FIRST IDOLATRY—FIRST WORSHIPPING OF IMAGES—ANCIENT MYTHOLOGY—INFIDELITY, ... 149

CHAPTER XXXVI.
ANCIENT TRADITIONS—CREATION—CHAOS—SABBATH—GARDEN OF EDEN—MAN, ONE FAMILY—EARLY GOLDEN AGE—DETERIORATION OF THE RACE—THE FALL—SATAN—THE SERPENT—THE DELUGE—MOUNTAINS—CHERUBIMS—TOWER OF BABEL—EARLY GIANTS—END OF THE WORLD—AFRICAN TRADITIONS, ... 160

CHAPTER XXXVII.
DOCTRINAL TRUTHS RETAINED AMONG THE HEATHEN—ONE GOD—THE TRINITY—THE WORD OF GOD, THE CREATOR—GOD MANIFEST IN THE FLESH—THE IMMORTALITY OF THE SOUL—GHOSTS—AN ATONING SACRIFICE, . . 170

CHAPTER XXXVIII.
THE ANCIENT ORACLES—THE SIBYLLINE BOOKS, ... 179

CHAPTER XXXIX.
THE ANCIENT MYSTERIES—FREEMASONS, ... 186

CHAPTER XL.
FIRST HEATHEN POETS—HOMER—HESIOD, ... 190

CHAPTER XLI.
FIRST HEATHEN PHILOSOPHERS—THALES—PYTHAGORAS—SOCRATES—PLATO—ARISTOTLE—ZOROASTER—LAOU TZE—CONFUCIUS, ... 195

CONTENTS.

CHAPTER XLII.

FIRST THEATRES—FIRST ACTORS—FIRST TRAGEDIES, ... 206

CHAPTER XLIII.

FIRST MONEY—ANCIENT COINS, ... 211

CHAPTER XLIV.

TYPES AND SYMBOLS IN CREATION, HISTORY AND REDEMPTION, . . . 224

CHAPTER XLV.

ANALOGIES IN CREATION AND THE COURSE OF NATURE TO REVEALED RELIGION, ... 233

CHAPTER XLVI.

NEW MANIFESTATION OF GOD—THE GREATEST EVENT IN HISTORY—THE MOST WONDERFUL BEING, THE LORD JESUS CHRIST, THE SON OF GOD AND THE SON OF MAN—FOUNDATION OF A NEW UNIVERSAL KINGDOM, . . 239

CHAPTER XLVII.

THE NEW KINGDOM—ITS WONDERFUL PROGRESS, ... 247

CHAPTER XLVIII.

THE HOLY GHOST—THE UNPARDONABLE SIN, ... 250

CHAPTER XLIX.

FIRST THINGS IN THE VISIBLE CHURCH UNDER THE NEW DISPENSATION—INTRODUCTION OF MEMBERS—CHILDREN AND HOUSEHOLDS, MEMBERS—THE LORD'S SUPPER—MODE OF BAPTISM—NEW SABBATH—FIRST FOREIGN MISSIONS—NEW WAY TO GOD—NEW PRIESTS—CHURCHES—FIRST SAVED—FIRST ENTRANCE INTO HEAVEN—CONCLUSION, ... 256

INDEX TO PLATES.

	PAGE
EGYPTIANS MOVING A COLOSSUS, ... *Facing Title-page*	
PLAYING ON THE HARP. From a Painting found in a Tomb at Thebes,	73
EGYPTIAN ENTERTAINMENT,	73
EXTINCT ANIMALS,	92
FRONT OF THE GREAT TEMPLE OF ABOO-SIMBEL, NUBIA,	113
ASSYRIANS MOVING A HUMAN-HEADED BULL,	120
ASSYRIAN KING SUPERINTENDING THE REMOVAL OF A COLOSSAL BULL,	124
HEAD OF THE GREAT SPHINX AND PYRAMIDS OF GIZEH, EGYPT,	127
CENTRAL AVENUE OF THE GREAT HALL OF COLUMNS, KARNAK, THEBES,	129
RUINS OF PETRA, IDUMEA OR EDOM,	148
ANCIENT COINS—SARDIS,	211
" ÆGINA,	211
" PERSIAN DARICS,	211
" PHILIP II. OF MACEDONIA,	211
" ALEXANDER THE GREAT,	211
" SYRACUSE,	211
" BYZANTINE—MICHAL DUCAS,	211
" TARENTUM, *Incused*,	211
" TITUS—CONQUEST OF JUDEA,	212
" MILETUS,	216
" JEWISH SHEKEL,	218
" PTOLEMAIC COPPER,	218
" ANTHONY AND CLEOPATRA,	218
" ROMAN ÆS,	219
" ROMAN FAMILY TITURIA—RAPE OF THE SABINES,	220
" ÆMILIA,	220
" TIBERIUS CÆSAR,	220
" NERO,	220
" EARLY GAULISH AND BRITISH,	221
ANCIENT METHOD OF WEIGHING MONEY,	214
TYPES IN CREATION,	224

NOTE.—Several of the above are introduced, without being particularly described, to illustrate some of the colossal works of the ancients.

The colored plates are taken from Roberts' splendid work, "The Holy Land, Idumea, Egypt," etc.

THE

FOUNDATIONS OF HISTORY,

A SERIES OF

FIRST THINGS.

CHAPTER I.

INTRODUCTORY.

IN looking at a history of the world in a small compass, we may well exclaim, A history of the world, in two or three small volumes! The world! composed of vast empires and of many nations; why the history of the decline of a single empire has filled many volumes! The world! having twelve hundred millions of inhabitants, and having had a hundred generations of hundreds of millions of people! Many volumes have been written on the life of one man. Enough books have been written on the world's history to make a large library.[1] A full history of the world in all its bearings we shall have time to read only in eternity. It is all recorded. John says, "I saw the dead, small and great, stand before God: and the books were opened: and the dead were judged out of those things which were written in the books, according to their works."[2]

In such a history, therefore, we can do little more than take a bird's-eye view of the world: soaring over it as if in a balloon, seeing plainly the great nations, and the great men, which rise up, here and there, like the mountain-tops; dipping occasionally down to the valleys; catching a glance at the cities; and now and then at the gatherings of men. We shall see the earth covered by a dark, heavy, moral cloud, like a funeral pall: through that cloud we shall see

---

[1] More than half a century ago, Müller, the Swiss historian, in laying the foundation of his Universal History, made extracts from the writings of one thousand seven hundred and thirty-three authors of ancient and modern times.   [2] Rev. xx. 12.

the beams of the Sun of Righteousness breaking, growing brighter and brighter, and carrying life to all nations. We shall hear an almost universal wail of woe, which has been going up continually for six thousand years from the earth's inhabitants. But gradually rising above this, we shall hear shouts of praise, growing louder and louder, as the "good tidings of great joy, to all people, that a Saviour is born, which is Christ the Lord," are spread through the earth.

As we soar through six thousand years, we shall see the lights and shadows of a beautiful picture both in nature and morals. While studying it, shall we forget the Great Painter and Architect? Him "who hath measured the waters in the hollow of his hand, and meted out heaven with the span, and comprehended the dust of the earth in a measure, and weighed the mountains in scales, and the hills in a balance. That stretcheth out the heavens as a curtain, and spreadeth them out as a tent to dwell in: that bringeth the princes to nothing. Lift up your eyes on high, and behold who hath created these things."[1]

In looking into the history of man and of nations, we behold a vast and complicated machinery in continued motion; and the more we look into it, the more wonderful do we find it in all its parts. Its movements are beyond our comprehension. Who made it? Why was it made? Is it left to regulate itself? Suppose we were looking at an immense piece of mechanism, made with admirable finish; its parts fitting together, and moving with a velocity and a power which, if uncontrolled, would carry destruction to itself and to every thing near it. Could we believe it made itself? Could we believe that it moved without having power communicated to it? Could we believe that the Maker *had no purpose in view* when he made it? Let us endeavor, then, in studying the history of the world, to learn why it was made; for we have a personal interest in knowing why.

[1] Isaiah xl. 12, 22, 26.

Our bird's-eye view, taking in the whole at a glance, will enable us to see everywhere the controlling hand of God; and his providence, like a golden thread, running through all time, and interwoven in all the affairs of man. Let us follow that thread, or else we shall be lost in a labyrinth.

And here, to help us on our journey, let us take a hint from an old negro, known as "The African preacher,"[1] formerly a slave in Virginia. The old African, while exceedingly humble and respectful, was jealous of his heavenly Master's glory, and answered scoffers accordingly. An individual of large fortune, who was accustomed to treat the subject of religion rather sportively, and who at the same time prided himself on his morality, said to him, "I think, old man, I am as good as need be. I can't help thinking so, because God blesses me as much as he does you Christians, and I don't know what more I want than he gives me; and yet I never disturb myself about preaching or praying." To this the old preacher replied with great seriousness: "Just so with the hogs. I have often seen them rooting among the leaves in the woods, and finding just as many acorns as they needed, and yet I never saw one of them look up to the tree from which the acorns fell." As we journey through the world's history, let us not think too much of the acorns; nor have our attention taken up too much with the noisy, quarrelsome hogs, or those that have gathered the most acorns; such as Alexander the Great, Crœsus, or Cæsar.

They are not the really great, whose influence and empires perish with their own short lives. The real conquerors of the world are those heroes of the Lord's hosts, who, although they have been dead thousands of years, are still assisting, by their example and writings, to extend the empire of the King of kings, with a power and influence which will be extending and increasing till the end of time.

[1] The African Preacher. *Presbyterian Board of Publication.*

Let us seek, therefore, first to become acquainted with the Creator of the world, and he will give us the key to open its history; and also enable us to look at it with the eye of Him who controls it. Let us learn from Him why He made the world, and what is to be the end of it; we shall then the more readily understand its history, and shall be better prepared to fill the place which we must each occupy in that history.

CHAPTER II.

FIRST HISTORIES OF THE WORLD—FIRST HISTORIANS—FIRST POPULAR LECTURERS.

BEFORE entering on our journey, let us examine the guide-books we have to direct us in our course. As regards creation, and the history of the world for the first thirty-five hundred years of its existence, the only reliable account that we have is that given by God himself, and contained in the Holy Scriptures. That history, written for the benefit of the people of God, is almost exclusively a history of the Church. As the Church, however, is in the world, and has always been in conflict with it, we find in that history accounts of persons and nations outside of the Church.

It is true those accounts are few and far between; but we have the satisfaction of knowing that they are true: while most of the later histories written by man are doubtful, and many are false. And we may be sure, that as much of the early history of the world has been revealed to us as is for our good. The old world became so exceedingly sinful, that we may almost say the less we know about it the better.

So far as we can learn, the world was twenty-five centuries without any written history. Moses, the first historian, wrote about B. C. 1500. From that time to about B. C. 445, the divinely inspired writers of the Bible are the only historians. There was not much need of written histories when men lived nearly a thousand years. It only required three or four persons to carry history, by word of mouth, from

Adam to Moses. That method of instruction, from father to son, is often referred to in the Bible.

> "Remember the days of old,
> Consider the years of many generations:
> Ask thy father, and he will shew thee;
> Thy elders, and they will teach thee."
>
> DEUT. xxxii. 7.
>
> "Tell ye your children of it,
> And let your children tell their children,
> And their children another generation."
>
> JOEL i. 3.

The Old Testament history ends with the books of Ezra and Nehemiah. The last of the Old Testament Books was written B. C. 445. The same year, the first authentic history written by any of the world's historians, viz., by Herodotus, is said to have been made public.

Herodotus of Halicarnassus is not only the first, but is the prince of heathen historians. His history is divided into nine books, called by the names of the muses. It was compiled while traveling through the then civilized world; and though it contains many marvelous and incredible stories, gathered from among the nations he visited, it still holds a high place among scholars, not only for the information it imparts, but for the beauty of its style, fascinating variety, and its noble simplicity.

The first heathen poets, and historians, were the first popular lecturers in the world. Herodotus read his history, referring principally to the wars carried on between Europe and Asia, before an assembly of the people gathered at Athens at the festival of their tutelar goddess. While reciting his history, Herodotus observed a young man who betrayed marks of strong emotion: struck with his intelligent aspect, he advised the father of the young man to give him the education of a philosopher. The name of this youth was *Thucydides*. He became the second of the heathen historians. His history, though comprising a short period only, displays such profound thought, such knowledge of men and of States, such majestic eloquence, and so noble a style, that as an historian and orator, Thucydides has retained a place among the most illustrious.

Herodotus represented the gods as so jealous of man's happiness, that if they favored any mortal, they did so only to render his fall more calamitous. Thucydides, like many of the present day who would feel affronted to be called heathen, would not allow that the gods interfered in human affairs, either for good or evil; making man's prosperity or adversity depend entirely upon himself.

It is well here to notice the difference between the inspired historians and those merely human, as regards the end they each had in view. The word of God says:

"All Scripture is given by inspiration of God, and is profitable for doctrine, for reproof, for correction, for instruction in righteousness; that the man of God may be perfect, thoroughly furnished unto all good works."[1]

Herodotus, the first of the world's historians, says:

"To rescue from oblivion the memory of former incidents, and *to render a just tribute of renown* to the many great and wonderful actions of Greeks and barbarians, Herodotus of Halicarnassus writes this historical essay."

Thus taught, that human history glorifies man, whilst the divine corrects and instructs man, and glorifies God; let us endeavor to bear the objects of the writers in mind, as we cull from their histories: so that what we gather may profit us and give glory to Him to whom it is due.

[1] 2 Tim. iii. 16, 17.

CHAPTER III.

FIRST WRITING—FIRST WRITING-MATERIALS.

IT will be interesting now to examine into the origin and the progress of the art of writing ; which, next to speaking, influences the world. The writings of Moses are by far the most ancient of which we have any knowledge. In the book of Job, supposed to have been written by Moses, we read of Job's exclaiming : " Oh that my words were now written! Oh that they were imprinted in a book! That they were graven with an iron pen and lead in the rock for ever!"[1] Job evidently had some idea of writing, although the word "written" might be rendered drawn, and the word "book" may signify any memorial in writing. Excepting this, no reference is made to writing prior to the time of Moses. We notice that the transfers of property before his day, instead of being made by written deeds placed on town records, were made by verbal acknowledgment before witnesses; as in the case of the purchase of the field and cave of Machpelah by Abraham ;[2] and we also find, that when Abraham sent to his relatives for a wife for his son, he did not write. Some think that the first writing was the Ten Commandments, written on stone by the finger of God. We know, however, that the earliest writing in the world was given by inspiration of Him who "giveth knowledge to man ;" and also, that it was in the Hebrew letter and language.

From the Hebrew alphabet came the Phœnician; from that the Greek ; the Greek letters being evidently the Phœnician

---

[1] Job xix. 23, 24.   [2] Gen. xxiii. 17.

turned from right to left; thence came the Roman; and from them, the letters now in use among civilized nations.

ROMAN.	GREEK.	HEBREW.
A	A alpha	א aleph
B	B beta	ב beth
C	Γ gamma	ג gimmel
D etc.	Δ delta, etc.	ד daleth, etc.

When the Jews under Joshua, with the writings of Moses in their hands, were driving out the Phœnician tribes, some of these sought refuge in distant colonies. It was at this time that Cadmus, a Phœnician, miscalled the "father of letters," introduced the use of them, under new forms, into Greece. Giving the Grecians an alphabet, he not only laid the foundation of that literature which is the admiration of scholars to this day, but he also furnished a written language which will be always memorable; as that in which the New Testament was originally written.

The peaceful reign of Solomon, and his reputed wisdom, drew persons from all parts of the world to learn of him. The knowledge of letters, and some ideas of the true God, were thus extended to other countries.[1]

The use of signs would naturally be adopted by barbarous nations, from seeing letters which they could not understand used by the more civilized; and also from traditional ideas of writing, which their fathers might have lost in wandering from the light of truth into the darkness and degradation of heathenism.

The ancient Hebrew characters differed somewhat from those now used in writing that language. Time also introduced changes in the ancient Greek letters. These changes would naturally occur before printing was known, as men never speak or write exactly alike. The first writings were from right to left. The Hebrew is yet written in that way.

[1] 1 Kings iv. 34.

The Greeks, deriving letters from the Phœnicians, also originally wrote like them from right to left. The change appears to have been brought about by making alternate lines follow each other: the first line from right to left, and the second from left to right, and so on. This they called writing as oxen plow. The laws of Solon were written in this way.

The old Hebrew characters were written in this manner:[1]

The old Phœnician, according to *Scaliger*, were written thus:

And the Greek, according to the most ancient specimen, were written thus:

These were probably the first letters of the Greek alphabet, which were originally sixteen only. The following, which are found in the ancient Sigean inscription, were afterward added:

Job speaks of writing on stone. That material God used when writing the Ten Commandments. Brass, lead, and

---

[1] Shuckford's Connection of Sacred and Profane History.

other metals in time came into use; then ivory and wood; and afterward, the wooden tablet was spread over with wax, which by being exposed to heat could be used again and again. The prepared skins of animals were used at an early period; and the word *skins* was used by the Ionians to denote books, long after they obtained a better material. Instead of making bound volumes, they first wrote their successive pages, if we may so call them, on one long scroll; which was unrolled as read.

The better material discovered was papyrus, a part of an Egyptian water plant, which the Greeks called *byblus*. We take our word bible from the Greek *biblos*, which they used to signify book, after adopting the byblus plant for bookmaking.

The Papyrus plant threw up stalks from eight to sixteen feet high, and from two to four inches thick, with foliage at the top. The pith of the stalk was cut in very thin slices, which were laid side by side, slightly overlapping each other; these were moistened with gum-water, and another layer of strips was laid across them. Both layers were then pressed, dried, and polished. From the *papyrus* comes our word paper.

In the third century before Christ, it happened that differences having arisen between the king of Pergamos and the king of Egypt, the latter cut off the supply of papyrus from Pergamos. This brought out the invention of what was called *pergamena*, and is now known as parchment. Paul desires Timothy to bring him the books which he left at Troas, " but *especially the parchments.*"[1] Parchment was an invention made known to men when the word of God was about to be scattered throughout the world by the translation called the Septuagint, and under the Gospel dispensation; and when a more durable material was needed to preserve that word during the dark ages.

[1] 2 Tim. iv. 13.

We are reminded from the familiar expression of the *leaves* of books, that our ancestors wrote on leaves. Before the introduction of papyrus, the ancient Romans used the inner bark of trees; so that *liber*, bark, became the Latin word for book; and thence comes our word *library*, meaning a collection of books. Our Saxon forefathers wrote on the bark of the *bocco*, their name for beech-tree; and from that we have our word *book*.

Pencils or brushes were made from the branches forming the crown of the Papyrus plant, by sharpening them. The Romans called the sharp-pointed instrument with which they wrote on tablets, etc., a *stylus*. Julius Cæsar was using one of them when he was attacked by his assassins, and trying to defend himself with it, wounded one of his assailants badly. The word translated pen, Psalm xlv. 1, probably meant a reed, which is the rendering in the Greek and Latin versions. Our word pen is derived from the Latin *penna*, a feather. The root of the Hebrew word translated *ink*, Jer. xxxvi. 18, makes it appear that it was a black fluid that was then used. In the days of the Apostles ink was common.

Remembering that writing originally came to us by inspiration, and probably by direct revelation from God, how careful we should be to use it for His glory. If words spoken never die, but are brought up again at the judgment of the last day, how much more shall words written!

CHAPTER IV.

THE CREATOR OF THE WORLD—APPEARANCES AND MANIFESTATIONS OF THE CREATOR.

WHEN we are asked, Who made you? how readily we answer, God. What else did God make? All things. We answer thus, because we have been taught. How can a thing tell who made it, and what it was made for, unless the Creator should tell it? If God had not revealed it to us in his word, we should have been as wise as the heathen philosophers, who taught that matter was eternal; or as the Hindoos, who represent that the earth is sustained upon the heads of elephants, who, when they shake themselves, cause earthquakes. In this respect the veriest child, knowing the first chapter of the Bible, is wiser than all the heathen. He learns more in ten minutes than they, with all their philosophers, have learned in five thousand years.

How short the account is in that chapter; and yet, how grand! Were there ever sublimer words than, "God said, Let there be light: and there was light?"[1] They are only equaled by the words of Him, "who being in the form of God, thought it not robbery to be equal with God."[2] Hear him say to the leper, "I will; be thou clean;"[3] and to a buried corpse: "Lazarus, come forth."[4] Hear him rebuke a great storm of wind, and say unto the sea, "Peace, be still. And the wind ceased, and there was a great calm."[5] And hear those most wonderful words! "Thy sins are forgiven."[6]

[1] Genesis i. 3.
[2] Philip. ii. 6.
[3] Matt. viii. 3.
[4] John xi. 43.
[5] Mark iv. 39.
[6] Luke vii. 48; Matt. ix. 2.

Who but God can speak such words? Thanks be unto God! for the revelations He has made unto us. He "spake in time past unto the fathers by the prophets; and in these last days hath spoken unto us by his Son."[1]

The first sentence which God has given to us in his history of creation, contains a peculiar revelation of God himself, which has a bearing upon all the succeeding history of the world: that is, the revelation of the plurality of the persons in the Godhead. This great truth was only gradually revealed to man. It was thus, as we shall hereafter see, with the promises of a coming Messiah, and of the plan of redemption. Revelation was gradual and progressive, as is the light of the natural day: there was twilight, and a dawn, before the full light came. We read, "In the beginning God created the heaven and the earth."[2] In the original it reads "Gods," in the plural number; while the verb "created" is in the singular; thus indicating a plurality of persons in one.

The plural noun is thus used to indicate the true God, and is connected with a verb in the singular number, several hundred times in the Scriptures. Trinity in unity, or three persons in one God, was fully revealed when "God was manifest in the flesh;"[3] and when He sent his disciples "to teach all nations, baptizing them in the *name* of the Father, and of the Son, and of the Holy Ghost:"[4] observe, not names, but the single name; for "these three are one."[5]

In other parts of the Bible the different persons of the Godhead are said to have taken part in the creation of the world, and to be now directing its affairs. It is well to note this as we go on, that we may better understand why the world was created; and also better understand its history.

The Bible in speaking of creation says, "The SPIRIT of God moved upon the face of the waters."[6] "By his SPIRIT

---

[1] Heb. i. 1.
[2] Gen. i. 1.
[3] 1 Tim. iii. 16.
[4] Matt. xxviii. 19.
[5] 1 John v. 7.
[6] Genesis i. 2.

THE CREATOR OF THE WORLD. 15

he hath garnished the heavens."[1] And again, "The SPIRIT of God hath made me."[2] It also speaks in many places of the Lord Jesus Christ as the Creator ; so that "all should honor the Son, even as they honor the Father."[3] It says, "The word was God. All things *were made by him ;* and without him was not any thing made that was made. The word was made flesh and dwelt among us. He was in the world, and the world *was made by him*, and the world knew him not."[4] "Jesus Christ, *by whom are all things*, and we by him ;"[5] "*for by him were all things created*, that are in heaven, and that are in earth, visible and invisible, whether they be thrones, or dominions, or principalities or powers : all things were *created by him*, and for him ; and he is before all things, *and by him all things consist.*"[6]

The Creator revealed himself to man immediately after his creation ; making known to him His will and showing him the way of peace and happiness.[7] And ever since, as a father with his children, the Lord has held communion with His chosen people ; and while protecting, teaching, and leading them to glory, He has not only constantly manifested His presence, but He has repeatedly appeared to them : sometimes in visions ;[8] sometimes in dreams ;[9] sometimes making His presence known by fire ;[10] by an audible voice ;[11] or by a sign, as in the burning bush to Moses,[12] the thunders and lightnings on Mount Sinai,[13] and the cloud in the Tabernacle and in the Temple.[14] Sometimes He appeared as a man, as He did to Abraham ; talking freely with him, promi-

---

[1] Job xxvi. 13.
[2] Job xxxiii. 4.
[3] John v. 23.
[4] John i. 1, 3, 10, 14.
[5] 1 Cor. viii. 6.
[6] Col. i. 16–18.
[7] Gen ii. 16 ; iii. 8.
[8] Gen. xlvi. 2 ; Ezek. i. 1.
[9] Gen. xx. 3 ; xxxi. 24 ; 1 King iii. 5.
[10] Leviticus ix. 24 ; x. 2 ; 1 Kings xviii. 38.
[11] Exod. xix. 19 ; 1 Kings xix. 12 ; 1 Sam. iii. 4.
[12] Exod. iii. 4.
[13] Exod. xix. 18.
[14] Exod. xl. 38 ; Levit. xvi. 2 ; 1 Kings viii. 10, 11.

ising blessings and making known His purposes.[1] He lived and died as a man on earth in the person of the Lord Jesus Christ; who was "God manifest in the flesh, seen of angels;"[2] "who made the worlds; and who being the brightness of God's glory, and the express image of his person, and upholding all things by the word of his power, when he had by himself purged our sins, sat down on the right hand of the Majesty on high."[3] There, if we are his people, we shall see him as He is, and be like him.[4]

All these manifestations of God were through the Lord Jesus Christ; the Mediator between God and man. It was He who was with the children of Israel in the wilderness.[5] "No man hath seen God at any time; the only begotten Son, which is in the bosom of the Father, he hath declared him."[6] Jesus said, "He that hath seen me hath seen the Father."[7]

After the ascension of the Lord Jesus Christ to take possession of his throne, as Prince and Saviour, God has manifested himself in the third Person of the adorable Trinity; the Holy Ghost. According to promise,[8] He descended on the day of Pentecost.[9] Since that time the Church has enjoyed the "communion of the Holy Ghost."[10] Every member brought into it is a token of His presence; for he is "born of the Spirit."[11] And, as we shall notice hereafter, He is now personally present building up that Church which is forming the history of the world.

[1] Gen. xvii. 1, 22; xviii. 1; xxvi. 2.
[2] 1 Tim. iii. 16.
[3] Heb. i. 2, 3.
[4] 1 John iii. 2.
[5] 1 Cor. x. 4, 9.
[6] John i. 18.
[7] John xiv. 9.
[8] John xiv. 16, 26.
[9] Acts ii. 4.
[10] John xiv. 17; Rom. viii. 9; 2 Cor. xiii. 14.
[11] John i. 13; iii. 8.

CHAPTER V.

WHY THE WORLD WAS CREATED.

WE should never have known in this life why the world was made, if God had not revealed it to us. Men in all places, where that revelation has not been sent, are like the hogs rooting among the acorns. If the hogs could speak, and we were to ask them why acorns were made? they would reply, For hogs to eat. And then if we were to ask them why hogs were made? they would answer, To eat the acorns. So everywhere man says, The world was made for me, and I was made to use the world, and thus enjoy myself. But God the Creator says otherwise. Whilst man says, "Soul, thou hast much goods laid up for many years; take thine ease, eat, drink, and be merry," God says, "Thou fool, this night thy soul shall be required of thee; then whose shall those things be which thou hast provided?"[1]

We turn therefore from man and ask God why the world was created, and why with all its wickedness it is continued? We hear from heaven the voice of those who cast their crowns before the throne, saying, "Thou art worthy, O Lord, to receive glory and honor and power: for thou hast created all things, and *for thy pleasure they are and were created.*"[2] We hear the injunction to the dwellers on earth, "Whether therefore ye eat, or drink, or whatsoever ye do, *do all to the glory of God.*"[3] God tells us that He *reveals himself* in creation and in history: "For the invisible things of him from the creation of the world are clearly seen, being understood by the things that are made, even his eternal power and

[1] Luke xii. 19.   [2] Rev. iv. 11.   [3] 1 Cor. x. 31.

Godhead."[1] It was also to show his wisdom and power to other worlds; for through the gospel we understand " the mystery, which from the beginning of the world hath been hid in God, who created all things by Jesus Christ : *to the intent that now unto the principalities and powers in heavenly places might be known by the church the manifold wisdom of God.*"[2]

The history of the world therefore is only the fulfillment of God's purposes : even wicked men being sometimes used as instruments. This is clearly shown in such cases as His permitting the selling of Joseph into slavery by his brethren, and His sending the Assyrian king to chastise the Jews.[3] The crucifixion of our Lord was also a wonderful instance of this : " Him being delivered by the determinate counsel and foreknowledge of God, ye have taken, and by wicked hands have crucified and slain."[4]

We need, therefore, as provision for our journey through the world's history, the revelation God has made to us of Himself, and of his purposes ; we must carry with us his promises, his threatenings, and his prophecies ; they are all revealed to us in his word ; and as his manifold wisdom is to be made known *by the church,* we must watch the progress of the church. We must be careful not to separate that which God has joined together : the history of the world and the coming of the kingdom of the Lord Jesus Christ through his church.[5]

---

[1] Rom. i. 20.   [2] Eph. iii. 9.   [3] Isaiah x. 7.   [4] Acts ii. 23.
[5] For a separate " History of the Work of Redemption" the reader is referred to Edwards' justly celebrated work with that title.

CHAPTER VI.

CREATION—THE AGE OF THE WORLD.

THE Bible history commences by revealing certain great facts, and great truths, which, like immense foundation stones, underlie and are connected with all the future history of the world. The first chapters are thickly studded with wonderful facts, which unaided human reason could never have found out; and which can only be received by faith: when thus received, they are simple and clear. "Through faith we understand that the worlds were framed by the word of God, so that things which are seen were not made of things which do appear."[1]

The doctrine that all things were created by one Eternal God is peculiar to the Bible; it is found nowhere else. It places God, as the One All-sufficient Creator, on a height infinitely above every other being; it shows us our entire dependence on him, our obligation to live to His glory, and the importance of seeking His favor. Let us prayerfully study out some of those great foundation facts and truths which are found in the first chapters of the Bible. They show us the cause of all the crimes, the wars, and all the misery that have been in the world since it was made; and also the source of all the happiness, little as it has been, which the world has thus far enjoyed. They show us the Genesis, or the *beginning*, of the race of man, of laws, of government, and of religion.

While the great fact of how the world was made is so clearly stated, there is a difference of opinion among the learned as to the exact time when it was made. This can only be learned by adding together the years of the

---
[1] Heb. xi. 3.

lives of the patriarchs as recorded in the Bible. The Hebrew, in which the Bible was first written, differs in the number of years from the Greek or Septuagint version, when speaking of the birth or death of some of those patriarchs from the creation to the time of Jacob. The Septuagint version, made about 280 years before Christ, was in general use in the time of our Saviour; and its language was sometimes, not always, quoted by him and by the apostles, as our English version is used at the present day. The Septuagint version has always been highly esteemed; and some, following the dates given in it, make the world nearly 5,500 years old before the coming of the Lord Jesus Christ. The time generally received is, according to the computation made in the seventeenth century by the learned Archbishop Usher, from the Hebrew, that the world was created 4,004 years before the Christian era.

In the account of creation we are told very plainly that "in six days God created the heavens and the earth:" not indefinite eras, or periods of time, but evenings and mornings, days. For wise reasons the Creator took that time; instead of speaking all things into being in one instant, which He could as easily have done. We are constantly reminded of this great fact in the fourth commandment, and by each returning Sabbath. Let us remember this that we may "avoid the oppositions of science, falsely so called."[1] We must also remember that every thing when created was immediately complete in itself; trees, animals, and man, each when made were full grown, full size, and perfect. Each also having the wonderful faculty of perpetuating its species.

While describing the progress of creation the record states again and again, "God saw that it was good." "God saw every thing that he had made, and behold it was very good."[2] No wonder that at the completion of such a work, "the sons of God shouted for joy!"[3]

[1] 1 Tim. vi. 20.   [2] Gen. i. 10, 12, 18, 21, 25, 31.   [3] Job xxxviii. 7.

CHAPTER VII.

ANGELS.

BESIDE the things which are seen, the Bible reveals to us that God created a host of unseen beings; Spirits, active, intelligent and holy: and also, that he has been constantly using these Spirits or, as they are called, *Angels*, in administering the government of the world. These wonderful beings have often appeared, taking an active part in the world's history: and we are told they will continue to do so, till that history is closed. An immense host of them were created: "An innumerable company."[1] When the angel announced to the shepherds that the Saviour was born, a multitude of them was with him praising God, and saying, " Glory to God in the highest, and on earth peace, good will to men."[2] John says, "I beheld and I heard the voice of many angels round about the throne: and the number of them was ten thousand times ten thousand, and thousands of thousands."[3]

Some of them were allowed to sin, and thus to fall " from their first estate;"[4] and as they, also, take a prominent part in history, we shall speak of them hereafter. Those, kept holy by the power of God, are called " elect angels."[5]

There are different grades or ranks of them; and they are called by different names, as Gabriel, Michael, etc., and by various titles, such as, Angel, Archangel, Cherubim, Seraphim, thrones, dominions, principalities, powers, etc.[6]

" Michael, the great prince, which standeth for the people

---

[1] Heb. xii. 22.   [3] Rev. v. 11.   [5] 1 Tim. v. 21.
[2] Luke, ii. 13.   [4] Jude vi.   [6] Col. i. 16.

of God,"[1] is thought to be not a created angel, but our Lord and Saviour Jesus Christ ; who is the angel of the covenant. The " Angel of the Lord " or the angel Jehovah, is also considered to be the same glorious Being ; who took upon him the form of a servant ; who came not to be ministered unto, but to minister.

The Angels are *messengers* of God :

> "Before His feet, their armies wait,
> And swift as flames of fire they move,
> To manage His affairs of state,
> In works of vengeance or of love."

They are also "ministering spirits ; sent forth to minister for them who shall be heirs of salvation."[2] As such they frequently appear in history. Abraham, when sending his servant to get a wife for Isaac, tells him, "The Lord God shall send his angel before thee."[3] Two angels were sent to deliver Lot out of Sodom.[4] Daniel said, "My God hath sent his angel, and hath shut the lions' mouth, that they have not hurt me."[5] Angels ministered to Jesus after his fasting and temptation :[6] and an angel strengthened him while in his agony in the garden.[7] An angel told Cornelius that his prayers were heard, and his alms had in remembrance in the sight of God : and directed him to send for Simon Peter, that he might learn the way of salvation through faith in the Lord Jesus Christ.[8] The angel of the Lord by night opened the prison doors, and brought the apostles forth, when shut up by the High Priest and those with him :[9] and afterwards delivered Peter from prison ; his chains dropping off and the iron gate opening of its own accord.[10] Angels ministered comfort to the women at the sepulchre of Jesus ; and to the apostles when Jesus ascended into heaven.[11]

[1] Dan. xii. 1.
[2] Heb. i. 14.
[3] Gen. xxiv. 7.
[4] Gen. xix. 15.
[5] Dan. vi. 22.
[6] Matt. iv. 11.
[7] Luke xxii. 43.
[8] Acts x. 3.
[9] Acts v. 19.
[10] Acts xii. 7.
[11] Acts i. 10.

They are said to "excel in strength," and to be greater "in power and might"[1] than men. They can move with wonderful rapidity. At the beginning of one of Daniel's prayers, "the commandment came forth; and Gabriel, being caused to fly swiftly, touched Daniel while he was yet praying."[2]

If we are the children of God they are continually about us; for to him, who makes the Lord his refuge, the promise is, "He shall give his angels charge over thee, to keep thee in all thy ways."[3] The Lord Jesus tells us: "The angels of the little ones which believe in him, do always behold the face of his Father which is in heaven:"[4] and, that when Lazarus died, he was carried by the angels into Abraham's bosom.[5] The Lord Jesus also said, that when He shall come at the end of the world "with great power and glory, then shall He send His angels and shall gather together His elect."[6]

The angels are said to be deeply interested in what is going on in the world: "desiring to look into"[7] the revelation which God has made of Himself in Christ, and in the plan of redemption. "There is joy in the presence of the angels of God over one sinner that repenteth."[8] Paul says, "We are made a spectacle to angels and to men."[9] When "God was manifest in the flesh, and justified in the spirit, He was seen of angels."[10] "When he bringeth in the first begotten into the world, he saith, And let all the angels of God worship him."[11] Angels are spoken of as contending with the fallen spirits; "Michael, the archangel, when contending with the devil disputed about the body of Moses."[12] In the Revelation we read, "Michael and his angels fought against the Devil and his angels."[13]

[1] 2 Pet. ii. 11.
[2] Dan. ix. 21, 23.
[3] Ps. xci. 11.
[4] Matt. xviii. 6, 10.
[5] Luke xvi. 22.
[6] Matt. xxiv. 31: Mark xiii. 27.
[7] 1 Pet. i. 12.
[8] Luke xv. 10.
[9] 1 Cor. iv. 9.
[10] 1 Tim. iii. 16.
[11] Heb. i. 6.
[12] Jude 9.
[13] Rev. xii. 7, 8.

Angels have often made themselves visible. Sometimes appearing like men ; at other times, as glorious beings having great power. They have generally appeared as messengers of love and mercy ministering to the people of God ; then again, they act as ministers of God's vengeance ; as when they destroyed Sodom and Gomorrah with fire from heaven ;[1] and as when, " the angel of the Lord went out, and smote in the camp of the Assyrians an hundred, fourscore and five thousand : and behold, they were all dead corpses."[2] And also, as when " God sent an angel unto Jerusalem to destroy it." " And David saw the angel of the Lord stand between the earth and the heaven, having a drawn sword in his hand stretched out over Jerusalem."[3]

If we are heirs of salvation, the ministering of angels will form part of our own history.

[1] Gen. xix. 13.   [2] 2 Kings xix. 35.   [3] 1 Chron. xxi. 15.

CHAPTER VIII.

THE GARDEN OF EDEN, OR THE FIRST ABODE.

WHO has not had his imagination excited while thinking of the Garden of Eden? At once we associate with it every thing that can please the eye, the ear, and the taste. We look back to it with regret, almost feeling that we once enjoyed its delights. The name *Eden* in Hebrew means "a delight"—"The LORD God planted a garden and out of the ground made the LORD God to grow every tree that is pleasant to the sight, and good for food." A Paradise of delights was prepared for man when he was created holy. The word Paradise is from the Greek, and means "garden."

The location of the Garden of Eden is minutely described in the Bible. Some of the rivers mentioned as flowing from it, the Hiddekel or Tigris, and the Euphrates, still bear the same name. It is generally supposed to have been located near the source of those rivers in the highlands of Armenia, in Asia Minor. The curse on the ground for the sin of man, causing it to produce thorns and thistles, united perhaps with the effects of the flood, has obliterated all traces of the exact spot. Some of the districts in that region, however, are still celebrated for their fertility and their beauty. There was a district known as Eden in the time of Hezekiah.[1]

Many make the same mistake with respect to the Garden of Eden, that they do in their views of heaven. The natural heart, thinking only of gratifying the senses, pictures to itself a place, where it may repose on beds of flowers, enjoying their perfume without fear of thorns or noxious insects;

---

[1] 2 Kings, xix. 12.

listening to the music of birds; seeing the wolf dwelling with the lamb and the leopard lying down with the kid; with nothing to molest or make afraid; and with nothing to do but to reach forth the hand and pluck the most delicious fruits. They overlook the fact that in Eden there was a law to be obeyed, there was labor to be performed, and a constant loving communion had with God. Add these, and to the natural heart Eden is no longer Paradise, and Heaven ceases to be desirable.

In the midst of the garden grew the tree of life, and the tree of knowledge of good and evil.[1] The fruit of the latter was forbidden to man. What kind of fruit it bore we know not, excepting "that the tree was good for food, and that it was pleasant to the eyes."[2] The command made it a test of obedience with a fearful penalty attached. Its name was probably given to the tree on account of the consequences connected with the eating of the fruit. The sin causing an immediate and a fearful knowledge of evil. When the LORD drove out the man, "he placed at the east of the Garden of Eden Cherubims, and a flaming sword which turned every way, to keep the way of the tree of life."[3]

In Eden there was free intercourse between man and his Creator, speaking as it were face to face. "They heard the voice of the LORD God walking in the garden in the cool of the day."[4]

Another Paradise, where there is fullness of joy and pleasures forevermore, is prepared for those who are made holy by faith in the Lord Jesus Christ. He said to the dying thief, "This day shalt thou be with me in Paradise." Between these two gardens and closely connected with each, another, deeply interesting to us, appears in history: it is known as the garden of Gethsemane.

"Agonizing in the garden,
Lo! your Maker prostrate lies!"

[1] Gen. ii. 9.   [2] Gen. iii. 6.   [3] Gen. iii. 24.   [4] Gen. iii. 8.

CHAPTER IX.

THE FIRST MAN—THE FIRST WOMAN.

THE work of creation was progressive; on each of the first five days a higher order of beings was successively created. The close of the fifth day saw the mighty pedestal erected for the great "image" which was to stand upon it; the splendid mansion prepared, with waiting attendants, for the noble being who was to occupy it. On the sixth and last day the greatest wonder, where everything was wonderful, appeared. God made man, and creation was complete. Even the history of his creation is wonderful. God spake; and inanimate matter came into being. He said: "Let the waters bring forth abundantly the moving creature that hath life and fowl that may fly above the earth, and the waters brought them forth:" and again, "Let the earth bring forth cattle and creeping things and beasts of the earth, and it was so."[1] But when man was to be created, the Trinity are spoken of as taking counsel together. "And God said, Let us make man in our image, after our likeness."[2] "And the LORD God formed man of the dust of the ground, and breathed into his nostrils the breath of life; and man became a living soul." And from a rib taken from the man, woman, as the history says, was "builded." "So God created man in his own image." Alas! it was only an image; soon lost, and man was again dust.

The words *formed, builded,* as used by the great Creator, convey some idea of the wonderful being called man. "The

[1] Gen. i. 20–24.   [2] Gen. i. 26.

anatomy of man," says Galen, " discovers above six hundred muscles, and whoever only considers these, will find that nature must have, at least, adjusted ten different circumstances, in order to attain the end proposed; so that in the muscles alone, above *six thousand* several views and intentions must have been formed and executed." He calculated there are two hundred and forty-four bones; and the distinct purposes aimed at in their structure to be twelve thousand. Then consider the senses of touch, sight, etc.; and then, the structure of the mind of man, capable of directing and controlling all this machinery, and with powers almost boundless, fitted to subdue the world unto itself. Think also of the heart and immortal soul of man, capable of loving, serving, and enjoying God, and, alas! capable of hating Him. Consider man! with the destiny before him of living an everlasting life; or of dying an eternal death! So frail, that an atom can cause him agony; and with but a passing breath between him and his eternal state of happiness or woe! Well may we, with the Psalmist, exclaim, "I am fearfully and wonderfully made!"

Man was called Adam, that is, *red earth*, either from the clay, from which he was formed, or from his ruddy appearance or flesh tint. "Adam called his wife's name Eve, that is, *living*, because she was the mother of all living."[1] A fact worthy of remembrance; as we are apt to forget, through pride and the difference which sin, food, and climate have produced in the human family, that " God hath made of one blood all nations of men for to dwell on all the face of the earth."[2]

Infidels, denying God's history of creation and of the Fall, and rejecting his plan of salvation, try to make it appear that our first parents were only full grown infants. To carry out their idea that man is his own saviour, they teach that the savages of the earth ever have been, and still are, in a state

---

[1] Gen. iii. 20.   [2] Acts xvii. 26.

nearest the natural and original one of man; and also that all civilized nations have become so by their own power of improvement. If such had been the case, man would have been the only imperfect being created: he would have been inferior to the animals, whose natural instincts have been perfect from the first. History, as well as the word of God, shows this theory of the infidel to be false. No individual or tribe which was once in a savage state has ever risen from that to a civilized state without having had civilization brought to them.

The famous historian Niebuhr has recorded his full conviction, "that all savages are the degenerate remnants of more civilized races, which had been overpowered by enemies and driven to take refuge in the woods, there to wander seeking a precarious existence, till they had forgotten most of the arts of settled life and sunk into a wild state." Criminals who had fled from society to escape punishment, also trappers and hunters in wild regions, would, with their descendants, lose the restraints and the arts of civilized life, and in time would become savage.

In regard to the freedom enjoyed by man in a wild state, the pure simplicity, the magnanimity and generosity of character which he there exhibits, according to poets and romancing novel writers, Archbishop Whateley has well observed, "The liberty enjoyed by the savage consists in his being left free to oppress and plunder any one who is weaker than himself, and of being exposed to the same treatment from those who are stronger. His boasted simplicity consists merely in grossness of taste, improvidence and ignorance. His virtue merely amounts to this, that though not less covetous, envious, and malicious than civilized man, he wants the skill to be as dangerous as one of equally depraved character, but more intelligent and better informed." Surely such was not man as he came forth perfect from his Maker's hands, in the image of God, and only a little lower than the angels.

We have no account of the personal appearance of those who figured in the early part of the world's history. We cannot but think, however, that when Adam was first created, formed after the likeness of God, in knowledge and holiness, with a free will, and with dominion over the creatures, made at once full grown, with all his faculties, with a body not yet weakened and defaced by sin, and which had a power, even while under the sentence, "dying thou shalt die," to last nearly a thousand years, we cannot but think that when he was thus first made, a perfect work, pronounced "very good" by the Great Creator, Adam must have been in appearance the noblest specimen of a man that ever walked the earth.

> "Not out of weakness rose his gradual frame;
> Perfect from his Creator's hand he came;
> And, as in form excelling, so in mind
> The sire of men transcended all mankind." [1]

And Eve must have had concentrated in her person all that the world has ever conceived of as beautiful and lovely in woman. Humanly speaking we may well be proud of our first parents: and we may well be satisfied, that we had such a representative in whom we were to stand or fall, as Adam was, when created.

There is a second Adam,[2] spoken of in history, "who is the image of the invisible God,"[3] "the express image of his person,"[4] in whom "dwelleth all the fullness of the Godhead bodily."[5] He also is the head and representative of a people; but they shall never fall: for they will be forever perfect in Him, who is their head.[6] He is represented to us as having "his visage marred more than any man, a man of sorrows and acquainted with grief, having no form nor comeliness;

[1] Montgomery.
[2] 1 Cor. xv. 45.
[3] Col. i. 15.
[4] Heb. i. 3.
[5] Col. ii. 9.
[6] Eph. i. 23; iv. 16; v. 30; John xiv. 19.

THE FIRST MAN. 31

and when we shall see him there is no beauty that we should desire him."[1]

Adam, created at once a man, lived nine hundred and thirty years; and, according to the Hebrew text, was cotemporary with all the patriarchs down to Lamech, the father of Noah. Lamech was fifty-six years old when Adam died. Thus Noah could have heard from his father, who had received it from Adam, a history of the world from the creation.

How long Eve lived is not stated. It is a curious fact, that in sacred history the age, death, and burial of only one woman, Sarah the wife of Abraham, are distinctly noted. Woman's age ever since appears not to have been a subject for history or discussion.

[1] Isai. lii. 14; liii. 2.

CHAPTER X.

THE FIRST MARRIAGE.

ADAM did not long remain a bachelor. Even in Paradise he found, for a short time, that something was lacking, "For Adam there was not found an help meet for him."[1] "The Lord God said, It is not good that the man should be alone."[2] A wife was therefore provided for him; and on the first day of his manhood, the first day of his life, Adam was married.[3] There are several facts connected with this first marriage in the world deserving attention; as it was the great foundation of all the social relationships, and of all the dear family ties and joys which have ever been in the world. It was also the foundation of all government. And history, and the present experience of the world, show that so far as the plan of the first marriage has been followed, or departed from, so have men brought happiness or misery on themselves.

There is some truth in the old adage that "marriages are made in heaven." They are so very often for the children of God. It was so with the first marriage. The Lord chose the wife for Adam, and prepared her especially for him. Adam was not even consulted. In accordance we find that the people of God afterward selected wives for their children. Abraham chose a wife for Isaac, and sent his servant to get her, saying, "The Lord God shall send his angel before thee, and thou shalt take a wife unto my son from thence."[4] Isaac charged Jacob whom he should not marry, and directed him to take a wife of the daughters of Laban.[5] The custom

---

[1] Gen. ii. 20.   [2] Gen. ii. 18.   [3] Matt. xix. 4, 6; Gen. ii. 25.
[4] Gen. xxiv. 4, 7.   [5] Gen. xxviii. 1.

THE FIRST MARRIAGE.

of the Jews was for the parents to betroth their children even in early life. Truly, "A prudent wife is from the Lord."[1]

The Lord said, "I will make him an help meet for him."[2] The forsaking of this first principle of marriage, having "an help meet," has brought untold misery into the world. It promoted the great wickedness of the antediluvians; it caused the Church to disappear almost entirely from the earth, and thus brought the deluge upon it. "The sons of God saw the daughters of men that they were fair; and they took them wives of all which they chose."[3] The children of God, as the Lord's people are called throughout the sacred history, married with the children of the world. Instead of converting them, as many are apt to think may be the case with those in whom they may be interested, the result proved as God, when charging His people on this subject, says it will always be. His charge is, "Thy daughter thou shalt not give unto his son, nor his daughter shalt thou take unto thy son. For they will turn away thy son from following me, that they may serve other gods: so will the anger of the Lord be kindled against you, and destroy thee suddenly."[4]

There are no sinners so great as they who sin against light and knowledge. It is not strange therefore that the record goes on to say: "There were giants on the earth in those days:" monsters in iniquity. The children of the mixed marriages became "mighty men, men of renown. And God saw the wickedness of man was great."[5] The children of God are therefore again directed, "Be ye not unequally yoked with unbelievers,"[6] and when ye marry, marry "only in the Lord."[7]

Another noticeable feature in the first marriage was that the Lord gave Adam, the head of the race, only one wife. History shows that his posterity, when they forsook God,

[1] Prov. xix. 14. [2] Gen. ii. 18. [3] Gen. vi. 2. [4] Deut. vii. 3.
[5] Gen. vi. 4, 5. [6] 2 Cor. vi. 14. [7] 1 Cor. vii. 39.

also forsook this feature in marriage, as it was originally instituted. It also shows that God's chastisement or curse has invariably followed the alteration. Polygamy is first spoken of as occurring among the children of Cain : " And Lamech took unto him two wives."[1] Since then, as a general rule, with the introduction of polygamy, woman has been only a toy or a slave in all places where God is not acknowledged. By a trick of Laban, Jacob was persuaded to marry two wives. The consequence, was constant hatred and jealousy, almost resulting in murder, between his children : causing trouble which came nigh bringing his gray hairs with sorrow to the grave. David added to his wives, and the result among his children was rape and incest by one, the murder of his brother by another, an attempt to seize the kingdom by a third, and a fourth causing his brother to be put to death for doing so. All this is the natural result of polygamy.

At the first marriage the two were pronounced " one flesh."[2] We find afterward the marriage tie became so loose, even among God's people, that Moses made rules to regulate the severing of it. The Pharisees to tempt the Lord Jesus Christ quoted these commands of Moses. His reply is worthy of remembrance : " Have ye not read that He which made them at the beginning made them male and female, and said, For this cause shall a man leave father and mother, and shall cleave (original, *be cemented*) to his wife : and they twain shall be one flesh ? Moses, because of the hardness of your hearts, suffered you to put away your wives ; but from the beginning it was not so. What therefore God had joined together, let not man put asunder."[3] He then says that a wife may be put away for one cause only : and that without that cause, " whosoever shall put away his wife, and shall marry another, committeth adultery.[3] *No human law can set aside this law of God.*

[1] Gen. iv. 19.   [2] Gen. ii. 24.   [3] Matt. xix. 3–9.

Thus was celebrated the first marriage. He who made them one closed it with his blessing. "God blessed them, and God said, Be fruitful, and multiply, and replenish the earth and subdue it: and have dominion over every living thing upon the earth." A delightful residence had been prepared for them; and Adam received his bride arrayed with that garment of beauty, purity, and innocence, with which her Creator had adorned her. "They were both naked, the man and his wife, and were not ashamed."[1] Happy couple! with unclouded prospects, and yet their honeymoon, oh, how short!

It is well here to bear in mind the words of our Lord: "In the resurrection they neither marry, nor are given in marriage, but are as the angels of God in heaven."[2]

[1] Gen. ii. 25. [2] Matt. xxii. 30.

CHAPTER XI.

THE FIRST LANGUAGE.

IT appears that as soon as Adam and Eve were created they could talk. They were not only made able at once to speak, but with the power of speech they also received a language. This language was a gift direct from God: otherwise it could never have been discovered. It is now communicated from one to another; and is only acquired by imitation, and after long practice.

It is interesting to trace what this first language was, which the Great Creator gave to His children, and which He used in conversing with them: and to catch the sounds which our first parents used in their prayers and praises to their Father and their God, and to express their joys and sorrows to one another. This language was doubtless the noblest ever uttered by man: being transmitted to us through man degraded by the Fall, it comes down, having lost, perhaps, in some degree, its original purity.

The languages now in use in the world, like the traditions of the nations which have been perpetuated by language, are easily traced back to one fountain-head. Those of the Christian part of it came from the Roman and Greek; and they were derived from the Phœnician and Hebrew, their very alphabets and letters coming the same way. The Chaldee, Syriac, and Samaritan were dialects of the Hebrew. The principal languages of the heathen world, the Arabic, the Persian, and the Sanscrit show a relationship to the same source. In that language the oldest book, by nearly a thousand years, was written.

The first difference in language in the world took place when the descendants of Noah attempted to build the tower of Babel. Then " the whole earth was of one language and of one speech." To restrain those who began to build the tower, and to keep them from following out their imagination, the Lord said : " Let us go down, and there confound their language, that they may not understand one another's speech."[1]

This confusion of tongues occurred among those who had forsaken God, leaving the original language with His children—with those who retained His word and his worship. They never could lose the language which contained the knowledge of all that they held most dear ; the precepts and promises of their God ; and even the names by which He had made himself known to them, and which they constantly used in addressing Him. There was no reason why their language should be changed as in the case of Babel. And as long as the Church of God is in the world, which will be to the end of it, the Hebrew will be cherished as the first revelation of God through His word. Through it alone He spake to man for four thousand years : in it He gave the law written with His own finger ; and on the cross, our Lord used it in speaking those memorable words : " Eli, Eli, lama Sabacthani ?"—My God, my God, why hast thou forsaken me ?

The first names in the world, whether given to men, places, the Sabbath, or to religious rites, were associated with something connected with the object named ; and in many places of the sacred history the reason is recorded why the person or thing was so named. These first names are all Hebrew ; and the explanation or meaning of them is also in Hebrew, thus proving that it was the language used at the time they were so named. It was thus with the names of Adam, Eve, Cain, Seth, Noah, etc., which all have a meaning. The wonderful names by which God has con-

[1] Gen. xi. 6.

descended to reveal Himself to us, the great names JEHOVAH, and JESUS, or Joshua, are also Hebrew, and full of meaning.

It is remarkable, that the first confusion of tongues occurred in consequence of the evil imaginations of men; and that the first work of the Holy Ghost, when He descended on the day of Pentecost, was the gift of tongues to bring men back to God. We are told that in heaven, an innumerable company, gathered of all nations and tongues, unite in one voice, ascribing, "Salvation to God and unto the Lamb."[1]

The Jews had a tradition, that before the fall, animals could talk. Josephus, in his history, speaking of the temptation, says: "All living creatures had one language." Some of them certainly appear to have the organs of speech; and even birds can be taught to talk. While we have no positive knowledge of the matter, we know that animals have suffered a change with all creation since the fall. It does not appear that Eve was surprised that the serpent could speak; but she could not well be surprised at anything; for where every thing was new, nothing could be particularly strange.

It is interesting to trace words back from language to language to their source, and to see how original words in traveling through time expand and grow. For instance, from *caph or cap*, Hebrew, *the hollow of the hand*, comes the latin *captivus, captive*, a person held in hand; also, *cavus, cave*. The *tap* of the drum from the Hebrew *tap to strike, to beat*. Cypher, a mode of writing, also numbers; from *sepher, to count, to write*. Many of our words sound almost the same in both languages; as, *Auil*, evil; *Dum*, to be silent; *Hul*, to howl; *Sac*, sackcloth; *Kara*, to cry; *Sir*, a prince, etc. How natural it is for all infants in their first attempts to speak, to say *ab-bab-ab*, or *em-mem-em*. How few know that these words were used by the first children in the world to express words dear to all. In Hebrew, *Ab*, or *Abba*, means father, and *Em* means mother.

[1] Rev. vii. 9.

CHAPTER XII.

FIRST WORK — FIRST SABBATH — FIRST FOOD.

THE idea that most persons entertain that work is part of the curse, a consequence of sin and of the Fall, is a great mistake. History reveals to us that all holy beings work. The first verse of history, the first revelation of God speaks of Him as working. God *created* the heaven and the earth. Again it says, " On the seventh day God ended his *work*."[1] Our Lord used the same manner of expression in speaking to the Jews : " My Father worketh hitherto, and I work."[2] We have already seen that the holy angels are " ministering spirits." It should not be considered strange, therefore, that so soon as Adam was created, work was found for him even in Eden. The record says, " the LORD God took the man, and put him into the garden of Eden to *dress it and to keep it*."[3] Endowed with a mind of almost unlimited capacity, and a body prepared for work, and with an earth filled with treasures for his use and comfort, part of the blessing upon him was, " replenish the earth and subdue it."[4] We find, also, God bringing to his notice every living creature : and Adam gave names to them all.[5] Employment was found for hand and tongue, for mind and heart.

The command " Six days shalt thou labor," was thus first given to man in Paradise ; and like all the other commands of God, it is not a curse but in order for a blessing. For the commands of God are all given in love. The promises made to the diligent and universal experience show that

---
[1] Gen. ii. 2.   [2] John v. 17.   [3] Gen. ii. 15.
[4] Gen. i. 28.   [5] Gen. ii. 20.

our prosperity and our happiness are connected with work. And although we are saved by faith, yet we are told, that "Faith without works is dead."[1]

And now appears another of the great foundation-stones of history; one which the Word of God, the history of the world, and the varied condition of the nations now on the earth, abundantly prove to be connected with the highest interests of man. Joined to the command to work is another command: "Remember the Sabbath day, to keep it holy."

Many look upon this commandment as first given by Moses to the Jews at Mount Sinai; but it was not so. The Sabbath was instituted at creation, and was given to man in the garden of Eden. "On the seventh day God ended his work which he had made; and he rested on the seventh day from all his work which he had made. And God blessed the seventh day, and sanctified it: because that in it he had rested from all his work, which God created and made."[2]

The word *Sabbath*, means *rest*. The Hebrew word translated "rested" means rather *ceased;* being not opposed to weariness, but to action: as God can neither know fatigue or need rest. Thus God "blessed" the *first day* after creation was finished, and "hallowed it." The first day of man's life was the Sabbath. The fourth commandment does not institute the Sabbath but reminds us of it; and it tells us to "*Remember* the Sabbath day, to keep it holy," and uses the same words to enforce it, that God did when he sanctified it at creation. Man, the creature, was thus continually to be reminded of his Creator.

The Sabbath, as a sign between God and his people, has now additional claims; two other important facts in history, each causing a corresponding change of the day, have been connected with it. It is now a sign of creation, redemption, and sanctification. "I gave them my sabbaths, to be a sign

---

[1] James ii. 26.   [2] Gen. ii. 2.

between me and them, that they might know that I am the Lord that sanctify them."[1] Each seventh day after the first day of man's life, being to him the first day of the week, continued to be thus consecrated until the deliverance of the Lord's people from Egypt, when, with the change of the beginning of the year, the Sabbath was changed to the seventh day, the day of the Exodus, to commemorate that event. "Remember that thou wast a servant in the land of Egypt, and that the LORD thy God brought thee out thence through a mighty hand and by a stretched out arm ; therefore, the LORD thy God commanded thee to keep the sabbath day."[2] That day passed away, with the other types of the Jewish dispensation, when the Creator had accomplished the great deliverance of His people by the sacrifice of Himself. On the first day of the week, the work of redemption was completed. On that day the Lord rose from the dead ; and on that day he repeatedly appeared to his disciples as they were assembled together.[3] On that day, the day of Pentecost, the Holy Ghost descended. A change of the Sabbath consequently followed, and the first day of the week,[4] the first day of the life of the Church in Christ its head, again became the Lord's day, and was consecrated as the Sabbath. Upon the first day of the week, therefore, the disciples came together to commemorate the Lord's death at His table, and to attend preaching,[5] and upon that day " every one is directed to lay by him in store an offering to the Lord as God hath prospered him."[6]

We find that God hallowed not only the first of man's time, and the first day of the Church risen in Christ, but He also claimed of his people the first fruits of their fields, the first born of their beasts and their first born son.[7]

[1] Ezek. xx. 12 ; Exod. xxxi. 13.   [2] Deut. v. 15.   [3] John xx. 19, 26.
[4] The wording in Matt. xxviii. 1, is remarkable. In the original it reads, "In the end of the *Sabbaths,* as it began to dawn toward the first of the *Sabbaths*."
[5] Acts xx. 7.   [6] 1 Cor. xvi. 2.   [7] Exod. xiii. 12 ; Levit. xxiii. 10.

The division of time into weeks was continued, even in places where men had ceased to acknowledge Him who had hallowed the seventh day. Even the number seven was considered a sacred or mystical number. Laban speaks of weeks.[1] The ancient Assyrians, descendants of Shem; the Egyptians, descendants of Ham; the Arabians, descendants of Ishmael; the Phœnicians, and other idolatrous nations, retained the week of seven days. And now, among the different nations of the earth, almost every day of the week is observed by one or another as a weekly festival or holiday, as a seventh day or sabbath: the Christian keeping Sunday, the Jews Saturday, the Mahommedans Friday, etc.

The Sabbath is one of the greatest blessings ever conferred upon man; it is a necessity of his nature, body and soul both requiring it. Even working cattle need it, and will do more work by resting one day in seven. The Lord says: "The Sabbath was made for man."[2]

Both history and God's word teach us, that this law, connected with our creation and our redemption, never has been, and never can be, broken with impunity. Infidels, in their vain attempts to dethrone their Creator, have tried to put aside His day. In the French Revolution of 1793, the Convention abolished the Sabbath; appointed instead of it every tenth day a period of rest, and directed the measurement of time by divisions of ten days. This was preparatory to a general abolition of the Christian religion, and a substitution of the worship of Reason in its stead. The result was, a state of society too terrible and too horrible even for Infidels to bear. And France was soon compelled to retrace her steps. Brutality and crime, physical and moral degradation, always accompany the desecration of the Sabbath; and the wrath of God is visibly revealed.

What a day of joy and gladness the first Sabbath must have been to Adam and Eve! The first day after their

---

[1] Gen. xxix. 27.   [2] Mark ii. 27.

creation and their union, the light of the first morning they ever beheld, was the Sabbath; and it was given to them that they might, in sweet fellowship with one another, contemplate the wonderful works of their Creator, all ministering to their happiness; and that they might hold a day of uninterrupted loving communion with one another and with their Father, God. It was probably the only Sabbath they ever thus enjoyed.

The first food prepared for man, and given to him in his first estate, was plain and simple. Fruits and vegetables, in the abundance and variety, however, of the garden which God had planted, gratified his taste, while supporting his life. "Every herb bearing seed, and every tree, in the which is the fruit of a tree yielding seed; to you it shall be for meat."[1] The animals and the fowls of the air could then dwell together in peace without fear, for "every green herb" supplied their wants.

God selected that, which was to supply this daily recurring want of our nature, as a field in which to place a test of that faith, confidence and obedience, without which a creature cannot be happy. Our first parents were restricted from the fruit of only one tree; that one they were forbidden even to touch. They did not need it; they had no desire for it. They had no knowledge of evil, nor of that Evil Being who now appears in history.

[1] Gen. i. 29, 30.

CHAPTER XIII.

THE DEVIL—DEMONS—FAMILIAR SPIRITS.

THE history of angels and of men confirms the important testimony of God's word, that creatures left to the freedom of their own will, though created holy, will not continue so, unless constantly upheld by the grace and power of God.

In the history of angels we have the first revelation of God's grace ;. and, that as a sovereign, He dispenses that grace according to his own will. His "*elect* angels"[1] were upheld : the rest were allowed to fall. In the history of man we have the first intimation that God is a God of mercy, and that, in dispensing mercy, He is likewise sovereign. Some men are elected, called, justified, and saved ;[2] while the rest are left to their own will, and to follow their own wicked inclinations. "He hath mercy on whom he will have mercy, and whom he will he hardeneth." "Shall the thing formed say to him that formed it, Why hast thou made me thus ? Hath not the potter power over the clay ?"[3] Rather let us say with the Lord Jesus : "I thank thee, O Father, Lord of heaven and earth, because thou hast hid these things from the wise and prudent, and hast revealed them unto babes. Even so, Father ; for so it seemed good in thy sight."[4]

A great number of angels "kept not their first estate, but left their own habitation."[5] They are of different ranks, and are described as, "principalities, powers, rulers

---

[1] 1 Tim. v. 21.   [2] Rom. viii. 29.   [3] Rom. ix. 18, 20, 21.
[4] Matt. xi. 25.   [5] Jude 6.

of the darkness of this world, and spiritual wickedness, or wicked spirits."[1] Among them is one so preëminent, that while they are all called devils, or demons, he is known as *the Devil:* and the others are spoken of as his angels.[2] He is called "Beelzebub, the prince of the devils:"[3] and is said to have a kingdom.[4] The word *Devil*, from the Greek, *Diabolos*, means Calumniator or Accuser. Another name he bears, Satan, means Adversary or Accuser. Hence he is called "the accuser of the brethren."[5] His false accusations were the commencement of Job's trials. Satan came with the sons of God before the Lord, and said, "Doth Job fear God for nought? Put forth thine hand now, and touch all that he hath, and he will curse thee to thy face."[6] He is known also as the "prince of this world;"[7] "the god of this world;"[8] "the father of unbelievers, even though they be children of Abraham, a murderer from the beginning, a liar, and the father of it."[9] Though all the devils are deceivers and adversaries; and though the Bible says: "Some shall depart from the faith, giving heed to seducing spirits, and doctrines of devils;"[10] yet we are warned particularly against their great leader: "Be sober, be vigilant; because your adversary the devil, as a roaring lion, walketh about, seeking whom he may devour."[11] He is the great "deceiver, that deceiveth the nations:"[12] "the prince of the power of the air, the spirit that now worketh in the children of disobedience."[13]

"God spared not the angels that sinned, but cast them down to hell."[14] Our Lord said: "I beheld Satan as lightning fall from heaven."[15] From all accounts, Satan was probably the most intelligent, the most powerful, the greatest

[1] Ephes. vi. 12.
[2] Matt. iv. 5, 8; Rev. xii. 9.
[3] Matt. xii. 24.
[4] Matt. xii. 26.
[5] Rev. xii. 10.
[6] Job. i. 9, 11.
[7] John xii. 31; xiv. 30.
[8] 2 Cor. iv. 4.
[9] John viii. 44.
[10] 1 Tim. iv. 1.
[11] 1 Peter v. 8.
[12] Rev. xx. 3, 8, 10.
[13] Eph. ii. 2.
[14] 2 Peter ii. 4.
[15] Luke x. 18.

being ever created. His condemnation was pride.[1] He exalted himself against God, and his first temptation of man was telling him : " Ye shall be as God."

> " Pride, self-adoring pride; was primal cause
> Of all sin past, all pain, all woe to come.
> Unconquerable pride; first, eldest sin,
> Great fountain head of evil! highest source,
> Whence flowed rebellion 'gainst the Omnipotent.
> Whence hate of man, and all else ill.
> Pride at the bottom of the human heart
> Lay, and gave root and nourishment to all
> That grew above. Great ancestor of vice!
> Hate, unbelief, and blasphemy of God."—POLLOK.

Well might the prophet exclaim : " How art thou fallen from heaven, O Lucifer, son of the morning! how art thou cut down to the ground."[2] For fallen angels no Saviour, no redemption was provided : our Lord " took not on him the nature of angels."[3] "He hath reserved them in everlasting chains under darkness, unto the judgment of the great day."[4] We are told " the devils believe that there is one God, and tremble."[5] And Satan, the Devil, is said to have "great wrath, because he knoweth that he hath but a short time."[6]

Men little think what an influence the Devil and his angels have had in the history of the world, from creation to the present time. Even the children of God, as they are apt to forget the ministering of holy angels, also forget their constant exposure to the snares of evil ones ; and need continually to be told, " Watch and pray, that ye enter not into temptation." Happy are they that the great Shepherd watches over them! as He did over Peter when He said : " Simon, Simon, behold Satan hath desired to have you, that he may sift you as wheat : but I have prayed for thee that thy faith fail not."[7]

---

[1] 1 Tim. iii. 6.   [2] Isaiah xiv. 12.   [3] Heb. ii. 16.   [4] Jude 6.
[5] James ii. 19.   [6] Rev. xii. 12.   [7] Luke xxii. 31.

From the beginning we find, that the Devil has had a hand, and sometimes a controlling one, in all the most important events of the history of man. The word of God teaches us that devils can enter into men and dwell in them. That one may go out of a man and afterwards return and take " seven other spirits more wicked than himself and enter in and dwell there."[1] Out of Mary Magdalene seven devils were cast:[2] out of a Gadarene, Jesus cast out a " Legion : because many devils were entered into him."[3] When great ends were to be accomplished, the Prince of the Devils, " the tempter," himself acted. He tempted Eve : he "stood up against Israel, and provoked David to number Israel;"[4] he tempted our Lord in the wilderness. And in his greatest effort, when he tried to destroy Jesus, " Satan entered into Judas surnamed Iscariot,"[5] and moved him to betray his master. Little did Satan think that he was assisting to carry out " the purpose for which the Son of God was manifested, that he might destroy the works of the devil:"[6] and that the time predicted was then come, that his own head should be crushed.

During the four thousand years of the history which God has given to us, frequent reference is made to wicked persons having familiar spirits ; and consulting with them : and also to people seeking information from the dead. The word *necromancer*, Deut. xviii. 11, means " one who seeks enquiries of the dead." For such and other abominations the Lord destroyed the Canaanites.[7] About four hundred years afterwards, " Saul died for his transgression against the Lord, and also for asking counsel of one that had a familiar spirit."[8] The law of God to the Jews on this subject was, " A man or woman that hath a familiar spirit shall surely be put to death."[9] " The soul that turneth after such as have familiar

---

[1] Matt. xii. 45.
[2] Mark xvi. 9.
[3] Luke viii. 30.
[4] 1 Chron. xxi. 1.
[5] Luke xxii. 3; John xiii. 27.
[6] 1 John iii. 8.
[7] Deut. xviii. 12.
[8] 1 Chron. x. 13.
[9] Levit. xx, 27.

spirits, I will even set my face against that soul, and will cut him off from among his people."¹ We are told that wicked Manasseh, three hundred and fifty years after Saul, "dealt with a familiar spirit:² and afterwards that his grandson Josiah put away from the land, with other abominations, "the workers with familiar spirits."³ When our Saviour was on the earth, Devils frequently spoke through men, even acknowledging him "as the Holy one of God;" "Christ the Son of God."⁴ But he rebuked them and would not suffer them to speak or testify of him.⁵ In Philippi, "a damsel possessed with a spirit of divination, which brought her masters much gain by soothsaying, cried after the apostles, saying, These men are the servants of the most high God, which shew unto us the way of salvation. Paul being grieved, turned and said to the spirit, I command thee in the name of Jesus Christ to come out of her. And he came out the same hour."⁶

The casting of devils and evil spirits out of persons, is spoken of as occurring almost in every place visited by our Saviour, or the apostles. In all ages, we see that men are inclined to "seek unto them that have familiar spirits, and to the dead, rather than to God, his law, and his testimony."⁷ Abraham's answer to the man in hell who wanted to send one from the dead to convert his brethren is worthy of notice: "If they hear not Moses and the prophets, neither will they be persuaded, though one rose from the dead."⁸

Devils will take part in the history of man till the end of the world. We are told that in the millennium, that old serpent, which is the Devil, and Satan, shall be bound a thousand years; and when the thousand years are expired, Satan shall be loosed out of his prison, and shall go out to deceive the nations; to gather them, as the sand of the sea in number, to

---

¹ Levit. xx. 6.   ³ 2 Kings xxiii. 24.   ⁵ Mark iii. 12; Luke iv. 41.
² 2 Chron. xxxiii. 6.   ⁴ Luke iv. 34, 41.   ⁶ Acts xvi. 16.
        ⁷ Isa. viii. 19.   ⁸ Luke xvi. 31.

battle : and while they compass the camp of the saints about, fire shall come down from God out of heaven, and devour them.[1] And then shall be the judgment. God's history goes further, and says, that devils and some men shall be associated hereafter. "The King shall say to them on the left hand, Depart from me, ye cursed, into everlasting fire, prepared for the devil and his angels."[2]

As we look through the history of the world, let us notice the important place which the Devil and his angels take in every part of that history. Let us remember that he quoted the word of God when tempting our Saviour: and that to effect his purpose, "Satan himself is transformed into an angel of light, and his ministers, as the ministers of righteousness."[3] Paul tells us why we should know all this; "lest Satan should get an advantage of us: for we are not ignorant of his devices,"[4] and also that we may know, with what fearful beings we have " to wrestle :" so powerful, that Paul exhorts, "Put on the whole armor of God, that ye may be able to stand against the wiles of the devil."[5] The Christian is also told, "Resist the devil, and he will flee from you:"[6] "Be strong in the Lord," "taking the shield of faith, wherewith ye shall be able to quench all the fiery darts of the wicked." There is one way in which he is very easily overcome :

"Satan trembles when he sees
The weakest saint upon his knees."

Let us now return to the garden of Eden. Behold! the prince of the devils is there; and with that crafty, wicked Spirit, the gentle, confiding, and unsuspicious Eve is left alone.

[1] Rev. xx. 2, 7. 9.
[2] Matt. xxv. 41.
[3] 2 Cor. xi. 14, 15.
[4] 2 Cor. ii. 11.
[5] Eph. vi. 11, 16.
[6] James iv. 7.

CHAPTER XIV.

THE FIRST SIN — THE FALL — FIRST EFFECTS OF SIN — FIRST GOSPEL CALL.

THE "Prince of the devils" assisted in laying the foundation-stone which we have now reached; and to accomplish his purpose he entered into a serpent. On it he built "a kingdom;"[1] making himself the "God of this world."[2] It is the foundation of all the sin, suffering, and sorrow, under which the world has groaned for nearly six thousand years. How exceedingly short and simple, are the details of a fact, which led to the destruction of one world by a flood, and will lead to its destruction a second time by fire! that led even the Creator himself to take upon him our nature, and suffer and die, to redeem a people to himself!

The serpent " said unto the woman, Yea, hath God said, Ye shall not eat of every tree of the garden? And the woman said unto the serpent, We may eat of the fruit of the trees of the garden: but of the fruit of the tree which is in the midst of the garden, God hath said, Ye shall not eat of it, neither shall ye touch it, lest ye die. And the serpent said unto the woman, Ye shall not surely die: for God doth know that in the day ye eat thereof, then your eyes shall be opened, and ye shall be as gods (or as God), knowing good and evil. And when the woman saw that the tree was good for food, and that it was pleasant to the eyes, and a tree to be desired to make one wise, she took of the fruit thereof, and did eat, and gave also unto her husband with her; and he did eat."[3]

[1] Matt. xii. 24, 26. [2] 2 Cor. iv. 4. [3] Gen. iii. 1.

THE FIRST SIN. 51

A few words are spoken to a woman; she listens, reasons a moment, eats an apple, gives of it to her husband, and he eats. In an instant they are changed; they have lost their holiness, their spiritual life; and at once they begin to suffer the eternal death, "the dying thou shalt die."[1] This change is called by the expressive word, *the Fall*.

In consequence of the federal relation which Adam sustained to his posterity, as their head, a fountain of corruption was thus opened, which tainted all the race. All are "conceived in sin"[2] and "born unclean;"[3] "there is none righteous, no, not one!"[4] and thus "death passed upon all men, for in Adam, all sinned."[5]

Little did our first parents dream of the unutterable woe and misery they were bringing upon themselves and entailing upon the untold millions of their descendants. We, however, cannot condemn them. Knowing no sin they had no idea of fear, of suffering, or of death. Let those condemn them, who seeing and feeling the effects of sin, and knowing in some degree what death is, yet love sin, and choose to continue in it.

It is worthy of notice that the first sin combined "the lust of the eye," the woman "saw it was pleasant to the eyes;" "the lust of the flesh," it was "good for food;" and "the pride of life," it was "a tree to be desired to make one wise." It has been well remarked, that human reason has been a traitor since the fall. It was so, before the fall; they reasoned themselves into sin. It is also worthy of notice, the first sin was unbelief, or want of faith; therefore, the gospel message is, Believe; and salvation is by faith.

The immediate effect of the Fall as shown in Adam, and also in all his posterity, was a change from the spirit of love, to the spirit of the devil: fear, a desire to hide away from God; hatred of God (for what we dread, we hate), and

---

[1] Gen. ii. 17.   [2] Psalm li. 5.   [3] Job xiv. 4; xv. 14; Ps. lviii. 3.
[4] Rom. iii. 10.   [5] Rom. v. 12, 15, 18; 1 Cor. xv. 22.

a spirit of false accusation: excusing himself, and charging the woman, and even God, as the author of his sin: "The *woman* whom *thou* gavest to be with me, she gave me of the tree."[1] "Adam and his wife hid themselves from the presence of the Lord God amongst the trees of the garden."[2]

Blessed be God! He did not leave man to follow his own inclinations; to add sin to sin, and to go farther and farther away from God to eternity. "The Lord God called unto Adam, and said unto him, Where art thou?"[3] It was the first gospel call. God calling after a fugitive sinner to return to Him, to consider his sin, and to hear a promise, before pronouncing a curse.

[1] Gen. iii. 12.   [2] Gen. iii. 8.   [3] Gen. iii. 9.

CHAPTER XV.

THE FIRST PROMISE OF A SAVIOUR—FIRST EFFECTS OF THE CURSE—FIRST CLOTHING—EXPULSION FROM EDEN.

WE can almost hear Satan's shout of triumph when he found that he had succeeded in casting a blight over the fair creation which God had pronounced very good: and as the news reached the fallen angels that their leader had established a new kingdom; that man, the noblest work of God, had fallen into "the snare of the devil,"[1] henceforth to be the "slave of sin, to obey it;"[2] to be "the servant of corruption;"[3] and to be "taken captive by the devil at his will,"[4] we can almost hear the echoes of their demoniac laughter. We are told that when God's people "have tears to drink in great measure," "their enemies laugh among themselves:"[5] Satan's triumph, however, was very short.

In gaining his temporal kingdom, the Devil had earned the additional title of "that old Serpent,"[6] and also an additional curse. Man had incurred the penalty of an eternal "dying thou shalt die;" and all holy beings looked for the execution of the fearful penalty: for, until now, mercy and the forgiveness of sins were unknown. Neither fallen angels nor fallen man sought forgiveness; nor of themselves would they ever do so; for we are told "*Repentance* and the forgiveness of sins are given to Israel by Him whom God hath exalted to be a Prince and a Saviour."[7]

The Lord God called Adam and Eve to him; and after

---

[1] Gen. iii. 6; 2 Tim. ii. 26.   [2] Rom. vi. 16.   [3] 2 Peter ii. 19.
[4] 2 Tim. ii. 26.   [5] Psm. lxxx. 6.   [6] Rev. xx. 2.   [7] Acts v. 31.

hearing their wicked excuses, before passing sentence upon them, He pronounced a curse on the Serpent. As part of that curse " the LORD God said, I will put enmity between thee and the woman, and between thy seed and her seed ; it shall bruise thy head, and thou shalt bruise his heel."[1]

Here we reach the most wonderful foundation-stone in history. In this curse we get the first glimpse of the " Rock of Ages:" the first gleams of a coming redemption, seen dimly through the early dawn of revelation. Four thousand years passed before that revelation was completed. Then it was fully revealed that He "who worketh all things after the counsel of his own will,"[2] " declaring the end from the beginning, and from ancient times the things that are not yet done,"[3] had not only foreseen the Fall, but had also provided a remedy for it even before the world was made. A Redeemer was found ; and a people were " chosen in him *before the foundation* of the world :"[4] a people who "were to be saved, not according to their works, but according to God's own purpose and grace which was given to them in Christ Jesus *before the world began.*"[5]

In the curse upon the Serpent we have the first revelation of the Redeemer and his people. Thenceforth there were to be two seeds or races on the earth ;[6] the seed of the Serpent, those animated by his Spirit, all the natural seed of fallen man ; and the seed of the promise, the Saviour, and those chosen in Him who was to be born of the woman. There was to be enmity put by God himself between the two seeds. We shall see that enmity show itself between the first children, Cain and Abel ; and constantly appearing in the history of the church and of the world. The seed of the promise was to be persecuted by the seed of the serpent,[7] but it was finally to triumph ; and the Serpent's power was to be crushed by One who was afterwards more fully re-

---

[1] Gen. iii. 15.   [2] Eph. i. 11.   [3] Isaiah xlvi. 10.   [4] Eph. i. 4.
[5] 2 Tim. i. 9.   [6] Matt. xiii. 38 ; John viii. 44 ; 1 John iii. 10.   [7] Gall. iv. 29.

vealed not only as the Son of man, but also the Son of God: "that he might destroy the works of the Devil."[1]

In the course of history we see that several times, just as Satan had apparently reached the summit of his ambition and had almost the entire possession of the world, he was humbled. It was so at the first temptation; it was so when he got possession of the whole world, excepting Noah; when God sent the flood and destroyed the children of the devil and preserved His own: it was so when Satan combined the church and the state; the priest, Herod and Pilate, against Jesus: and it will be so in his last struggle; when he shall gather the nations of the earth against the saints, just before the day of judgment and his own final doom.[2]

Although a Deliverer was promised, God said to the woman, "I will greatly multiply thy sorrow;" and to the man, "cursed is the ground for thy sake; in sorrow shalt thou eat of it all the days of thy life; thorns also and thistles shall it bring forth to thee. In the sweat of thy face shalt thou eat bread, till thou return unto the ground; for out of it was thou taken; for dust thou art, and unto dust shalt thou return."[3] Thus a curse passed on all creatures for man's sin; and since then "the whole creation groaneth and travaileth in pain together until now,"[4] waiting to be "delivered from the bondage of corruption."

As a token of his faith in the promised Deliverer, Adam called his wife Eve, that is, *life*, "because she was the mother of all living."[5] Previously she had been "called *Isha*, woman, because she had been taken out of *Ish*, Man."[6] Eve also believed the promise; and, as we shall see hereafter, named her children accordingly. God had put enmity between her and the serpent.

Their faith was accepted: for the record goes on to say, "unto Adam also and to his wife did the LORD God make

[1] John iii. 8.
[2] Rev. xx. 9.
[3] Gen. iii. 16, 19.
[4] Rom. viii. 22, 21.
[5] Gen. iii. 20.
[6] Gen. ii. 23.

coats of skins, and clothed them."[1] These skins must have been the skins of animals offered in sacrifice : as animals were not given to man for food until after the flood.[2] We read afterwards of the " Lamb slain from the foundation of the world ;"[3] and also that Christ's people are clothed with his righteousness: " *God clothed them.*"[4]

Our first parents were then sent forth from the garden of Eden. They must have been there but a very short time : probably not one week, perhaps only one day ; for although part of the blessing in their estate of innocence was, " Be fruitful and multiply," their first children, Cain and Abel, were conceived and born in sin, after the Fall, and their expulsion from Eden.[5]

[1] Gen. iii. 21. [2] Gen. ix. 3. [3] Rev. xiii. 8.
[4] Isaiah lxi. 10; Rom. iii. 22. [5] Gen. iv. 1.

CHAPTER XVI.

THE FIRST CHILD—FIRST SACRIFICE—FIRST DEATH.

THE first exclamation of surprise recorded, is that which Eve uttered when Cain was born. Part of the penalty inflicted upon the woman for being led by the serpent into sin was, that her sorrows should be greatly multiplied in having children.[1] However, like most mothers since her time, Eve "remembered no more the anguish, for joy that a man was born in the world."[2] She exclaimed, "I have gotten a man from the LORD,"[3] or *I have gotten the man, Jehovah:* and she therefore called him Cain, that is, *gotten or acquired.* She doubtless thought he was the Messiah, the promised seed by whom the serpent was to be destroyed.

It appears the mother had the naming of the first child born into the world. We also find the wives of Jacob and others naming their children from circumstances occurring or connected with their birth. The hope that they should be the mother of the promised seed, of Him in whom all the nations of the earth were to be blessed, was one of the causes of the intense desire of having children, observable afterwards among the Jewish women.

Eve soon found, that, instead of being of the seed of promise, "her gotten," her "Cain was of that wicked one:"[4] was one of the seed of the serpent, one of "the children of the devil."[5] Finding she was mistaken, Eve thought that

[1] Gen. iii. 16.   [2] John xvi. 21.   [3] Gen. iv. 1.
[4] 1 John iii. 12.   [5] 1 John iii. 10.

her next son was the promised seed, though she had named him Abel, *vanity or sorrow*. And when again disappointed by his death, still clinging to the promise, she fixed upon another son, born when Adam was one hundred and thirty years old; or, according to the Septuagint, two hundred and thirty years old: and called him Seth, that is, *appointed or put:* "For God, said she, hath appointed me another seed instead of Abel."[1]

Although heirs of all the world, the first children were not brought up in idleness. Cain was a tiller of the ground, and Abel was a keeper of sheep. They had also a religious training, and were taught to make offerings to the Lord. "In process of time," or *at the end of days*, at the end of the year or week, most probably on the Sabbath, "Cain brought of the fruit of the ground an offering unto the Lord. And Abel, he also brought of the firstlings of his flock and of the fat thereof. And the LORD had respect unto Abel and to his offering: but unto Cain and to his offering he had not respect."[2] It is most likely "there came a fire out from before the Lord and consumed upon the altar the burnt offering and the fat"[3] of Abel's sacrifice: as was the case at special times with sacrifices which the Lord approved.[4] Abel's sacrifice appears to have been in compliance with a custom or form of worship already established.

Cain's offering of the fruit of his labors was rejected. How strange! Which of us would not prefer being presented with a basket of choice fruit or flowers, rather than have a lamb or a dove killed and burnt before us? It is common, however, for even earthly kings to dictate the way in which they are to be approached; thus we see the law of king Ahasuerus was, "That whosoever, whether man or woman, shall come unto the king into the inner court, who is not called, there is one law of his to put him to death, ex-

---

[1] Gen. iv. 25. [2] Gen. iv. 3. [3] Levit. ix. 24; 1 Kings xviii. 38.
[4] Levit. ix. 24; Judges vi. 21; 1 Kings xviii. 38; 1 Chron. xxi. 26.

THE FIRST SACRIFICE. 59

cept such to whom the king shall hold out the golden sceptre that he may live."[1] The King of kings in all times, has had an appointed way, in which only his rebellious subjects were to approach him. None were permitted to enter within the vail before the mercy-seat in the tabernacle, but Aaron the high priest ; and he at fixed times only, and with appointed offerings, under penalty of death.[2] The Kohathites, whose duty it was to carry the holy things, were thus warned : " They shall not go in to see when the holy things are covered, lest they die :"[3] and God's command was, " The stranger that cometh nigh shall be put to death."[4] " Nadab and Abihu offered strange fire before the LORD, which he commanded them not. And there went out fire from the LORD and devoured them, and they died before the LORD."[5] " Uzzah put forth his hand to the ark of God, and took hold of it ; for the oxen shook it. And the anger of the Lord was kindled against Uzzah ; and God smote him there for his error ; and there he died by the ark of God."[6] King Uzziah, in his pride, invaded the priest's office, and attempted to burn incense ; while in the act, the Lord smote him with leprosy.[7] Thanks be to God ! we are now permitted, and even directed through the Lord Jesus Christ, to " come boldly to the throne of grace, that we may obtain mercy, and find grace to help in time of need."[8]

Cain, it appears, did not believe the promise of God ; nor in the necessity of an atonement for sin. In the pride of unbelief he offered the unitarian offering of his own productions or works : and his offering was rejected. Abel believed the promise : for we are told, " *By faith* Abel offered unto God a more excellent sacrifice than Cain, by which he obtained witness that he was righteous, God testifying of his gifts."[9] He could not have offered it " by faith,"

---
[1] Esther iv. 11.   [3] Numb. iv. 20.   [5] Levit. x. 1.   [7] 2 Chron. xxvi. 16.
[2] Levit. xvi. 2, 13.   [4] Numb. xviii. 7.   [6] 2 Saml. vi. 6.   [8] Heb. iv. 16.
[9] Heb. xi. iv.

unless he knew that God had appointed the sacrifice and would accept it. God has always declared his abhorrence of such worship as is taught by the precepts of men, without being instituted by Him and in accordance with his word.[1]

The history of the religions which have been on the earth has filled volumes: but in reality there have been but two religions; the followers of the Lord, and the followers of the Devil.[2] Ever since the offerings of Cain and Abel, the descendants of Adam, in all places and in all ages, have been presenting offerings in religious worship. The seed of the woman, the line of patriarchs, prophets and martyrs, all the chosen people of God, whether Jew or Christian, have come to God with faith in the "Lamb that was slain," the Lord Jesus Christ: while the seed of the serpent have, as constantly, been making offerings and sacrifices of every description, according to their own inventions; and have been as constantly rejected. And such has been the result even when they went through the outward forms of the sacrifices appointed by God. The Pharisees were very punctilious in observing all the precepts of the laws of Moses, even tything mint, anise and cummin; but instead of seeking to be saved by faith in the sacrifice of the Lord Jesus Christ, they hated him, and put him to death. They depended on their own works, and therefore they offered the sacrifice of Cain. Though children of Abraham, and members of the visible church, yet they were of the seed of the serpent; for our Lord said to them, "Ye are of your father the devil."[3] We can easily tell of what seed we are: *Do we offer unto God the offering of Cain, or the offering of Abel?*

And here it is remarkable, that the Holy God, who is infinite in love, should have directed the killing and the offering in sacrifice of lambs and doves; the very emblems of innocence. Yet such was the fact: and, from the Fall to

---

[1] Isaiah xxix. 13; Matt. xv. 9.   [2] 1 John iii. 8, 10.
[3] John viii. 44; Rev. ii. 9.

the advent of the Lord Jesus Christ, guilty man could approach God in no other way. It is also remarkable, that the God of infinite justice should have allowed the only being who ever lived on earth "holy, harmless and undefiled," to suffer, and to be put to a cruel death. Why was it? *The sacrifices were one.* Man had sinned : " the wages of sin is death :"[1] " without shedding of blood there is no remission : "[2] " thus it behooved Christ to suffer : "[3] and He, " his own self bare our sins in his own body on the tree."[4]

The first deaths in the world were of animals; innocent animals slain by God himself, or according to his directions; slain in consequence of man's sin, and for man's benefit. They were the lambs offered in sacrifice, with whose skins God clothed Adam and Eve. Could they have looked on those sacrifices without being deeply moved on account of their sin?

[1] Rom. vi. 23.
[2] Heb. ix. 22; Lev. xvii. 11.
[3] Luke xxiv. 46.
[4] 1 Peter ii. xxiv.

CHAPTER XVII.

FIRST PERSECUTION — FIRST MARTYR — FIRST MURDER — BURIALS — FIRST DEATH PENALTY.

"CAIN was very wroth, and his countenance fell."[1] Instead of seeking mercy, he dared to be angry with God; and to dispute his right to dictate how a sinner should come unto Him. The LORD bore with him; and "said unto Cain, Why art thou wroth? and why is thy countenance fallen? If thou doest well shalt thou not be accepted?" What wonderful forbearance! what amazing condescension on the part of the great, the holy God, toward a rebel defying him! Instead of submitting to God, and seeking instruction from Abel, " Cain talked with Abel, his brother." It was the first controversy, the first persecution for religious opinion. In his hatred of the truth, Cain, unable to strike down the Almighty, rose up against the child of God, "against Abel his brother, and slew him." "And wherefore slew he him? Because his own works were evil, and his brother's righteous."[2] The wrath of the serpent, as has been the case often since, was thus instrumental in sending a redeemed soul the quicker to glory. The first of the seed of the promise died a martyr to his faith and as a witness for salvation by an atoning sacrifice; for it is expressly stated, that Abel "being dead yet speaketh."[3] Since the death of Abel how many have been compelled to suffer and lay down their lives on account of their faith.

Poor Adam and Eve! their first born, their "gotten," their noble, manly son, is a murderer; and what is worse,

---

[1] Gen. iv. 5.   [2] 1 John. iii. 12.   [3] Heb. xi. 4.

is of the seed of the Serpent; is rejected of God. Their second, their lovely Abel, is murdered because he bears the image of God. What multiplied sorrows! far greater than the loss of Eden. What fruits from merely eating an apple! Was that all? *Is any sin little?* "Sin, when it is finished, bringeth forth death:"[1] and "the wages of sin are death."[2]

We have no account of the manner of Abel's burial. The first burial of which we have an account is that of Sarah, in the Cave of Machpelah, which was bought for a burial place by Abraham.[3] A favorite mode of burial with the Jews was in sepulchers hewn out of the rocks—our Lord was thus buried. Deborah and Rachel, having died while Jacob was journeying, were buried by him in graves.[4] A pillar or tombstone was placed by Jacob over Rachel's grave for a memorial of her. Both modes of burial were, doubtless, used from the beginning.

The punishment of a murderer forms a part of the history as well as of the law which God has given to us. Cain was fool enough to think he could hide his crime even from God. When "the Lord said unto him, Where is Abel thy brother?" he had the audacity to reply, "I know not: am I my brother's keeper?" The family of our first parents were spared the additional sorrow of being compelled to put their son and brother to death as a murderer. The Lord himself became the avenger. The Lord said to Cain, "The voice of thy brother's blood crieth unto me from the ground. And now art thou cursed from the earth." A curse passed upon his occupation, the fruit of which he had brought as an offering. "When thou tillest the ground, it shall not henceforth yield unto thee her strength; a fugitive and a vagabond shalt thou be in the earth." Cain knew that his doom was sealed. In agony he exclaimed, "Thou has driven me out from the face of the earth; and from thy face shall I be hid; and I shall be a fugitive and a vagabond in the earth; and it shall

[1] James i. 15.   [2] Rom. vi. 23.   [3] Gen. xxiii. 9.   [4] Gen. xxxv. 8, 19, 20.

come to pass, that every one that findeth me shall slay me. My punishment is greater than I can bear." It appears the Lord gave him a special mark or token, "lest any finding him should kill him."

It is remarkable that after the flood, when God blessed Noah and his sons, and gave all things into their hands, and for the first time gave them permission to eat flesh, saying, "Every moving thing that liveth shall be meat for you; even as the green herb have I given you all things," he adds: "the blood thereof, shall ye not eat. And surely your blood of your lives will I require; at the hand of every beast will I require it, and at the hand of man; at the hand of every man's brother will I require the life of man. Whoso sheddeth man's blood, by man shall his blood be shed: for in the image of God made he man."[1] This law was given to Noah as the second head of the race. Since then, in all places and in all ages of the world, the murderer has been pursued with death; even where there has been no law, the relatives of the murdered one, or a lawless mob, have always been constrained to carry God's sentence into execution. No human law can abrogate the death-penalty for murder. Woe to the community that attempts it! For the people have taken, and always will take the law in their own hands: and while the murderer will certainly be slain, violence and bloodshed will be increasing, until God's law is again honored.

[1] Gen. ix. 3-6.

CHAPTER XVIII.

CAIN—FIRST CITY—POWER OF THE SEED OF THE SERPENT—FIRST POLYGAMY.

AFTER "the Lord had set a mark upon Cain, lest any finding him should kill him; Cain went out from the presence of the Lord and dwelt in the land of Nod, on the east of Eden."[1] The land of Nod was so called from *Nad*—*a vagabond*, which Cain was thenceforth to be. Like all places, the resort of vagabonds, its population increased rapidly; for nearly all of Adam's children were of that class. In the childhood of the world, as we have before noticed, the Lord manifested his presence in many ways. Cain went away from the place where the Lord was worshiped; and where He thus revealed himself.

The first city in the world was built by Cain. Violence and fear banded men together, and led them to fortify places to defend themselves, or from which they could go out to attack others. The pride of the bloody men called conquerors, also caused them to build the first cities, before and after the flood, and gave names to them. Cain called his city after the name of his son Enoch.

It is worthy of remark, that for thousands of years the seed of the serpent, though under a curse, built the great cities, furnished the kings of the earth, and had the power of the world; while the seed, to whom all blessings of this life and that to come were promised, had to live by faith; as heirs of an inheritance not yet received. Cain, under a curse, became a ruler and built a city. The first great cities

[1] Gen. iv. 16.

after the flood, Babylon, Nineveh, etc.,[1] were built by Nimrod, the mighty hunter, a mighty one in the earth, although Nimrod was descended from Ham, who was under a curse; and was, with his descendants, to be "a servant of servants, unto his brethren."[2] The descendants of Esau, who was hated of God and was to serve Jacob, furnished generations of dukes ruling cities; while the descendants of Jacob, the seed of the promise, from whom kings were to be born, were in slavery in Egypt. There was some truth in the assertion of the Devil, while tempting our Lord, when he said, "All the power of the kingdoms of the world is delivered unto me;" but he lied when he added, "And to whomsoever I will I give it."[3] Pilate boasted to our Lord, "Knowest thou not that I have power to crucify thee?" Jesus answered, "Thou couldest have no power against me, except it were given thee from above."[4] Pharaoh, while holding the chosen people in slavery, is told by the Lord, "Even for this purpose have I raised thee up, that I might shew my power in thee."[5] Happy are we that we know and can say to our Father in heaven, "Thine is the kingdom and the power."

How long Cain lived we are not told. As the ground was not henceforth to yield her strength to him, like a vagabond he lived on others. According to Josephus, "He did not accept of his punishment in order to amendment, but to increase his wickedness; for he only aimed to procure every thing that was for his own bodily pleasure, though it obliged him to be injurious to his neighbors. He augmented his household substance with much wealth by rapine and violence; he excited his acquaintance to procure pleasure and spoils by robbery; and became a great leader of men into wicked courses. He also introduced a change in that way of simplicity wherein men lived before, and was the author of measures and weights. And whereas they lived inno-

---

[1] Gen. x. 8, 10, 11.   [2] Gen. ix. 25.   [3] Luke iv. 6.
[4] John xix. 10.   [5] Exod. ix. 16; Rom. ix. 17.

cently and generously while they knew nothing of such arts, he changed the world into cunning and craftiness. He first of all set boundaries about lands; he built a city and fortified it with walls, and he compelled his family to come together to it." An old Jewish tradition represents him as having at last become insane, in which state he wandered about more like a wild beast than a man. As in those days men lived nearly a thousand years, Cain doubtless had many descendants. Several of them became celebrated, as we shall see hereafter, for their inventions.

Lamech, one of these descendants, is the first who is mentioned as having taken unto him two wives. The changing of God's plan of marriage, and introducing polygamy and all its evils in its place, was a fit invention for a descendant of Cain. The natural fruits of polygamy we have already noticed.

CHAPTER XIX.

FIRST INVENTIONS—FIRST MUSICIANS—FIRST ARTIFICERS—
EARLY KNOWLEDGE OF THE ARTS.

THE history of inventions is nearly coeval with the existence of man, and forms a very important part of the history of the world; as the Disposer of events has often produced great changes in the world by communicating the knowledge of "an invention" at a time suited to the accomplishment of His purpose. We are too apt to lose sight of God, and of his special providence, in these so-called *inventions*.[1] We have also little idea of the vast provision which the beneficent Creator has made to supply our wants. Think, for instance, of the immense stores of iron, and also of coal, the use of which has only lately been discovered. See one little island, Great Britain, producing about eighty millions of tons of coal yearly; yielding, besides many other things, almost enough coal and iron to form an island of respectable size every year! Think again of the vast hidden power put in matter for the use of man; that a pint of water and a pound of coal originate a power and sustain a motion which would soon wear out the human system of the strongest man; and that with the aid of a little water and coal and iron, the labor of one individual is made equal to that of the combined efforts of two hundred and twenty-six persons. A steam engine of one hundred horse power is estimated as equal to

---

[1] Many thoughts were gathered for this chapter, making it almost a compilation from an interesting and able work by Rev. John Blakely, entitled "The Theology of Inventions, or Manifestations of the Deity in the Works of Art."

the strength of eight hundred and eighty men; and the machinery of Great Britain, as doing the work of five hundred millions of men. What a vast amount of human toil is thus mitigated, and of human misery alleviated! What a wonderful provision to increase our comforts we find laid up in but a small part of the earth with larger supplies found elsewhere.

When God blessed Adam and Eve in Eden, He gave them dominion over all creatures moving upon the earth; and told them "to replenish the earth and subdue it."[1] He did the same to Noah and his sons immediately after the flood, saying, "into your hand are they delivered."[2] The animal and vegetable and mineral kingdoms were thus placed at man's disposal. We go into a factory, and are content with being a little surprised at the sight of complicated machinery; and with knowing that it is a cotton, woollen, or some other factory. We are too often like the rustic, who can see nothing to admire in nature's beauty.

"The primrose by the river's brim
A *yellow* primrose is to him,
And it is nothing more."

But examine the machinery, and we find the bowels of the earth have contributed iron or brass; the surface of it has furnished wood or cotton and other vegetable products; while the animal kingdom has furnished the leather, the bone, the hair, the grease, etc. These materials have no natural relation, no chemical affinities; but drawn from three kingdoms, they are by a mechanical combination made to assume a new form, and to accomplish a new purpose for man's use and benefit. Then turn to the man who is called "the inventor;" we have already noticed what a wonderful piece of mechanism he is: prepared to subdue the world; not able to create; yet with powers of body and of mind able to

[1] Genesis i. 28.   [2] Genesis ix. 2.

make every thing else tributary to his wants and to his pleasure. The hand alone of the artisan is a combination of wonders: constructed to seize and handle bodies of every form and shape; and with sensibilities so acute and so varied that a touch can almost determine their nature; whether hard or soft, rough or smooth, fine or coarse, heavy or light, hot or cold.

The earth being created as the theatre of redemption, it was prepared accordingly by the Creator and Redeemer: not only with all things necessary for man while upright in Eden, but also with those things which he so much needs in his fallen estate. The Fall was foreknown, and provision was made accordingly; not only for the redemption of man, but for his wants while that redemption was being accomplished. Materials were created with certain qualities and powers, all fixed in the mind and in the purpose of God. The knowledge how to use those materials has been imparted from time to time, by Him who "teacheth man knowledge," in such measure only, and at such times as He had determined before they were created. We need not be surprised, therefore, that the uses of some things apparently the most simple, and of powers which have existed since creation, have been only lately discovered. God had so willed it. The art of navigation was known to the ancients; but for thousands of years they had to keep near shore and make short voyages, until a few centuries since, when the use of the mariner's compass was discovered, and a way across the oceans opened. Yet the polarity of the magnet existed from creation; and iron was known shortly after the fall.[1] The steam engine in its elementary principles has also existed since the beginning. The water, the fire, and the minerals, with the powers contained in them, were prepared and ready for use. Water could always be converted into steam; and for thousands of years steam had shown its power in raising the lid of the

[1] Genesis iv. 22.

teakettle, before the thought how to use that power was carried successfully into execution. The telegraph simply applies a power which electricity has always possessed. The art of printing was imparted about the time of the Reformation, to assist in spreading the kingdom of God. And it is a gratifying fact that the Bible was the first work printed with movable metal types. The Book containing God's message to man, which Popery had kept as a sealed volume for nearly a thousand years, was thus brought within the reach of all. No wonder that the sudden lowness of the price, and the multiplicity and uniformity of the copies, caused the first seller of them to fly for his life to avoid being executed for witchcraft.

The knowledge of some of the greatest inventions has been imparted in our day, just as the time foretold in prophecy of the fall of the man of sin and of the false prophet is at hand, when the twelve hundred and sixty years spoken of are expiring, when Popery and Mohammedism are to come to an end,[1] and the "everlasting Gospel is to be preached to every nation and tongue."[2] Daniel was told that at the "time of the end, many shall run to and fro, and knowledge shall be increased."[3] We are now seeing these great prophecies being fulfilled. The world has been opened to the Gospel, and its uttermost parts are brought near, through the knowledge given to man enabling him to subdue it.

What tools Adam had in Paradise we do not know. Although thorns and thistles were not yet, as the ground was not yet cursed,[4] still he would have needed some tools to "dress the garden and to keep it;" as well as to "subdue the earth." The first invention recorded is that of making clothes after the Fall. "They sewed fig leaves together and made themselves aprons."[5] God, however, provided a better material and condescended to teach them how to use it,

---

[1] Rev. xii. 6; xiii. 5; Dan. xii. 7.   [2] Rev. xiv. 6, 8.
[3] Dan. xii. 4.   [4] Gen. iii. 18.   [5] Gen. iii. 7.

for "unto Adam and to his wife did the Lord God make coats of skins and clothed them."[1] "Cain was a tiller of the ground," and necessarily must have had some implements to do it with. Abel, when he "brought of the firstlings of his flock and of the fat thereof,"[2] as an offering unto the Lord, must have used tools in preparing his sacrifice. Cain afterward builded a city.[3] The preparation of the materials to build a city, the erection of buildings, and the necessary occupation and wants of those living in cities, at once convey the idea of an advanced stage in knowledge of tools, of machinery, and of the arts, even in that early age of the world.

It is a truism, incidental, however, to fallen nature only, that "Necessity is the mother of invention." Had man not sinned, all his powers, created, as they were perfect, would have been constantly and joyfully alive and active with immortal energy. A blight, part of the "dying death," passed upon those powers at the Fall; and it has required necessity, or the grace of God, to keep them alive. It is a curious fact, that the first inventions spoken of were after man had sinned; and were to supply wants occasioned by sin: and also that the first inventors spoken of were of the descendants of Cain, and of the "seed of the serpent."

In inventions, reason shows its superiority over animal instincts; the latter making no progress.

> "The winged inhabitants of Paradise
> Wove their first nests as curiously and well
> As the wood minstrels of our evil day."

Yet fallen man has doubtless been compelled to look to inferior creatures and receive suggestions from them. Using his reason, he will

> "The art of building from the bee receive,
> Learn of the mole to plow; the worm to weave;
> Learn of the little nautilus to sail,
> Spread the thin oar, and catch the driving gale."—Pope.

[1] Gen iii. 21. [2] Gen. iv. 4. [3] Gen. iv. 17.

FROM A PAINTING, FOUND IN A TOMB AT THEBES.

EGYPTIAN ENTERTAINMENT. (From a Painting in the British Museum.)

Endicott & Co. Lith. N.Y.

FIRST INVENTIONS. 73

However, in this, as in all other ways of obtaining knowledge, man is dependent upon God. He claims not only to have created the iron and the coal, but also the artificer. Speaking to His Church, He says: "Behold, I have created the smith that bloweth the coals in the fire, and that bringeth forth an instrument for his work; and I have created the waster to destroy."[1] The iron, the smith, the weapon formed, and the waster, are all His. He therefore can well add, "No weapon that is formed against thee shall prosper."[2]

In the brief history of Cain and his descendants we have a record of several inventors and inventions, showing a great knowledge of the arts in the first days of the world; and also that the luxuries of life, such as musical instruments, etc., were early introduced. Jabal "was the father of such as dwell in tents, and of such as have cattle."[3] To be a father implies an originator or inventor. Abel had kept sheep; but Jabal must have introduced some system in rearing and taking care of cattle, and also tents and tentmaking. Paul nearly four thousand years after worked as a tentmaker, being of that craft.[4] Jubal, a brother of Jabal, is recorded as being "the father of all such as handle the harp and the organ."[5] Both stringed and wind instruments are here spoken of; and also a father or teacher of musical composition and mechanical harmony. From Jubal probably comes the word jubilee, first celebrated with the sound of the trumpet. The Psalmist, when calling upon all things that hath breath to praise the Lord, adds: "Praise him with stringed instruments and organs."[6] The seed of Cain first invented musical instruments; though afterward used to assist in praising the Lord, it is a sad fact that the seed of the Serpent now often uses them, even in the Lord's house, for the very purpose of robbing Him of his praise.

The next verse of the narrative shows us a much more

---

[1] Isaiah liv. 16.   [3] Gen. iv. 20.   [5] Gen. iv. 21.
[2] Isaiah liv. 17.   [4] Acts xviii. 3.   [6] Ps. cl. 4.

extensive knowledge of the arts and sciences. Tubal-Cain, a member of the same family, was "an instructer of every artificer in brass and iron."[1] He is supposed to be the Vulcan of the ancients, one of their fictitious deities often mentioned. It is the same name, simply shortened; and the occupations of both were the same. To be a teacher of every artificer, he must have had a thorough knowledge of ores and of metals; of the art of smelting and of mixing them; and of moulding or beating them into the required form: and also a considerable acquaintance with chemistry. By tradition, Vulcan was celebrated as a manufacturer of arms and armor. As Tubal-Cain was a descendant of Cain, living among his followers, and the earth becoming filled with violence, we may well suppose that he introduced their manufacture and excelled in making them.

A Jewish tradition ascribes to Naamah, sister of Tubal-Cain, the introduction of ornaments in female dress. It is not improbable that Cain's city was the Paris of the world, and that his children led the fashions, for it appears they drew all the world after them.

We may infer from the simple directions given when the ark was built, that many things in relation to ship-building were then already known. The cities built shortly after the flood show that the arts had not been lost, but that the knowledge of them must have been preserved by those in the ark. The ruins of those cities surprise us with their magnitude and grandeur. The huge stones used in their buildings, the immense statues and columns of their temples, as also the pyramids, etc., show that they were accustomed to mammoth works.

In the account of the preparation of the materials for the tabernacle, we have a comprehensive exposition of the arts in almost every department. "There was the hewing, sawing, planing, joining, carving and gilding of wood. There

---

[1] Genesis iv. 22.

was the melting, casting, beating, boring, and engraving of metals. There was the spinning, weaving, dyeing, bleaching, sewing, and embroidering of fabrics; the tanning and coloring of skins. There was work in gold, silver, and brass; in blue, purple, and scarlet; in fine linen and in goats' hair. There was the polishing and engraving of precious stones," etc., etc. The Lord not only gave special directions how the tabernacle and every thing pertaining to it were to be made, but He also prepared and called the workmen: "The Lord spake unto Moses, saying, See, I have called by name Bezaleel, the son of Uri, the son of Hur, of the tribe of Judah; and I have filled him with the Spirit of God, in wisdom, and in understanding, and in knowledge, and in all manner of workmanship." "And I, behold, I have given with him Aholiab, the son of Ahisamach, of the tribe of Dan: and in the hearts of all that are wise hearted I have put wisdom, that they may make all that I have commanded thee."[1]

When we remember that all this was over three thousand years ago, and that nearly three thousand years before that there were teachers of the arts and of music in the family of Cain, we must acknowledge that in the early days of the world they knew more than we are apt to give them credit for. In fact the ancients were acquainted with arts which are now lost. Let us also bear in mind that a knowledge of the arts and civilization, have no power in themselves to purify the heart or to improve society. The descendants of Cain, while making the greatest progress in worldly knowledge, were growing greater monsters in crime. Education, without Christianity, makes men more powerful and more cunning in carrying out their evil designs, and therefore makes them more dangerous.

[1] Exodus xxxi. 2, 6.

CHAPTER XX.

THE CHURCH—ITS PRESERVATION A CONSTANT MIRACLE.

LET us now turn to watch the progress of that perpetual wonder in the world, the Church : in which, above all other things, the Creator has always taken the greatest interest ; as a theatre for which He created the world ; that by it He might make known his manifold wisdom to principalities and powers in heavenly places.[1] The progress, the very existence of that church in the world, is a wonder. Its preservation is a perpetual miracle : indeed, every soul added to it is such ; for that soul is "born again ;"[2] is raised from the dead ;"[3] and is a "new creation,"[4] in which has been displayed " a working of the mighty power, of the exceeding greatness of the power"[5] of the Almighty.

In looking back through the six thousand years of the world's history, we see a litle band, like a few straggling sheep journeying through a wilderness filled with wolves, weak, defenseless, tottering, surrounded by enemies, and at times so few in number that they are to be found only in a single family. It is the seed of the promise, reduced just before the flood to part of a family of eight persons, while the seed of the serpent numbered perhaps a thousand millions. Out of the successive generations on the earth, they are for twenty-three hundred years to be found only in a single line from father to son ; and then for seventeen hundred years after, they count only a few in a single nation, out of the many nations of the world.[6] They were a very

---

[1] Eph. iii. 9. [3] Eph. ii. 1. [5] Eph. i. 19.
[2] John i. 13; iii. 3. [4] Eph. ii. 10; 2 Cor. v. 17. [6] Rom. ix. 6; xi. 3.

"little flock"[1] in the time of our Saviour. And each member of that flock is so weak, so prone to sin and death, as to be continually forced to cry out, "O wretched man that I am! who shall deliver me from the body of this death?"[2] and yet so strong in the Lord as to be able at the same time to shout, "I thank God, which giveth us the victory, through Jesus Christ our Lord."[2]

We have seen the first member added to this flock murdered for his faith by his own brother. The record, four thousand years afterwards, in speaking of the faith and trials of some of the members of this flock, as during that long period it had been journeying through the world, hated by all men, says: "others were tortured not accepting deliverance; that they might obtain a better resurrection: and others had trial, of cruel mockings and scourgings, yea, moreover of bonds and imprisonments: they were stoned, they were sawn asunder, were tempted, were slain with the sword: they wandered about in sheepskins and goatskins; being destitute, afflicted, tormented (of whom the world was not worthy): they wandered in deserts,"[3] etc., etc. Read the experience of Paul before he was put to death; what he calls "light affliction, being but for a moment, and working for him a far more exceeding and eternal weight of glory." "We are troubled on every side, perplexed, persecuted, cast down, alway delivered unto death for Jesus' sake; in stripes above measure, in prisons frequent, in deaths oft. Of the Jews five times received I forty stripes save one. Thrice was I beaten with rods, once was I stoned,"[4] etc., etc. We see from time to time the most powerful monarchs of the greatest empires of the world trying to annihilate them with fire and sword; and if possible to blot out their very name from the earth. We see Satan and his angels, with increasing malignity, using all their arts to tempt, to

---

[1] Luke xii. 32.
[2] Rom. vii. 24, 25; 1 Cor. xv. 57.
[3] Heb. xi. 35, 36.
[4] 2 Cor. iv. 8, 9, 17; xi. 23

corrupt and destroy them; at times to effect his purpose, getting "his children"[1] in possession of the high places of the visible church, and even entering himself into some of its members,[2] as he did when Jesus was betrayed. We see the visible church procuring the death of the Shepherd of this flock, then stoning Stephen under pretence of blasphemy;[3] and then causing a great persecution; the high priest himself for this purpose giving letters to a man "breathing out threatenings and slaughter against the disciples of the Lord."[4]

We see antichrist in the church itself, having obtained power over the kingdoms of the world twelve hundred and sixty years, endeavoring to destroy the followers of the Lord Jesus wherever they could be found, by massacres, by wars, and by the inquisition. Truly, long since would the church have disappeared from the earth, and all knowledge of God been banished from it, and the world have become a hell, had not God in his sovereignty and his mercy determined otherwise. As ten righteous men would have saved Sodom,[5] so the presence of the Church of Jesus Christ, "the salt of the earth,"[6] now saves the world. When the last member of it is gathered in, the world will be burned up.

We see all this malice of the seed of the serpent overruled and even made subservient to God's purposes of saving and extending his church. "Herod and Pontius Pilate, with the Gentiles and the people of Israel, were gathered together against the Lord and against his Christ, for to do whatsoever God's hand and counsel determined before to be done."[7]

We see the provision made for the salvation of that church by the Saviour giving himself for her: and then giving her His Word, the ministry, and the sacraments for her edification. We see that there always has been but one true

---

[1] John viii. 44.   [2] Luke xxii. 3.   [3] Acts vi. 13.   [4] Acts ix. 1.
[5] Gen. xviii. 32.   [6] Matt. v. 13.   [7] Acts iv. 26, 28; ii. 23; viii. 4.

church, and but one way of salvation from the beginning; and that is by faith in the testimony of God and in the sacrifice of the Lord Jesus Christ.

That church has always had a government and a form of worship which separated it from the world; making it a visible church. The members of it in all ages have been known as the Lord's people; and have "called themselves by the name of the Lord."[1] They now call themselves after His name, Christians.[2] The true members of that church—"for they are not all Israel which are of Israel"[3]—are called "the chosen," "the elect," "the sons of God;" "the sheep for whom the Shepherd laid down his life,"[4] and whom He leads through the wilderness "like a flock,"[5] etc., etc. While Cain and the seed of the serpent have always fled from the face of the LORD, the church has always enjoyed the special manifestations of His presence: sometimes visibly, as in the cloud in the wilderness, and when "God was manifest in the flesh."[6] He has said, "Where two or three are gathered together in my name, there am I in the midst of them,"[7] "Lo, I am with you alway, even unto the end of the world."[8] After the ascension of our Lord, the Holy Ghost the promised Comforter, came to abide with the flock for ever.[9] And since the day of Pentecost the Church has enjoyed His presence and His teachings. Every true member of it is a "temple of the Holy Ghost,"[10] and has angels ministering to him or her: for the angels are "sent forth to minister for them who shall be heirs of salvation."[11] Even heaven was created for them: for at the judgment "the King shall say unto them, Come ye blessed of my Father, inherit the kingdom prepared for you from the foundation of the world."[12]

---

[1] Gen. iv. 26, margin.
[2] Acts xi. 26.
[3] Rom. ix. 6.
[4] John x. 15.
[5] Ps. lxxviii. 52.
[6] 1 Tim. iii. 16.
[7] Matt. xviii. 20.
[8] Matt. xxviii. 20.
[9] John xiv. 16, 26.
[10] 1 Cor. iii. 16; vi. 19.
[11] Heb. i. 14.
[12] Matt. xxv. 34.

Happy flock! amid all your trials, temptations, and sufferings, while

> "Marching through Immanuel's ground,
> To fairer worlds on high,"

ye may well "rejoice, and be exceeding glad; and leap for joy, when men shall hate you, and revile you, and persecute you, for the son of man's sake."[1] "Fear not, little flock, for it is your Father's good pleasure to give you the kingdom."[2]

> "Weak as you are, you shall not faint,
> Or, fainting, shall not die;
> Jesus, the strength of every saint,
> Will aid you from on high."

"All things work together for your good."[3] Because you are "children of God, then heirs:"[4] "all things are yours; and ye are Christ's; and Christ is God's;"[5] The Creator is your Redeemer and Saviour. You may well exclaim, "If God be for us, who can be against us? Who shall lay any thing to the charge of God's elect?"[6]

---

[1] Matt. v. 12; Luke vi. 23.
[2] Luke xii. 32
[3] Rom. viii. 28.
[4] Rom. viii. 17.
[5] 1 Cor. iii. 22.
[6] Rom. viii 31, 33.

CHAPTER XXI.

FIRST GATHERING OF THE CHURCH — VISIBLE CHURCH, CHILDREN AND SLAVES MEMBERS — FIRST PUBLIC WORSHIP — FIRST REVIVAL OF RELIGION — FIRST PRAYER MEETING.

WE have seen the first step in gathering the Church; " God called unto Adam" while he was trying to flee from him. He also called Abraham: " by faith Abraham, when he was called to go out into a place which he should after receive for an inheritance, obeyed."[1] He called and converted Paul, when full of hatred he was seeking to destroy the Church.[2] The Scripture says, " Whom He did predestinate, them He also called."[3] The Gospel is now the call of God. The next step was the commencement of revelation, the promise of the great Deliverer; the Seed of the woman which was to bruise the head of the serpent;[4] promises, prophecies, and commandments, being afterwards added from time to time until the word of God was complete; and a curse recorded against any man who should add to it.[5] Then came public worship; and, as an act of faith, the offering of a lamb in sacrifice: and a lamb was slain continually in the Church of God from the time of Abel's sacrifice for the space of four thousand years; until He who was " the Lamb slain from the foundation of the world,"[6] " a lamb without blemish and without spot; who verily was foreordained before the foundation of the world,"[7] was offered on Calvary. Since then, the Lord's supper commemorates the same sacrifice; and is, by way " of remembrance," " to show the Lord's

---

[1] Heb. xi. 8.   [2] Acts ix. 4.   [3] Rom. viii. 30; i. 6.   [4] Gen. iii. 15.
[5] Rev. xxii. 18.   [6] Rev. xiii. 8.   [7] 1 Peter i. 19.

death till he come."[1] The reading of the word of God, preaching, prayer, and praise, have also always formed part of public worship.

The visible church, according to God's own appointment, has always embraced not only his people, but their households: their children and their slaves. God said unto Abraham "Thou shalt keep my covenant, thou, and thy seed after thee in their generations."[2] "He that is born in thy house, or bought with thy money must needs be circumcised."[3] And he that is not, "that soul shall be cut off from his people; he hath broken my covenant."[4] "The Lord said unto Moses and Aaron, this is the ordinance of the passover: There shall no stranger eat thereof: but every man's servant that is bought for money, when thou hast circumcised him, then shall he eat thereof. A foreigner and a hired servant shall not eat thereof."[5] When the Jews were separated from other nations, as the visible church of God, the stranger that wished to unite with them could do so. For circumcision and the feast of the Passover there was "one ordinance both for the stranger and for him that was born in the land:"[6] as now, the stranger born out of the visible church may be baptized and partake of the Lord's Supper. In all generations the covenant of the Lord has been, "I will be a God unto thee, and to thy seed after thee."[7] The children of our first parents were therefore named in faith, and were trained to make offerings to God. God's covenant with Abraham and his descendants brought a whole nation into the communion of the visible church, and made them his peculiar people. Throughout the Old and New Testaments they were directed to teach their children the reason for the sacraments; as showing God's wonderful works in saving his people.[8] God's statutes and commandments were "to them,

---

[1] 1 Cor. xi. 25.   [2] Gen. xvii. 9.   [3] Gen. xvii. 12, 13.   [4] Gen. xvii. 14.
[5] Exod. xii. 44, 45.   [6] Num. ix. 14; Exod. xii. 48.
[7] Gen. xvii. 7; Acts ii. 39; 1 Cor. vii. 14.   [8] Ex. xiii. 8, 14; Deut. iv. 9.

their sons, and their sons' sons:" and they were to "teach them to their children diligently;"[1] and to "bring up their children in the nurture and admonition of the Lord:"[2] not to it, but as already in it. Thus we find Abraham, Jacob, Joshua, etc., circumcising and consecrating their households; likewise, the jailer at Philippi "was baptized, and all his straightway;"[3] also Lydia and her household,[4] and the "household of Stephanas."[5]

In all ages God has required from his people a public recognition of the covenant made with them and their seed. The Jewish child was in early infancy to be publicly brought into covenant with the visible church by the sacrament of circumcision; as the child of the Christian is now by baptism. If he forebore to join in the celebration of the Passover feast when grown, he was to be "cut off from among his people."[6]

The first public worship, and the first revival of religion mentioned, was at the birth of Enos, the son of Seth, born when Adam was two hundred and thirty-five years old. "Then began men to call upon the name of the LORD."[7] In the margin it reads "men began to call themselves by the name of the Lord." They acknowledged the Lord as their God; and called themselves, and were called by Him, his people. They felt their dependence on God; and Seth named his son accordingly, Enosh, man *in weakness*. Individually, Adam, Abel, and Seth, had before this called upon the Lord with their sacrifices. Adam had begotten sons and daughters; they also had been multiplying; and as they grew up had forsaken the worship and the face of the Lord. When Enos of the third generation was born, there appears to have been the first public gathering of the visible church. It could have consisted only of Adam, Eve, and such of their younger children as they could control, and Seth and his

---

[1] Deut. vi. 2, 7. [2] Eph. vi. 4. [3] Acts xvi. 33. [4] Acts xvi. 15.
[5] 1 Cor. i. 16. [6] Num. ix. 13. [7] Gen. iv. 26.

family. Possibly some of Adam's other children may have joined them; but from the record it is doubtful: if they did, they could not have continued with them, as it appears the whole world, excepting those named in the one line of father to son, became corrupt.

They began to "call upon the name of the Lord;" it was the beginning of prayer-meetings. The names which the Lord has assumed, such as, the Almighty, the Lord thy God, the Father, Jesus, the Saviour, the Comforter, the God of Jacob, the Hearer of Prayer, etc., etc., not only make known to us His nature, attributes, and covenant relationship with His people, but they are also the foundation of their prayers. In all ages the Lord's people have called upon His name: relying upon His promises, that when they gather together in His name, "He will be in the midst of them,"[1] and "that whatsoever they ask in His name, He will do it."[2]

[1] Matt. xviii. 20. [2] John xiv. 13, 14.

CHAPTER XXII.

FIRST CONSECRATION OF PROPERTY—FIRST PROPHETS—FIRST TRANSLATION OF THE BODY—FIRST PREACHERS.

THE giving or consecration of property to the LORD, was connected with and was part of the first act of worship. Cain, " a tiller of the ground, brought of the fruit of the ground an offering unto the LORD." Abel, a keeper of sheep, " brought of the firstlings of his flock and of the fat thereof." The sacrifices were of their most valuable property. How early the custom of devoting one tenth to the Lord was introduced we cannot tell. Abraham " gave tithes of all" to Melchizedek, " the priest of the most high God,"[1] more than four hundred years before the Lord claimed the first born " among the children of Israel, both of man or beast," saying : " It is mine :"[2] beside demanding a tenth " of the produce of the land, of the fruit of the tree, of the herd and of the flock."[3] Jacob vowed a vow, saying, " If God will be with me," etc., " of all that thou shalt give me I will surely give the tenth unto thee."[4] The church in the time of the Jews, in addition to the tenth, were directed to give the first fleece and the first fruits of the land ;[5] and also to offer many particular sacrifices beside their free-will offerings.[6] They were constantly to remember the Levites, as the Lord's ministers who had no portion in the land ; and also to consider the poor. Three times each year, at their great feasts, every male was to appear before the Lord in the appointed place, and the charge to them was, " They shall not appear before

---

[1] Gen. xiv. 18, 20. [3] Levit. xxvii. 30, 32. [5] Deut. xviii. 4.
[2] Exod. xiii. 2. [4] Gen. xxviii. 20, 22. [6] Ezra iii. 5.

the Lord empty: every man shall give as he is able, according to the blessing of the LORD thy God which he hath given thee."[1] One of the first acts recorded of the church after the ascension of Christ, was selling their possessions and laying the proceeds down at the apostles' feet.[2] The command of the Lord now is, "Upon the first day of the week let every one of you lay by him in store, as God hath prospered him,"[3] for the Lord's use: an offering willingly made by the renewed heart of the redeemed, whose first cry constrained by a Saviour's love is, "Lord what wilt thou have me to do?"[4]

Prophesying was early in the church. In fact, every believer in the first promise was a living witness, by his life and his manner of worship, for a Saviour to come. "For the testimony of Jesus is the spirit of prophecy."[5] Special revelations, however, were made to the church, from time to time, giving clearer views of God's sovereignty and of his purposes. Prophets were raised up to comfort the church and increase her faith; and, as we shall see hereafter, foretelling the destruction of the powerful empires of this world, as well as that of all sinners in the world to come. The first specially mentioned as a prophet is Enoch, born in the seventh generation, in the year 622. He prophesied of "the coming of the Lord with ten thousand of his saints, to execute judgment upon all, and to convince all that are ungodly among them of all their ungodly deeds, and of all their hard speeches which they have spoken against him."[6] He doubtless referred to the coming flood, as well as to the last great day.

Enoch not only thus prophesied of the judgment, and that "them also which sleep in Jesus will God bring with him;"[7] but he was himself also a witness to the resurrection of the body: for after walking with God till he was three hundred and sixty-five years old, when he had lived only about one

---
[1] Deut. xvi. 16.   [2] Acts ii. 45, iv. 35.   [3] 1 Cor. xvi. 2.   [4] Acts ix. 6.
[5] Rev. xix. 10.   [6] Jude 15.   [7] 1 Thess. iv. 14.

third of the usual length of men's lives in those days, "by faith Enoch was translated that he should not see death ; and was not found, because God had translated him : for before his translation he had this testimony, that he pleased God."[1] There was a proof of the glorious change to take place in the bodies of believers in each important era of the Church ; Enoch in the patriarchal, Elijah in the Jewish or prophetical, and the Saviour and the bodies of the saints raised after his resurrection, in the Gospel era.

Preaching has always been in the Church. The patriarchs were not only the priests, elders, and rulers in the church, but were the teachers of the children.[2] In the Jewish church, in lieu of the first born sons, the Lord took the tribe of Levi, and the Levites were specially consecrated to the Lord's service. Part of their duty was to preach ; they were " to teach Jacob God's judgments, and Israel his law :"[3] "they taught all Israel :"[4] "they read in the book in the law of God distinctly, and gave the sense, and caused them to understand the reading."[5] We wonder when we think that for four thousand years the knowledge of the true God, and of the way of salvation by faith, was confined to the line of a single family and to a single nation : that thousands of millions of men, in successive generations, had died without God and without hope, before the injunction was given to the Church, " Go ye into all the world, and preach the Gospel to every creature."[6] We can only say, "Even so, Father : for so it seemed good in thy sight."[7] Yet when we consider men's hatred to God, to the Gospel, and to those who preach it, we are the more surprised that it is sent to them at all.

Enoch must have preached when he prophecied. Noah is expressly spoken of, as " a preacher of righteousness."[8] His preaching, however, was only a constant " savour of death

---

[1] Heb. xi. 5.   [3] Deut. xxxiii. 10.   [5] Neh. viii. 8.
[2] Gen. xvii. 23; xviii. 19.   [4] 2 Chron. xxxv. 3.   [6] Mark xvi. 15.
[7] Matt. xi. 26.   [8] 2 Peter ii. 5 ; 1 Peter iii. 19, 20.

unto death;"[1] for it is worthy of notice that he preached and warned men a hundred and twenty years, while building the ark, without to our knowledge making a single convert. In gathering his elect, "it pleased God by the foolishness of preaching to save them that believe."[2] For "faith cometh by hearing, and hearing by the word of God."[3] Paul asks, "How shall they believe in him of whom they have not heard? and how shall they hear without a preacher."[3] It is a fearful fact that the Gospel is also to be preached as a testimony against men; as it was in the days of Noah, and when it was preached to Chorazin and Bethsaida; although, as then, men will reject it. Our Lord says, "this gospel of the kingdom shall be preached in all the world for a witness unto all nations; and then shall the end come."[4]

The Lord's word to Ezekiel, when He sent by him a message to the visible church, is remarkable: showing that the duty of preachers, as "ambassadors for Christ," is simply from their heart to deliver His message, and leave the results with Him. The LORD said unto Ezekiel, "Get thee unto the house of Israel, and speak with my words unto them. For thou art not sent to a people of a strange speech, and of an hard language, but to the house of Israel. Surely, had I sent thee to them, they would have hearkened unto thee. *But the house of Israel will not hearken unto thee.*" "Fear them not, neither be dismayed; all my words that I shall speak unto thee receive into thine heart, and speak unto them and tell them, Thus saith the LORD GOD: whether they will hear, or whether they will forbear."[5]

---

[1] 2 Cor. ii. 16. [2] 1 Cor. i. 21. [3] Rom. x. 14, 17.
[4] Matt xxiv. 14. [5] Ezek. iii. 4 to 11.

CHAPTER XXIII.

FIRST LENGTH OF HUMAN LIFE—INCREASE OF POPULATION AND DECREASE OF THE CHURCH—MIXED MARRIAGES—FIRST GIANTS—GIGANTIC ANIMALS.

A VERY remarkable feature of the period before the flood was the extraordinary length of men's lives. They lived nearly a thousand years. Had men continued to live that long, the fathers of the men now living might have conversed with the Saviour when he was on the earth, and their great-grandfathers could almost have talked with Adam. We have a record of but a few persons who lived before the flood, and those in two distinct lines only : that of some of the descendants of Cain, the age of none of whom is given, and that of Seth and some of his descendants, probably not the oldest sons, but such as were chosen to be the seed of the promise and to be the progenitors of the Lord Jesus Christ.

Adam lived nine hundred and thirty years, equal however to a longer life, as he never was a child. Methuselah, whose age is the longest recorded, lived nine hundred and sixty-nine years. Most of the others lived nearly as long. Noah was six hundred years old at the time of the flood, and lived three hundred and fifty years after it, making his age at the time of his death nine hundred and fifty years. He was probably the oldest man that has been in the world since the flood ; as after it men's lives were gradually shortened, until Moses, a few generations afterward, was constrained to write,

"The days of our years are three-score years and ten; and if by reason of strength they be four-score years, yet is their strength labor and sorrow; for it is soon cut off, and we fly away."[1] However, the life even of Methuselah was only as a dream or a vapor; for it is as easy to look back a thousand years as eighty, they are both as yesterday when they are past. The record, in the fifth chapter of Genesis, of the lives of the patriarchs before the flood is wonderfully concise.

The increase of the population of the world before the flood must have been very rapid. Jacob's descendants increased, while in Egypt, only two or three hundred years, to millions. What must have been the population of the world, when men lived nearly a thousand years begetting sons and daughters!

The church diminished in numbers as the world increased in population. The patriarchs saw the millions of their descendants, with one or two exceptions, in one immense, continuous stream, separating themselves from God, joining the children of the world, and going to perdition. Methuselah, Noah's grandfather, who died the year of the flood, lived seven hundred and eighty-two years after his son Lamech was born, and "begat sons and daughters." "Lamech lived after he begat Noah five hundred and ninety-five years, and begat sons and daughters." Noah must therefore have had a vast number of brothers and sisters, uncles, aunts, and cousins, religiously trained; they, with their children and their children's children, probably numbered millions when Noah entered the ark, yet not one of them was saved. Truly, "they which are the children of the flesh, these are not the children of God,"[2] even although they enjoy the benefits pertaining to "the adoption, and the glory, and the covenants, and the service of God, and the promises, and the fathers, of whom as concerning the flesh Christ came, who is

---

[1] Psalm xc. 10.   [2] Rom. ix. 8.

over all God blessed for ever. Amen."¹ With all these advantages, how many have perished!

The Bible history gives one reason for the apostacy of the children of the church. The people, or sons of God, married with the children of the world, or unbelievers. "The sons of God saw the daughters of men that they were fair; and they took them wives of all which they chose."² This led them to worldliness, to idolatry, and to destruction. Such marriages have always been forbidden by the Lord. We have already noticed that, to avoid this, Abraham and Isaac sought wives for their children from among their relatives; and also that the Lord gave a reason to the Jews, when forbidding them to let their children contract marriages with the heathen:—"For they will turn away thy son from following me, that they may serve other gods: so will the anger of the Lord be kindled against you, and destroy thee suddenly."³ By these marriages, and the fruits of them, the Lord was provoked, and "said, My Spirit shall not always strive with man;" remembering, however, "he is flesh," in his mercy he added, "yet his days shall be an hundred and twenty years:"⁴ thus foretelling the destruction of the world and giving space, all that time, for repentance, till the ark was built. The flood, however, came without one of them repenting, believing, or being saved.

Some of the children of these mixed marriages became mighty men, men of renown; and, as is generally the case with those who sin against light and knowledge, they became giants or monsters in iniquity and crime.

"There were giants in the earth in those days." We read also of families and even nations of giants among the descendants of Noah after the flood—men of great stature and strength. The spies, sent by Moses to explore the land of Canaan, said, "We saw giants, the sons of Anak, which come of the giants; and we were in our own sight as grass-

¹ Rom. ix. 4.   ² Gen. vi. 2.   ³ Deut. vii 3, 4.   ⁴ Gen. vi. 3.

hoppers, and so we were in their sight."[1] The LORD gave to the Ammonites for a possession a land previously " occupied by giants; a people great, and many, and tall, called Zamzummims : "[2] and He gave to the Moabites the land of the Emims, also " accounted giants." The iron bedstead of Og, the king of Bashan, one of the remnants of giants, is described as being nine cubits, or about fifteen feet, long, and four cubits, or about six feet, wide.[3] Goliath, slain by David, was about ten feet high. Since his time men have occasionally attained to about the same height. Climate and food will change the size of men and animals. Some of the Patagonians now would be giants to the Laplanders. As the term giants is applied only to a few, it is probable that men before the flood did not differ much from those after it, either in size or wickedness.

The fossil remains of gigantic animals, some of which are probably antediluvian, are frequently discovered buried in the earth, and they may be seen in the various museums. Some of these apparently belong to species the whole race of which is extinct. They may have been destroyed by the flood, or by violent convulsions of the earth causing a change of climate. Some of them may have been exterminated by the smaller animals, or by man. As the earth becomes more populous, and is subdued by man, it is likely other large animals, which man may not want to use, will disappear from it.

NOTE.—Prepared restorations of many of these animals, as they are supposed to have appeared, are exhibited at the Crystal Palace, Sydenham. From copies of these, the annexed plate has been prepared. Some of the largest of them are—

The *Iguanodon*. A gigantic Lizard, estimated length, thirty to sixty feet.

The *Megalosaurus*. Another Lizard, supposed to have been carniverous, and probably twenty-five to thirty feet long.

[1] Numb. xiii. 33.   [2] Deut. ii. 20.   [3] Deut. iii. 11.

SUPPOSED FORMS OF EXTINCT ANIMALS AND THEIR COMPARATIVE SIZES WITH THAT OF MAN.

GIGANTIC ANIMALS. 93

The *Hylæosaurus.* A combination of the Crocodile and Lizard, covered with scales, and having a row of long spines along the back. Length twenty to thirty feet.

The *Ichthyosaurus.* According to Mantell, "had the beak of a porpoise, the teeth of a crocodile, the head and sternum of a lizard, and the paddle of a whale."

The *Plesiosaurus.* Having the head of a lizard, the teeth of a crocodile, a neck of enormous length, like the body of a serpent, a body and tail of the proportions of an ordinary quadruped, and the paddles of a turtle or whale. Length twelve or fifteen feet.

The *Glyptodon.* A gigantic Armadillo, about fourteen feet long.

The *Megatherium.* A gigantic Sloth, much larger than the elephant; its body about twelve feet long and eight feet high; its feet were more than three feet long, and terminated by immense claws.

The *Dinotherium.* A gigantic Tapir, much larger than the Mammoth; supposed length eighteen feet.

The *Mastodon* or Mammoth. In the year 1800, the remains of one, with the flesh on, was discovered in the ice in Northern Russia. It was covered with reddish wool and with hair eight inches long. The skeleton, now in St. Petersburg, is nine and a half feet high, and the body sixteen feet in length. It must have been twice the size of the existing elephant. For some years the flesh of this animal was cut off for dog-meat by the people around, and bears, wolves and foxes fed upon it until the skeleton was cleared of its flesh.

CHAPTER XXIV.

THE FIRST VESSEL—FIRST DESTRUCTION OF THE WORLD—THE DELUGE—CRADLE OF THE WORLD AND OF THE CHURCH.

"GOD saw the wickedness of man was great in the earth, and that every imagination of the thoughts of his heart was only evil continually." "The earth was filled with violence. And God looked upon the earth, and behold it was corrupt; for all flesh had corrupted his way upon the earth."[1] It would be so now, were it not for the grace of God. There was, however, one exception: all had gone astray, "but Noah found grace in the eyes of the Lord. He was a just man, and walked with God."[2] The Lord communicated to him the fact that He was about to destroy all that lived upon the earth; and directed him to build an ark in a certain manner and of a certain size. Noah believed God, for "by faith Noah, being warned of God of things not seen as yet, prepared an ark to the saving of his house; by the which he condemned the world, and became heir of the righteousness which is by faith."[3]

The Ark is the first vessel spoken of, although it is likely small boats had been previously built. It was several times larger than any vessel ever known, until the late wonder, the "Great Eastern," was built. The length, breadth, and height of both these vessels do not vary much; but the Ark must have had much greater capacity, as it was built squarer,

---

[1] Gen. vi. 5, 11.   [2] Gen. vi. 8, 9.   [3] Heb. xi. 7.

THE FIRST VESSEL. 95

being designed simply to float on the water and to carry a large cargo, while the Great Eastern tapers at the ends and toward the keel, to give her speed. The cubit is variously estimated from seventeen and one-half to nearly twenty-two inches. Estimating it at the latter, the Ark was about five hundred and forty-seven feet long, ninety-one feet wide, and fifty-five feet high.

We can easily imagine how much ridicule the Ark must have excited while it was building. Had there been lunatic-asylums in those days, Noah would probably have been shut up in one, and other persons put in charge of his property. To build the Ark and to provide a year's supply of " of all food that is eaten " not only took the labor of one hundred and twenty years, but must also have required a very large sum of money. When Lot urged his sons-in-law to escape with him from Sodom, he appeared unto them " as one that mocked," and was treated as such. We are told that there will be scoffers in the last days before the world is destroyed the second time by fire.[1] Seeing such an immense vessel building far away from the sea, which of us would not have attempted to sneer? Hear one say, Well, old man, when are you going to launch her? How much are you going to ask for a passage? Hear another exclaim, " He thinks he is elected to be saved and the rest of the world is to be damned ; I am thankful I don't believe in so unmerciful a God." The constant preaching of Noah, his godly, self-denying life, and his steady, continued efforts in following God's directions, so that he and his family might be saved, must have made some serious at times, and perhaps made some try to do some good works to buy God's favor in case a flood should come. The miracle of all kinds of animals, birds, creeping things, &c., going " two and two unto Noah into the ark " must have caused some to wonder for a moment. Some even may have felt a little solemn, when all had gone in, with Noah, and his wife, and

[1] 2 Peter iii. 3.

his sons, and their wives; and "the Lord had shut him in."[1] Happy is it for the people of God that they "are kept by the power of God through faith unto salvation,"[2] "their lives hid with Christ in God."[3] It is well for them that the Lord shuts them in, otherwise they would not stay there. The mass of the world, however, went on as usual; "eating and drinking, marrying and giving in marriage, until the day that Noah entered into the ark."[4] "The same day were all the fountains of the great deep broken up, and the windows of heaven were opened. And the rain was upon the earth forty days and forty nights." Doubtless some began to be frightened when it began to rain; while others perhaps laughed at them, saying, We have seen it rain before. Doubtless, as the storm and the waters rose, many began to pray; but it was too late. Perhaps some of Noah's carpenters begged to be admitted into the ark, urging that they had helped to build it. What other reply could he make to them, but, You were paid for it; I can not save you. They who are now helping to build churches and spread the gospel, without seeking to be saved by faith in the Lord Jesus Christ, may well ponder the question, "What became of Noah's carpenters?"

In forty days the waters had risen fifteen cubits, or about twenty-three feet, above the highest mountains; which would be, on an average, a rise of about seven hundred feet each day. "And all flesh died; every living substance was destroyed that was upon the face of the ground, and the fowl of the heaven. And the waters prevailed on the earth an hundred and fifty days."[5]

There is no fact in history better attested, independent of the Word of God, than the flood; and none more universally acknowledged by all nations. Many evidences of it exist at the present day. The highest mountains, in every part of

[1] Gen. vii. 16.   [2] 1 Peter i. 5.   [3] Col. iii. 3.
[4] Matt. xxiv. 38.   [5] Gen. vii. 23.

the earth where search has been made, furnish abundant proofs that the sea has spread over their summits, shells, skeletons of fish and sea monsters being found on them. The universality of the flood is shown by the fact that the remains of animals are found buried far from their native regions. Elephants, natives of Asia and Africa, have been found buried in the midst of England; crocodiles, natives of the Nile, in the heart of Germany; shell-fish never known in any but the American seas, and also skeletons of whales, in the most inland counties of England, &c.

The waters, after prevailing on the earth one hundred and fifty days, began slowly to return to their accustomed channels. In a short time the ark rested upon the mountains of Ararat, in Armenia; and some months after that, when the earth was dried, Noah and his family, who had been just one year in the ark, went out of it to take possession of a new world. Western Asia thus became a second time the birthplace of the human family. This region, a small spot on the world's surface, was not only the cradle of two worlds, but also of the Church. While the rest of the world was left in spiritual darkness, it enjoyed the special manifestations of God's presence, and the revelations of his will, continuously for four thousand years, until the Creator more signally honored it by making it the place of his residence while in the flesh.

"A circle, with its center at Haran, and a radius of four hundred miles, will embrace Eden and Ararat; Babylon and Nineveh, the early seats of learning and science; Mesopotamia, where God revealed himself to Abraham; Phœnicia, where commerce and many of the arts of peace arose; and Palestine, the birth-place of the prophets, apostles, and evangelists innumerable, and the scene of the birth, labors, and death of our blessed Lord. Over this wonderful district, where life was once so abundant, darkness and death have brooded for centuries."

CHAPTER XXV.

CHRONOLOGICAL TABLE, BEFORE THE FLOOD, ACCORDING TO ARCHBISHOP USHER.

From the Creation to the Deluge, Sixteen Hundred and Fifty-six Years.

A. M.	B. C.	
1	4004	The creation of all things in six days. The fall of Adam, and the promise of a Saviour.
2	4003	The birth of Cain. Birth of Abel.
129	3875	Murder of Abel, and curse on Cain.
130	3874	Birth of Seth, Adam his father being 130 years old.
235	3769	Enos born. Seth 105 years old. Revival of religion. Visible Church formed, and called by the Lord's name.
325	3679	Cainan born, Enos his father 90 years old.
395	3609	Mahalaleel born, when Cainan is 70.
460	3544	Jared born, when Mahalaleel is 65.
622	3382	Enoch born, Jared being 162.
687	3317	Methuselah born, Enoch being 65.
874	3130	Lamech, father of Noah, born, Methuselah being 187 and Adam 874 years old.
930	3074	Adam dies, aged 930 years. Lamech, father of Noah, having lived 56 years cotemporary with Adam.
987	3017	Enoch is translated, aged 365 years.
1042	2962	Seth dies, aged 912 years.
1056	2948	Noah is born, Lamech his father being 182.

CHRONOLOGICAL TABLE. 99

A. M.	B. C	
1140	2864	Enos dies, aged 905 years.
1235	2769	Cainan dies, aged 910 years.
1290	2714	Mahalaleel dies, aged 895 years.
1422	2582	Jared dies, aged 962 years.
1536	2468	Deluge foretold. Noah commanded to build the ark 120 years before the flood came, and preaches that time.
1556	2448	Japhet born, his father Noah being 500 years old.
1558	2446	Shem, the second son of Noah, born.
1560	2444	Ham, third son of Noah, born.
1651	2353	Lamech, father of Noah, dies, aged 777.
1656	2348	Methuselah, the oldest man, dies, aged 969 years. In the same year, and in the six hundredth year of Noah's age, the flood comes upon the earth and destroys all living on it excepting those with Noah in the ark.

CHAPTER XXVI.

FIRST THING DONE AFTER THE FLOOD—FLESH FIRST GIVEN FOR FOOD—FIRST OCCUPATION—FIRST DRUNKENNESS.

SAVED from the wreck of a world, the first thing Noah did after leaving the ark was to build an altar unto the LORD, and offer burnt offerings on it. These sacrifices, like Abel's, were with the shedding of blood; and as Abel's, they were accepted by the Lord as "a sweet savour."[1] He said, "I will not again curse the ground any more for man's sake; for (or though) the imagination of man's heart is evil from his youth; neither will I again smite any more every living thing as I have done." He added, "While the earth remaineth," seed-time and harvest, etc., shall not cease. Thus, immediately after the flood, an intimation was given that the earth itself was to remain for a certain time only. The rainbow was then set in the cloud as a token that all flesh should not be again destroyed by a flood.

Blessing Noah and his sons, God put the fear and dread of them on all things that moved, and delivered all creatures into their hands. He also gave them the flesh of every living thing for meat, even as before he had given the green herb for their food. He forbade the eating of blood; a law which was again given to the Church in the time of the Jews,[2] and yet again by the apostles.[3] God told them blood was the life of the flesh. It is a strange fact that the circulation of the blood, as the life of the flesh, was lost sight of for over three thousand years; when it was again discovered

---

[1] Gen. viii. 21.   [2] Levit. iii. 17.   [3] Acts xv. 20.

by Dr. Harvey, A. D. 1628. The fathers of the new world, as representatives of the race, were also told : " At the hand of every man's brother will I require the life of man. Whoso sheddeth man's blood by man shall his blood be shed : for in the image of God made he man." [1]

Like all the covenants of God with His people, the promises and covenants He made with Noah and his sons embraced their descendants, " Behold I establish my covenant with you, and with your seed after you." [2]

The history that God has given us here again reminds us that all men are of one family. It says that of the three sons of Noah, Shem, Ham, and Japhet, " was the whole earth overspread." [3]

We do not read of the gathering of any of the treasures of the old world from the ruins caused by the flood. Although the owner of a world, Noah went at once to work, and " began to be an husbandman, and he planted a vineyard." The next act recorded of him is not so creditable : " he drank of the wine, and was drunken ; and he was uncovered within his tent." Poor human nature ! Noah, now an old man over six hundred years old, a believer, a "preacher of righteousness," exposing himself, drunk and naked. How faithful is the history God has given us ! showing us not only the faith, but also the falls, and even the crimes of those whom He has made heroes and saints in his church.

· The different effects on the children of God, and on the seed of the Serpent, which the knowledge of those sins causes, were shown by the children of Noah : as they have been shown by their descendants ever since. The sins of the Lord's people, and their punishment, as recorded in the Scriptures, " happened unto them for ensamples ; and they are written for our admonition. Wherefore let him that thinketh he standeth take heed lest he fall." [4] Believers are

---

[1] Gen. ix 5. See First Murder, chap. xvii. [2] Gen. ix. 9.
[3] Gen. ix. 19. [4] 1 Cor. x. 11.

thus led to be humble, to watch, and to pray. Unbelievers, on the contrary, act exactly the reverse. Ham, instead of mourning at his father's fall, exposed him. Thus, the enemies of the Lord, to this day, take advantage of David's crime, and make it "an occasion to blaspheme;" as it was foretold they would do.[1] How many there are now building their hopes for eternity on the sins of some professing Christians around them, making them their bridge to heaven! How many expect to be saved by *believing in Judas!*

[1] 2 Sam. xii. 14.

CHAPTER XXVII.

FIRST GOVERNMENT—FIRST DESPOTISM—FIRST SLAVERY—FIRST SLAVEHOLDER—DIVINE INJUNCTIONS TO MASTERS, SLAVES, AND SUBJECTS—THE FOUNDATIONS OF FREEDOM.

THE first government in the world was parental. This foundation of all government the Lord has not only made a necessity in our social relations, but he has recognized it in the fourth and fifth commandments, and confirmed it, with repeated injunctions to parents and children, throughout the Bible. From it grew the patriarchal, the parent becoming the head of a tribe of descendants bearing his name. Afterward, when gathered into communities, these heads of families, or some chosen from them, became rulers, under the title of elders. This name has been a badge of honor and authority in all ages and in nearly all languages. Thus the words *senior, señor, signor, seigneur, senator,* expressing dignity and authority, come from the Latin word senior, or elder. So also the title alderman or eldermen. Unhappily, in many places, the title, as well as the power associated with it, has been given to men unworthy of the name, and unfitted both by age and character to rule.

The rulers and judges of the first nation, whom the Lord called His people, and to whom He gave a constitution and laws, were appointed as follows: "The Lord said unto Moses, Gather unto me seventy men of the elders of Israel, whom thou knowest to be the elders of the people, and officers over them," " and I will take of the spirit which is upon thee, and will put it upon them, and they shall bear the burden of the people with thee."[1]

According to the express directions of the Lord, the visi-

[1] Numbers xi. 16, 17.

ble Church has always been under the government of elders. When Moses was sent to deliver the Israelites out of Egypt, he was sent first with a message to the elders of Israel.[1] And the elders ruled in Israel until they assisted in putting our Lord to death. The office was continued in the Christian church. Even the apostles called themselves elders, and met with the elders in council when decrees were to be issued.[2] Directions were given to appoint elders in every church,[3] and they were called *bishops* or *overseers*, the word in the original Greek being the same.[4] Sin was the cause of the introduction of other governments, both in the church and in the state ; and with the change of government came anarchy, despotism, and slavery.

Noah's fall was the occasion not only of displaying the different characters of his sons, but also of a prophecy, showing what was to happen to their descendants, a prophecy which the history of the world ever since has proved to have been inspired. While Ham mocked, Shem and Japhet avoided the sight of their father's nakedness, and respectfully covered him. When Noah awoke from his wine, and knew what Ham had done unto him, he said, "Cursed be Canaan [the son of Ham] ; a servant of servants [or the most degraded of slaves] shall he be unto his brethren."[5] Thus the first human slavery spoken of in history was prophesied, as a consequence of sin. Slavery, as a curse, descending upon the sinner and his children.

One of the sure consequences of sin has always been degradation and slavery. The first kingdoms and despotic governments in the world were founded by the descendants of Ham. When the Jews rejected the reign of God, they sought a king ; as a consequence, God gave them one, saying, Their king should tyrannize over them.[6] Even civil law

---

[1] Exod. iii. 16, 18 ; iv. 29.
[2] Acts xv. 2, 6, 23 ; 1 Peter v. 1 ; 2 John 1.
[3] Titus i. 5, 6, 7 ; Acts xiv. 23.
[4] Acts xx. 28 ; Phil. i. 1.
[5] Gen. ix. 25.
[6] 1 Sam. viii. 7, 11.

makes criminals labor in state-prisons as slaves. All of us, being sinners by nature, are slaves: we are "servants of sin,"[1] and are "in the snare of the Devil, taken captive by him at his will."[2] When Moses told the children of Israel what should happen to them after they ceased to obey God, among other curses which should fall upon them, he said, "Ye shall be sold unto your enemies for bondmen and bondwomen, and no man shall buy you."[3] And so it proved: when they forsook the Lord, "He delivered them into the hands of spoilers that spoiled them, and he sold them into the hands of their enemies."[4] This happened no less than six times during the government of the Judges, and repeatedly afterward;[5] till, after the crucifixion of the Lord Jesus, when Jerusalem was destroyed by the Romans, those Jews who escaped from the great slaughter were sold into slavery; and such numbers were offered for sale that thousands perished, because purchasers could not be found for them all. Whenever His people repented and returned unto Him, the Lord delivered them from their bondage; and then, He generally punished those whom He had used to chastise his people, because they did it with wicked intent.[6]

History, in every age, agrees with what is the fact in all parts of the world now, that, where men have forsaken the Lord, and where his Word has not free course and is not glorified, there the masses, already slaves of Satan, become slaves of their fellow-men. They fall under the iron rule of a military, civil, or of an ecclesiastical despotism, the last the worst of them all, bringing soul and body into slavery. Civil liberty does not of itself make men free; nor does the fact of their being citizens of a republic make them so.

"Peoples may not rise, though kings may fall."

The people of Great Britain are free, and live in security

---

[1] Rom. vi. 17. [2] 2 Tim. ii. 26. [3] Deut. xxviii. 68. [4] Judges ii. 14.
[5] 2 Chron. xxviii. 5; xxxvi. 5; xxiv. 24; 2 Kings xvii. 6; etc.
[6] Judges iii. 9; Isaiah x. 6, 12.

under a monarch; while the people of France, during the republic of 1793, were slaves under a "reign of terror." Few nations have thus far ever existed on the earth where the masses have been free; or where they were fit to be free; or where they could have continued free, if made so.

"Men unfit for freedom can't be free."

The United States enjoy civil and religious liberty, because they were settled by God-fearing men, and because their laws and constitutions were framed by such men. Let the public heart, however, become infidel and corrupt, and soon, like the so-called South American republics, they will be free only in name: a degraded people, they will select or become the prey of unprincipled rulers; "the wicked will walk on every side, when the vilest men are exalted,"[1] and there will then be constant revolutions and civil wars, till despotism will follow anarchy. The nations of the world will not be fit for universal suffrage until the millennium.

The first slaveholder spoken of is Abraham, the chosen "friend of God," "the father of all them that believe."[2] When, in obedience to the word of the Lord, he left his kindred and his country, he took with him Sarai, his wife, and Lot, and all their substance that they had gathered, and the *souls* that they had gotten in Haran.[3] Driven by a famine into Egypt, he received from Pharaoh, while there, sheep and oxen, *men-servants and maid-servants*.[4] When he went to rescue Lot, he armed "three hundred and eighteen trained servants, *born in his own house*."[5] Afterward, Abimelech "took sheep, and oxen, and *men-servants, and maid-servants*, and gave them unto Abraham."[6] Constantly increasing in wealth, Abraham must have had thousands of slaves; and these are spoken of among the *blessings* given him by God. His pious servant, in speaking of his master to Laban, said, "God hath blessed my master greatly." "He hath given

[1] Psalms xii. 8.
[2] Rom. iv. 11, 12.
[3] Gen. xii. 5.
[4] Gen. xii. 16.
[5] Gen. xiv. 14.
[6] Gen. xx. 14.

him flocks and herds, and silver and gold, and *men-servants and maid-servants*,"[1] etc. When Canaan, through Ham, was cursed to be a servant of servants unto his brethren, a part of the *blessing* upon Shem and Japhet was that Canaan should be their servant.[2]

And what is surprising, heathen masters sometimes received blessings from holding the Lord's people in slavery. Naanan the Syrian, was cured of his leprosy through the instrumentality of a Hebrew captive, a slave of his wife.[3] Potiphar, a descendant of Ham, bought and held Joseph as a slave, and made him overseer in his house. From that time, "the Lord blessed the Egyptian's house for Joseph's sake; and the blessing of the Lord was upon all that he had."[4]

The Lord has always recognized and sanctioned the relationship of master and slave thus instituted. It has a perpetual recognition in two of the Ten Commandments, the fourth and the tenth. The masters were not only blessed by the relationship, but in some cases, as we have already noticed, slavery proved a blessing also to the slave: by bringing him, with his master's children, into the visible church; into the covenant which God made with his believing or Christian master, the slave being made, with him, a partaker of the ordinances, sacraments, and privileges of the Church.[5]

Slavery appears to have been common in the time of Abraham. It was the custom then, as it has been in some parts of the world ever since, for the victors in war either to put all the conquered to death or to make slaves of them. Our own ancestors, the Anglo-Saxons in England, when conquered by the Normans, were made slaves. Among the heathen it has also been common for parents to sell their children. The Lord refers to this custom, when, in one of his many touching appeals to his people, He said, "Which of

---

[1] Gen. xxiv. 35.   [2] Gen. ix. 26, 27.   [3] 2 Kings v. 3.
[4] Gen. xxxix. 5.   [5] Gen. xvii. 12, 13; Exod. xii. 44, 45.

my creditors is it to whom I have sold you? Behold, for your iniquities have ye sold yourselves."[1] Persons were often sold, and children were liable to be taken for debt;[2] others would go voluntarily into servitude. As the Lord has done in regard to all relationships not in themselves sinful, so in all ages of the Church, the Lord has given rules regulating the relationship of masters and servants, or slaves. His law to the Church in the time of the Jews was, "He that stealeth a man and selleth him," "he that be found stealing any of his brethren of the children of Israel and maketh merchandise of him, he shall surely be put to death."[3] They could, however, hold their brethren as slaves, getting them by purchase or otherwise according to law, for a term of six years, when the Hebrew slave was to be again free, unless he or she declared before the judges that they wished to remain with their masters, in which case their ears were to be bored, and then they could not recover their liberty until the year of jubilee.[4] The case was different with those taken in war, or bought of the heathen. "Of the heathen that are around you, of them shall ye buy bondmen and bondmaids. Ye shall take them as an inheritance for your children after you, to inherit them for a possession; they shall be your bondmen forever."[5] Directions were also given in regard to the treatment of their slaves.[6] In those directions, in speaking of the slave, these words are used, "for he is his money."[7]

In the New Testament, connected with injunction to husbands and wives, and parents and children, the respective duties of Christian masters, and of Christian slaves, whether having Christian or heathen masters, are repeatedly and very clearly laid down.[8] The directions to Timothy, and through

---

[1] Isaiah l. 1. [2] 2 Kings iv. 1. [3] Exod. xxi. 16; Deut. xxiv. 7.
[4] Exod. xxi. 2, 6; Levit. xxv. 40. [5] Levit. xxv. 45, 46.
[6] Exod. xxi. 20, 26, 27, 32; Deut. xvi. 11, 14. [7] Exod. xxi. 21.
[8] Col. iv. 1; Eph. vi. 9; 1 Tim. vi. 1, 2; Eph. vi. 5; Col. iii. 22; Titus ii. 9; 1 Peter ii. 18.

him to all ministers, are: "These things teach and exhort."[1] In regard to this, as in other reforms, the Church then, as it is at the present day, was troubled by false teachers, and pretended reformers, who arrogated to themselves more wisdom, and greater philanthropy, than the Lord, and his Apostles. The character of those who teach otherwise respecting the duties of masters and slaves, is then given, and also how such are to be treated. "If any man teach otherwise, and consent not to wholesome words, even the words of our Lord Jesus Christ, and to the doctrine which is according to godliness; he is proud (or a fool), knowing nothing, but doting about questions and strifes of words, whereof cometh envy, strife, railings, evil surmisings, perverse disputings of men of corrupt minds, and destitute of the truth, supposing that gain is godliness: *from such withdraw thyself.*"[2]

It is worthy of remark, that when these injunctions were given, there were about sixty millions of slaves in the Roman empire alone; and a large portion of the slaves in the world were white; and also, that their heathen masters had not only the power of life and death over them; but they often exercised that power with the greatest cruelty. Vedius Apollo, an intimate friend of Augustus, fed his fishes with the flesh of his slaves. The governments of the world in the days of the Apostles were most arbitrary and tyrannical. The deceitful Tiberius, with absolute power, was bringing the world into slavery, when the Lord uttered those memorable words: "Render to Cæsar the things that are Cæsar's, and to God the things that are God's."[3] The detestable, bloodthirsty Nero was emperor, when Peter wrote, "Honor the king." "Submit yourselves to every ordinance of man for the Lord's sake; whether it be to the king, as supreme;"[4] etc.

There is no sin in having power; but in the abuse of it. The government of God is most absolute; yet, without sin.

[1] 1 Tim. vi. 2.   [2] 1 Tim. vi. 3, 5.   [3] Mark xii. 17.   [4] 1 Peter ii. 13, 17.

When the Roman centurion urged the Lord to heal his slave simply by a word, he used as an argument, that the Lord could control diseases, even as he himself had power over his slave to send him where he pleased. Our Lord, instead of telling him he sinned, in having and using such power, gave him this great commendation ; " I have not found so great faith, no, not in Israel."[1] Woe! to them who make a wrong use of power. Woe! to that individual, or to that state, which, by its laws, uses power to keep degraded and debased any whom Christ came to save. Woe! to them, who, instead of seeking to break every yoke, and loose every bond, endeavor to tighten them. They must render an account to their Master, who is no respecter of persons.

The Scriptures tell us, " The powers that be are ordained of God. Whosoever, therefore, resisteth the power resisteth the ordinance of God."[2] To carry out His designs, God sometimes raises up and gives power, for a season, to wicked men ; even to usurpers, wading through blood to a throne. In consequence of Solomon's idolatry, God sent a message to Jeroboam, which made him king of the ten tribes after their revolt.[3] He sent Elijah to " anoint Hazael to be king over Syria : and Jehu to be king over Israel :"[4] though they would obtain those kingdoms by killing the sovereigns then reigning over them. He said to Pharaoh : " For this cause have I raised thee up, for to shew in thee my power."[5] Speaking of the conquering king of Assyria as " the rod of His anger," God said, " I will send him against an hypocritical nation, to take the spoil and to tread them down like the mire of the streets. Howbeit, he meaneth not so, neither doth his heart think so. But it is in his heart to destroy and cut off nations, not a few."[6] Our Lord said to Pilate : " Thou couldest have no power against me, except it were given thee from above."[7] We are directed to honor

---

[1] Matt. viii. 10.　　[2] Rom. xiii. 1.　　[3] 1 Kings xi. 9, 31.　　[4] 1 Kings xix. 15.
[5] Exod. ix. 16.　　[6] Isaiah x. 6.　　[7] John xix. 11.

the authority even of such rulers; and to pay tribute and custom to whom they are due: for such were in authority when these injunctions were given. When a deliverer is sent, or when the people have the power given to them to throw off the yoke; then, they are "the powers that be," and are to be respected as such. In all history an unsuccessful rebellion is counted as treason; a successful one, is honored as a revolution.

The Gospel is the only remedy for any evil connected with any human institution or government. It fits men to be free; *and it will make them so.* The Egyptian master put all that he had into the hands of Joseph, a slave; and this slave, afterwards, was raised to be the ruler of all Egypt. Why? "The Lord was with Joseph, and the Lord made all that he did to prosper."[1] Thus Daniel, a captive, is made first president over an hundred and twenty princes ruling a kingdom:[2] and the captive Mordecai is made next to king Ahasuerus over the greatest kingdom then in the world.[3] The wicked king Ahaz was forced to become a servant to the powerful king of Assyria.[4] His son Hezekiah was enabled to throw off the yoke. How? Hezekiah "trusted in the Lord God of Israel: he clave to the Lord and departed not from following him. And the Lord was with him; and he prospered whithersover he went forth."[5] Afterwards when the king of Assyria came against him with an overwhelming host, Hezekiah carried the blasphemous message which had been sent to him, and spread it before the Lord with a prayer for deliverance. The answer sent to that prayer, as recorded, 2 Kings xix. 20, showing how the Lord controls heathen kings, and protects His own people for His own name's sake, is sublime! The result was: "the angel of the LORD went out that night and smote in

---

[1] Gen. xxxix. 3, 4.   [2] Dan. v. 29; vi. 1.   [3] Esther x. 3.
[4] 2 Kings xvi. 7, 18.   [5] 2 Kings xviii. 5, 7.

the camp of the Assyrians an hundred and four score and five thousand."

The Lord's people may be called to suffer and to die for his name's sake; but they "have the promise of the life that now is, as well as of that which is to come."[1] They cannot be kept slaves. They must become rulers. Among the many blessings promised by the Lord to his people, if they walked in his statutes and kept his commandments, was: "The Lord shall make thee the head, and not the tail: and thou shalt be above only, and thou shalt not be beneath."[2] "Five of you shall chase an hundred, and an hundred of you shall put ten thousand to flight: and your enemies shall fall before you."[3] And this was literally true in all the history of the Jewish nation for fifteen hundred years:[4] and it has been verified with Christian nations again and again ever since.

The preface to the ten commandments continually reminds the people of God that once they were slaves: and also, who made them free. "I am the Lord thy God, which have brought thee out of the land of Egypt, out of the house of bondage."[5] The same motive to love and good works is taught throughout the Epistles, "For ye are bought with a price: therefore glorify God in your body and in your spirit, which are God's."[6] The burden of the "new song" of praise and thanksgiving in heaven is, "Thou wast slain, and hast redeemed us to God by thy blood," "and hast made us unto our God kings and priests: and we shall reign on the earth."[7]

Part of the mission of the Lord Jesus Christ was "to preach deliverance to the captives, to set at liberty them that are bruised."[8] Hence, our constant prayer should be, "Thy kingdom come."

---

[1] 1 Tim. iv. 8; 1 Cor. iii. 22. [2] Deut. xxviii. 13. [3] Levit. xxvi. 8.
[4] Gen. xiv. 15; Judges vii. 2, 19; 1 Sam. xiv. 6; 1 Chron. xi. 11, 20.
[5] Exod. xx. 2. [6] 1 Cor. vi. 20; vii. 23; 2 Cor. v. 15; Titus ii. 14.
[7] Rev. v. 9. [8] Luke iv. 18.

CHAPTER XXVIII.

DESCENDANTS OF HAM—FIRST KINGDOMS—NIMROD—FIRST CITY AND FIRST BUILDING AFTER THE FLOOD—BABEL OR BABYLON—FIRST ASTRONOMICAL OBSERVATIONS.

HAM signifies *black* or *burnt*. His descendants dwelt in the tropical or hot regions of the earth. The Cushites settled in the southern regions of Asia; in time spreading over Arabia to Egypt. The land of Cush is translated in the Bible the "land of Ethiopia:" and its inhabitants "Ethiopians." We must bear in mind that generally those referred to by that name in the Bible are inhabitants of Arabia, and not of the land now known as Ethiopia, south of Egypt.[1] The sons of Canaan settled in Palestine and Syria; and the sons of Mizraim and Phut in Egypt, and Lybia in Africa.

Neither Ham nor his descendants became degraded slaves immediately. In fact his descendants for many years were more powerful than the children of the other sons of Noah, who were to inherit the blessing. Although they were to be the slaves of Shem, yet some of them, the Egyptians, held the Israelites, the best of Shem's children, in the most cruel slavery for generations.

The first great conqueror spoken of was a grandson of Ham; the first cities built after the flood, the first kingdoms established, the first immense buildings erected, and the first great works, the remains of some of which are among the wonders of the world to the present day, were built by the children of Ham. Nations of giants were descended from

---

[1] Numb. xii. 1; Exod. ii. 21, etc.

him : races of men of immense stature and power.[1] Like the descendants of Cain and the "seed of the Serpent" before the flood, his descendants were for many years the mighty men of the world ; while the "children of the promise" were dwelling in tents and in comparative obscurity. How they must have scoffed at the prediction of the coming judgment upon them. How natural that one of them, Goliath, "defied the armies of the living God!"[2] How sad the fact, that "because sentence against an evil work is not executed speedily, therefore the heart of the sons of men is fully set in them to do evil."[3] But God's word and His purposes are sure : though to men they may appear slow in their execution.

The first kingdoms after the flood being established by the descendants of Ham, made them, while conquering others, the slaves of absolute rulers. The devoted nations, which, when the cup of their iniquity was full,[4] God commanded the Israelites to destroy, those not destroyed being made the hewers of wood and the drawers of water,[5] were descended from Canaan : and so were the Phœnicians and the Carthaginians afterwards subjugated and destroyed by the Greeks and Romans. The Africans, bought and sold like beasts for three thousand years to the present day, are descendants of Ham.

Nimrod, the meaning of whose name is *rebellion, impiety*, was a son of Cush and grandson of Ham. "He began to be a mighty one in the earth. He was a mighty hunter before the Lord."[6] The Septuagint calls him the Giant Hunter. According to his name, he was doubtless a bold rebel, fearing neither God nor man ; like those hunters of whom Micah speaks, when he says, "They lie in wait for blood ; they hunt every man his brother :" for Nimrod's conquest must have been over his relatives. "The beginning of his kingdom was Babel, and Erech, and Accad, and Calneh, in

---

[1] Numb. xiii. 33; Deut. ii. 20; iii. 11. [2] 1 Saml. xvii. 36, 45.
[3] Eccles. viii. 11.   [4] Gen. xv. 16.   [5] Joshua ix. 21, 27.   [6] Gen. x. 8.

the land of Shinar." According to some he also founded Nineveh and the Assyrian empire; although this appears to have been done by Asshur when driven by Nimrod out of Shinar.[1] The ruins of some of the cities built by Nimrod still remain; and his name, proverbial in the time of Moses, is to the present day familiar to the Arabs. A remarkable mound on the site of ancient Babylon is now known among them as the "Hill of Nimrod." He is thought to have reigned one hundred and forty-eight years, and to have died B. C. 2099.

Belus succeeded Nimrod and was the second king of Babylon. According to Pliny, he was the inventor of the Chaldean astronomy. He was a student, and spent his time in improving his people. He reigned sixty years, and died B. C. 2039. Before ascending the throne he was probably cotemporaneous with Nimrod, and was perhaps older than he.

Some think that Nimrod and Belus were the same person. A passage of Eupolemus seems to make Belus to be Ham. While another would make it appear that Phut, one of the sons of Ham, also had the name. It was probably a title given to several of the early kings. Eusebius well says, " It must be confessed the ancient writers have very much confounded these ancient names with one another."

We have no reliable accounts of the nations existing from the time of Noah to Abraham, excepting such as we can glean from the Bible. In those days the population of the earth increased, as it did before the flood, marvelously fast; as the descendants of Noah for several generations lived nearly five hundred years. Even when human life was shortened, Jacob went down into Egypt with his family numbering only seventy souls: and his descendants when they left Egypt, two hundred and fifteen years after, numbered over six hundred thousand fighting men: thus making their whole number more than three millions. However, a numerous seed

---

[1] Genesis x. 11.

was part of the blessing promised to Abraham : and Goshen was given to them as the best of the land of Egypt.¹ It was the most fruitful district of the most fertile part of the world; even the women, according to Aristotle, having sometimes three, four, and even five children at a birth.² The promised land did not embrace much territory : yet the Israelites in taking possession of it destroyed seven nations, whom Moses describes as greater and mightier than they were.³ These powerful nations were some of the descendants of Ham. They had "cities great and fenced up to heaven;" and were "a people great and tall."⁴ Before that time, the Emims, the Horims, and the Zuzims, nations of giants, also descendants of Ham, had been destroyed by the posterity of Lot and of Esau.⁵ Thus for a period of about eight hundred years from the building of Babel to the conquest of Canaan, the great nations and kingdoms of the world were the descendants of him, upon whose children a curse was resting to be fulfilled in due time.

We have already noticed that the first city after the creation and the first cities after the flood were built by the enemies of the Lord, by Cain and by Nimrod, and their followers. The first city built after the flood was Babel or Babylon. Founded in rebellion and pride, Babylon has always been opposed to the Lord's people : excepting only when the Lord, in a few instances, specially interposed by directing the hearts of its monarchs otherwise. And although even the traces of the city have long since been almost obliterated from the earth, still the name, significant of heresy, pride, and persecution of the Lord's people, has been given in the prophesy of the Revelation to Rome and the Papacy :⁶ and Babylon exists and will continue till Rome shall be destroyed.⁷

[1] Gen. xlvii. 6.   [2] Hist. Anim, 1, vii.   [3] Deut. vii. 1; iv. 38.
[4] Deut. ix. 1, 2; i. 28.   [5] Deut. ii. 10, 20, 22.
[6] Rev. xiv. 8; xvii. 5, 18; xviii. 10.   [7] Rev. xviii. 10, 21, 24.

FIRST BUILDING.

Babel or Babylon, the same in the original, meaning *confusion*, was founded about one hundred years after the flood; B. C. 2247. The earth till that time had but one language. To check the building of the tower, and to humble its builders, God confounded their language. The place became afterwards the famous city of Babylon. The tower, it is supposed, afterwards became the tower of Belus in that city. Herodotus visited this tower, and describes it as a square pyramid six hundred and sixty feet in length and breadth, or half a mile in circumference at the base, from which arose eight towers one above another, decreasing in size to the summit, which was reached by a broad road winding up around the outside, wide enough for carriages to pass each other, and even to turn. Strabo says it rose to the same height, six hundred and sixty feet.

The tower was used for astronomical observations. The first record we have of these being made was at Babylon. It is remarkable that Calisthenes sent to Aristotle a register of astronomical observations, made at Babylon, extending back from the taking of that city by Alexander the Great, nineteen hundred and three years, which goes back to about fourteen years after the tower was built. It was, however, chiefly devoted to the worship of Bel or Baal, whose temple contained immense treasures, including several statues of massive gold, one of which was forty feet in height. Here was deposited the sacred golden vessels brought from Jerusalem, 2 Chron. xxxvi. 7; Jer. li. 44. It ruins are supposed to be the present Birs Nimroud, six miles south-west of Hilleh, the modern Babylon; an immense mound of coarse sun-dried bricks, laid with bitumen, strewn with fragments of pottery, etc., fused by some intense heat. It is one hundred and ninety feet high, with a tower on the top thirty-five feet high and ninety feet in circumference, rent at the top as if by lightning.[1] "Let us make us a name," cried the builders.[2]

[1] Bible History.   [2] Genesis xi 4.

And so men are still striving to do; although time is constantly proving the truth of the declaration of the Lord, that every high tower, and the haughtiness of men, shall be made low, and the Lord alone shall be exalted.[1]

From the time of the confusion of tongues, Babylon figures very little in history, until the ambassadors of Merodach-baladan came to Hezekiah, B. C. 712, to congratulate him on his miraculous recovery from sickness: a period of about fifteen hundred years; during a part of which period Nineveh had been the seat of empire. It would be out of place, therefore, to do more than to take a glance at its growth, till under Nebuchadnezzar it attained the summit of splendor, with walls sixty miles in circumference, three hundred feet high, and seventy-five feet wide, having on each side twenty-five brazen gates, from which roads crossed to the opposite gates. The king's palace was in an enclosure of six miles in circumference, in which were the hanging gardens, sustained by arches upon arches four hundred feet high, terraced off for trees and flowers, and watered from the river by concealed machinery.

Many centuries before this, a "goodly Babylonish garment" was so coveted that one of them, with a little gold, tempted Achan to bring defeat on Israel, and destruction upon himself and his family.[2] See her the Paris of the world! furnishing it with perfumes and fashions. See her renowned for her learning, her manufactures, and her skill in the arts; renowned also for her wealth, her luxury, and her licentiousness. See her just as she is becoming the seat of empire and the proud mistress of all nations, and then listen to the fearful denunciations of Isaiah, the prophet of the Lord, uttered more than a century before Babylon reached the summit of its greatness. We hear the echoes of his words: "Babylon, the glory of kingdoms, the beauty of the Chaldees' excellency, shall be as when God overthrew Sodom and

---

[1] Isaiah ii. 11, 15; Rev. xvi. 19.   [2] Joshua vii. 21.

Gomorrah. It shall never be inhabited, neither shall it be dwelt in from generation to generation: neither shall the Arabian pitch tent there : neither shall the shepherds make their fold there : but wild beasts of the deserts shall lie there ; and their houses shall be full of doleful creatures ; and owls shall dwell there, and satyrs shall dance there. And the wild beasts of the islands shall cry in their desolate houses, and dragons in their pleasant palaces."[1] And hearing these words, we have the exact description of Babylon as it is at the present day; and also a standing witness that the Lord rules among the nations and directs the end from the beginning.

[1] Isaiah xiii. 19; xiv. 22; xlvii.

CHAPTER XXIX.

NINEVEH—THE ASSYRIANS—SEMIRAMIS.

NINEVEH, the capital of Assyria, was founded shortly after Babel or Babylon, about two hundred and eighty miles north of that city, on the east bank of the river Tigris. The Bible account is, " Out of that land (Shinar) went forth Asshur (one of the sons of Shem) and builded Nineveh, and the city of Rehoboth,[1]" etc. In the margin it reads, Nimrod after building Babylon and Calneh in the land of Shinar, went out into Assyria and builded Nineveh and Rehoboth, *the streets of the city* or the great public or market places. A tradition declares that Nineveh took its name from Ninus ; and that Ninus was the son of Nimrod : this, however, could not well have been, as Micah speaks of the land of Asshur and the land of Nimrod as two distinct countries ;[2] and besides, according to received history, Ninus, the second king of Assyria, conquered the Babylonians and united the two kingdoms.

The Assyrians were the descendants of Asshur, the second son of Shem. His territory in Shinar appears to have been invaded by Nimrod the giant hunter of his brethren before (or in the face of) the Lord. Nineveh was probably first built as a fortress. The kingdom of Assyria was inconsiderable when Ninus began to reign. He soon enlarged it by his conquests and laid the foundations of a mighty empire. He was ever restless and ambitious, and, according to Justin, began the first general wars, and thus broke the peace of the world. He died B. C. 1987, after reigning fifty-two years.

[1] Gen. x. 11.   [2] Micah, v. 6.

ASSYRIANS PLACING A HUMAN-HEADED BULL. (Partly restored from a bas-relief at Kouyunjik. From Layard's Nineveh.)

ASSYRIA. 121

The Assyrian empire was founded, B. C. 2059, and lasted till the reign of Sardanapalus, the thirty-first sovereign, B. C. 747, a period of about 1300 years. Little is known of Nineveh or Assyria during nearly the whole of that period. The first king of Assyria mentioned by name in Scripture is Pul, supposed to have been the father of Sardanapalus. Pul invaded Israel in the days of Menahem, B. C. 769 :[1] having been "stirred up by the God of Israel" to do this, because Israel had forsaken the God of their fathers.[2] Before this we have a partial history of Nineveh in the book of Jonah, B. C. 862; in which it appears that "Nineveh believed God,"[3] when He sent a prophet with a message threatening its destruction. As the result of that faith, we behold all the inhabitants of a great heathen city humbling themselves before God : proclaiming a fast ; and, from the king down, the greatest to the least, putting on sackcloth ; sitting in ashes ; repenting of sin ; and crying mightily unto God. It is not strange that God heard them.

It was by the king of Assyria that the Lord removed Israel out of his sight for their sins.[4] From that time the ten tribes disappeared. It was a king of Assyria that sent the blasphemous message to Hezekiah ; and it was to his dwelling at Nineveh that he returned, after the angel of the Lord had smitten in one night, in the camp of the Assyrians, a hundred and fourscore and five thousand.[5]

Of Assyrian history, written by natives, nothing remains excepting some fragments of Berosus the Babylonian, who wrote in the fourth century before Christ, and is quoted by Josephus. The history of Assyria, said to have been written by Herodotus, is lost. Outside of the Bible, little dependence can be placed on any history, written by the ancients, of occurrences which took place before their day. When they speak of such events, they not only do not agree, one

---

[1] 2 Kings xv. 19.   [2] 1 Chron. v. 25, 26.   [3] Jonah iii. 5.
[4] 2 Kings xvii. 5, 23.   [5] Isaiah xxxvii. 37.

with another, but they also blend truth and fiction, tradition and superstition, so together, as to make the sifting difficult, and at times impossible. For instance, few names are more celebrated than that of Semiramis, described by some as queen of Babylon, and by others as queen of Nineveh : while there are some who, on account of the difficulty of ascertaining who she was, when she lived, and what she accomplished, go so far as to doubt whether there ever was such a queen at all ; and suppose that it was the name of a tribe. As to the age in which she lived, Syncellus, a Byzantine historian, gives the date 2177 B. C., while Herodotus places her about B. C. 713 ; and Dr. Usher, B. C. 1215. Different authors make her the wife, daughter, mother, and some the step-mother of Ninus. There may have been several queens by the name of Semiramis, each adding to the celebrity of the name, and also tending to add to the obscurity of ancient history. Semiramis removed her court from Nineveh to Babylon : and her name may be associated thus with both cities.

The vast works attributed to this ancient queen are the great walls of Babylon, and the first bridge over the Euphrates. She is described as leading her armies to battle, and as a conqueror penetrating India and Bactria. The accounts of her death are as various as those of her life. According to one, she was turned into a dove, and worshipped under that form in Assyria ; another tells us that she burned herself, at Babylon, in a fit of grief at the loss of a favorite horse ; a third states that she was murdered by the command of her step-son Ninyas. She is said to have come into notice in this way : Ninus was unsuccessful in an attack on some fortress ; Semiramis, the wife of one of his soldiers, promised to gain it for him. Being allowed to take the command, by her skill and courage she not only took the fortress, but so gained for herself the admiration of Ninus, that he took her from her husband, and made her the partner of his empire ; and when he died, he left the whole, with

Ninyas, his son, under her care. Ninus was buried by Semiramis, according to one tradition, in a very singular manner. She caused his own palace to be converted into his tomb, by having it entirely covered over with a vast mound of earth, said to be the only memorial of the site of Nineveh after its destruction. This token of affection and mode of burial are disputed by two other traditions, one of which says he was buried at Babylon, and another, that he ended his days at Crete, whither he fled on being dethroned by Semiramis. Ninyas, the reputed murderer of his stepmother, is described by some as a very weak and sensual character; and his successors, showing little of the spirit of Nimrod, became proverbial for sloth and luxury; leaving no names worthy of record. According to others, Ninyas, making no wars, regulated his extensive dominions with such wisdom, that he laid the foundations of an empire which lasted over a thousand years; a record more creditable than if he had made many wars and conquests.

Strabo says that Nineveh was much larger than Babylon. Diodorus Siculus describes it as about twenty miles long, twelve miles broad, and sixty miles in compass. This agrees with the prophet Jonah, who speaks of it as " an exceeding great city of three days' journey," [1] twenty miles a day being the common computation for a pedestrian. It was surrounded by large walls 100 feet high, so broad that three chariots could drive abreast on them, and defended by 1,500 towers, 200 feet in height. Nineveh is made important in scripture, by having two of the books of the minor prophets, Jonah and Nahum, making reference almost exclusively to it. In the latter, a perfect poem, the threatenings against Nineveh are continued, says Dr. Adam Clarke, " in a strain of invective, astonishing for its richness, variety, and energy. One may hear and see the whip crack, the horses prancing, the wheels rumbling, the chariots bounding after the gallop-

[1] Jonah iii. 3.

ing steeds, the reflection from the drawn and highly polished swords, and the hurled spears, like flashes of lightning dazzling the eyes, the slain lying in heaps, and horses and chariots stumbling over them!" A little more than a hundred years after Nahum's prophecies of its destruction, Nineveh was destroyed, B. C. 606 or 612. From that time no mention is made of Nineveh by any of the sacred writers; and the most ancient of the heathen authors speak of it, as a city once great, but now destroyed. For about two thousand years even the traces of Nineveh were lost to the world; so utterly "Nineveh is laid waste."[1]

Much interest has lately been excited by the wonderful discoveries of Mr. Layard, and the museums of the world are being enriched by means of the excavations made by him on the site of ancient Nineveh. Palaces buried under the sand for twenty-four centuries are brought to view; with their walls partly faced with alabastar slabs, nine to twelve feet long, covered with paintings and sculptures; serving the double purpose of ornament, and of historical annals, by commemorating battles and great events. In these the king is always represented as much larger than other men, and is foremost in hunting scenes, battles, sieges, triumphs, and religious ceremonies; all of which are painted on the walls in great variety, and in gorgeous colors. Nimrod, the giant hunter, may have been represented; or the impression may have started from him that kings were to be thought of as giants. The immense winged bulls and lions with human heads, standing ten to sixteen feet high at the doorways, the space covered, and the thickness of the walls, in some places fifteen feet, give us some idea of the grandeur of the palaces; while the paintings and relics found reveal their national and domestic manners, their character, and religious condition: all agreeing with such accounts of them as we find in the Bible.

[1] Nahum iii. 7.

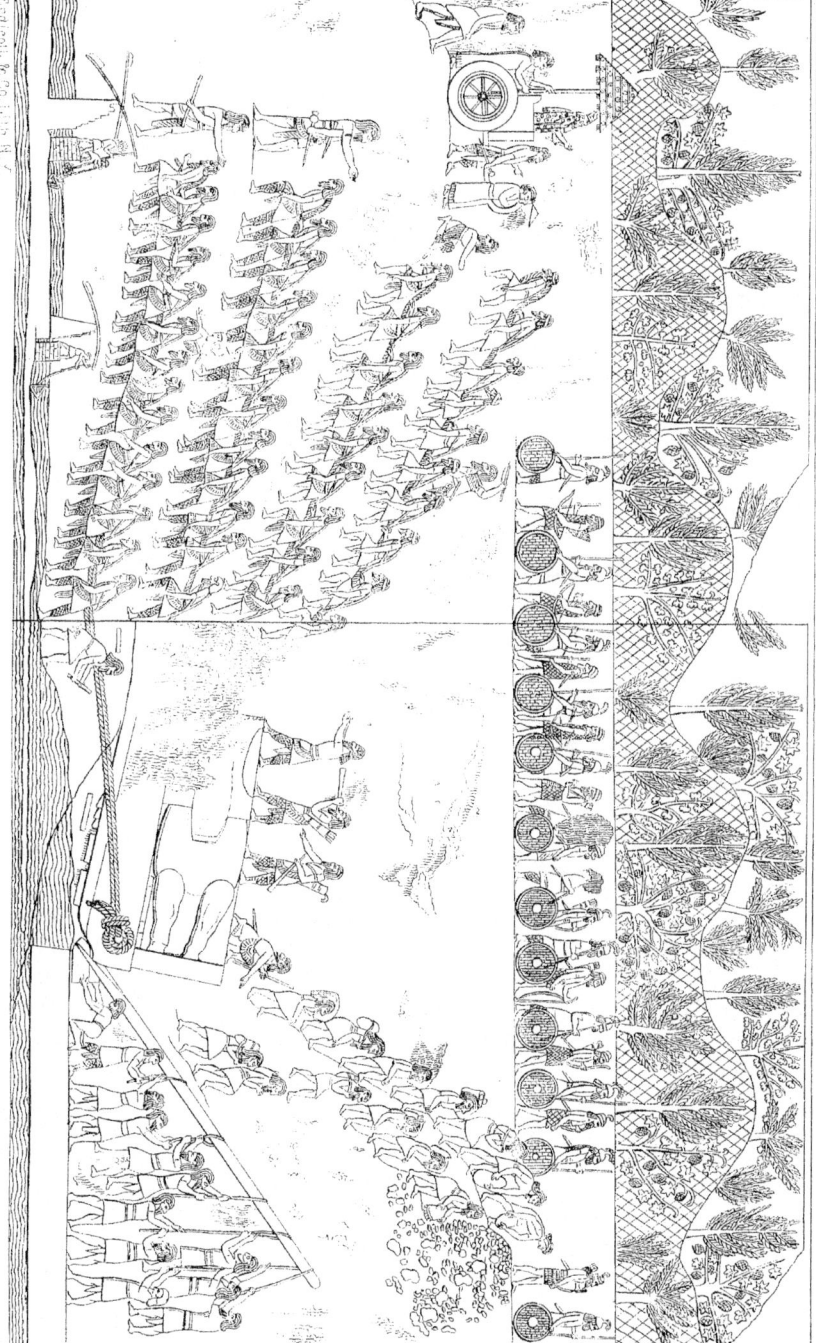

KING SUPERINTENDING REMOVAL OF COLOSSAL BULL, KOUYUNJIK (from Layard's Nineveh.)

NINEVEH. 125

In regard to luxury and "the pride of life," the ancients doubtless equaled the present day. Mr. Layard says, that the Assyrians, "in form, color, ornament, and artful disposition of attire, and in careful decoration of their person, seem to have given the pattern of luxury to all other people; and it appears as if they could never be outdone. An ancient Assyrian, in the very height of the mode in his day, painted his eyebrows and his cheeks, whitened his complexion, sometimes even washed in milk, and had the whole skin rubbed over to make it smoother and softer. He curled his long hair with the greatest exactness, as also his mustaches, and even curled or carefully plaited his beard. If natural hair was wanting (theirs was usually abundant) its place was supplied, as among the Egyptians, by false hair. From his sandals to his cap, from his dagger-hilt to the point of his sword-sheath, all was labored ornament; necklaces, earrings, amulets, seals, &c., displayed the ingenuity of the Assyrian artisan, and the pride and riches of the Assyrian noble. The same may be said of household furniture. Silver and gold abounded; the chair, the footstool, the couch, the bed, the throne, shone with the precious metals, or displayed the most delicate and tasteful workmanship in wood or ivory. Even the pottery was of elegant forms, and the use of glass was known."

From their peculiar forms, the Assyrian letters are usually called cuneiform, that is wedge-shaped; they have also been termed arrow-headed or nail-headed. It is said that these letters were formed with the thorns of the Acacia, arranged and cemented to a block, which was then used to stamp the bricks.

The exact fulfillment of the prophecies foretelling the degradation of Egpyt; the dispersion, and also the preservation of the Jews;[1] the destruction of Babylon, and of Nineveh; the state in which the ruins of those cities were

[1] Deut. xxviii. 64; iv. 27.

to remain, and in which they have remained for more than two thousand years, is much more wonderful than their first growth and grandeur. What would be thought, should a man speak in the name of the Lord, and threaten the total destruction, and the complete and continued desolation of London and Paris, or of New York, and assert that the very sites of those cities should become the dwelling places of wild beasts, and should even become unknown! As we read the ancient prophecies, and see their fulfillment, let us not forget to acknowledge Him, who says, " Remember the former things of old ; for I am God, and there is none like me, declaring the end from the beginning, and from ancient times the things that are not yet done, saying, my counsel shall stand, and I will do all my pleasure." [1]

[1] Isaiah xlvi. 9, 10.

CHAPTER XXX.

EGYPT—-ITS EARLY PROSPERITY—ITS ABASEMENT—HIEROGLYPHICS—SESOSTRIS.

EGYPT was settled shortly after the flood by Mizraim, one of the sons of Ham; and very probably by Ham himself. The origin of the name is unknown. We get it from the Greeks and Romans, who called it Egyptus. The Egyptians called their country Cham or Chamia, after Ham. The Hebrew word for it in the Bible is Mizraim; and the Turks and Arabians still call it Mizr, after Mizraim. It is repeatedly called in the scriptures "the land of Ham."[1] Like Cain under the curse, Ham probably went away from his father, and from the place where the true God was worshipped. Josephus ascribes to him the first introduction of idolatry after the flood. Bringing up his children godlessly, they were led to look back to him as their god, and after his death worshipped him. The most ancient of the gods of Egypt was called Amm, or Amoun, who is recognized by scholars as the Zeus of the Greeks, and the Jupiter of the Romans.

From the first, Egypt has occupied an interesting place in history. A long, narrow strip of land, about seven hundred miles in length; shut in by the Red Sea and the desert, east and west, and by the Mediterranean and the mountains, north and south; made exceedingly fertile by the annual overflowing of the celebrated river, the Nile; trading with other countries, through caravans obtaining the productions of Asia,[2] and enriched by the spoils of war, Egypt speedily

---
[1] Psalms cv. 23, 27; lxxviii. 51; cvi. 22.   [2] Gen. xxxvii. 25.

became powerful and prosperous. With a cloudless sky, an atmosphere almost too brilliant for the eye, a burning sun, and trees which hardly cast a shade; the land, long since would have become a desert, had it not been for the regular annual inundations of the Nile, which more than takes the place of rain. These inundations, so mysterious in the view of ancient ignorance and superstition, are caused by periodical rains in the countries farther south. The river begins to rise about the middle of June, overflows its banks in August, and reaches its highest point early in September. From the middle of August till towards the end of October, the most of the land of Egypt resembles a great lake or sea, in which the towns appear as islands. The land is not only by this means watered; but, when the waters recede, a deposit is left on the soil of thick slimy mud, which serves as a rich coat of manure, causing it to be exceedingly fruitful. In place of the flood, almost immediately, a beautiful garden appears.

Egypt had its princes and its Pharaoh in the time of Abraham;[1] many cities in the time of Joseph;[2] and its immense standing army of chariots and horsemen in the time of Moses. It was said afterwards to have contained twenty thousand cities. Some of them, No-Ammon or Thebes, Zoan, On or Heliopolis, Noph or Memphis, etc., will always live in history. Of Thebes, Homer wrote, nearly three thousand years ago:

> "The world's great empress on the Egyptian plains,
> That spreads her conquests o'er a thousand states,
> And pours her heroes through a hundred gates."

The historical pictures on the walls of the palaces in Thebes, although painted three thousand years since, are as bright in their colors, and as fresh in their appearance, as if just finished. On the outer wall of one of these palaces, are pictures extending eight hundred feet in length. Like the

---

[1] Gen. xii. 15.   [2] Gen. xli. 48.

paintings in Nineveh, the king is represented as a giant in size, and as performing most wonderful deeds.

With Egypt, we at once associate the touching story of Joseph and his brethren, one of the first instances showing how God overrules the evil designs of men to carry out his own purposes ; in that case, " to preserve his people and to save their lives by a great deliverance." [1] We think also of the fearful plagues sent upon it when the Lord would deliver his people—the destruction of Pharaoh and his host— its myriads of mummies—its pyramids, its immense statues, and its vast ruins ; those of the temples of Luxor, and Karnac, and of the city of Thebes being the wonder and delight of travelers to the present day. We remember its seats of literature and learning—its celebrated Alexandrian library—its first and great translation of the Bible, from the Hebrew into the Greek, known as the Septuagint—its Pharaohs,[2] its Ptolemies, and its fascinating Cleopatra.

Standing on its foundation by Ham and Mizraim, and looking forward from this starting point, we see Egypt having growth, and power, and great monarchs of its own, for a period of nearly seventeen hundred years—the distant cloud, containing the lightning of God's wrath, continuing so small as to be almost imperceptible to the human eye. We see Egypt twice used to preserve the chosen seed ; Jacob and his household, and Jesus, the Son of God, taken down into Egypt to preserve them alive, and brought up thence according to the word, " Out of Egypt have I called my son."[3] We hear one of its proud monarchs, Pharaohhophra, or Apries, boasting of having established his kingdom so surely, that it was not in the power of any god to dispossess him of it ;[4] and, while he is speaking, we hear Ezekiel proclaiming the word of the Lord ; foretelling not

---

[1] Gen. xlv. 7.
[2] Pharaoh—Egyptian Phra, *the king ;* *ra* signifies *sun* and *king.*
[3] Hosea xi. 1 ; Matt. ii. 15.   [4] Herodotus lib. ii. cap. 169.

only the destruction of the proud king, but also, that Egypt "shall be the basest of the kingdoms; neither shall it exalt itself any more among the nations."¹ "And there shall be no more a prince of the land of Egypt."²

Egypt first appears in history in the time of Abraham, enjoying not a very creditable reputation. Abraham driven there by famine, had just grounds to fear that the Egyptians would kill him for the purpose of taking his wife away from him.³ Their reputation in this respect, however, was not much worse than that of some of the other descendants of Ham, the Philistines, a hundred years after, when Isaac was driven, by another famine, to dwell among them.⁴ Of the previous history of Egypt, and of most of its subsequent history for a thousand years, we have no reliable record. The history of Joseph, and that of the deliverance of the children of Israel about four hundred years after Abraham's visit, give us a glimpse of the country and of the people; and then we again lose sight of Egypt in history for five hundred years; when reference is again made to it in the reign of David; and shortly after, we read of Solomon's making affinity with Pharaoh, King of Egypt, and marrying his daughter.⁵

The Egyptians from the first were idolaters. Their religion, beside the worship of Ham, consisted, also, in the worship of the heavenly bodies and the powers of nature. It had the peculiarity of adopting living animals as symbols of the real objects of worship; holding many of them sacred, keeping them in temples, and worshipping them with sacrifices as gods. Their priests, as usual, the most powerful and honored of the castes in which the people were divided, cultivated at the same time astronomy and astrology. Of this class were, probably, the wise men, sorcerers, and magicians called by Pharaoh to compete, by their enchantments, with

---

¹ Ezek. xxix. 2, 15; Jerem. xlvi. 24, 25.   ² Ezek. xxx. 13.
³ Gen. xii. 12. 14.   ⁴ Gen. xxvi. 7.   ⁵ 1 Kings iii. 1.

Moses.[1] We shall have occasion to refer again to the early religion of Egypt in the chapter on first idolatry.

Nearly fourteen hundred years after the history given by Moses, Manetho, an Egyptian priest, B. C. 150, by command of a Greek king then reigning in Egypt, wrote a history of Egypt in Greek. He said it was compiled from the annals kept by the priests in the temples, and from the legends and laws of his country. This history, unreliable as it must have been, is lost. Fragments of it have been preserved in the writings of Josephus, Eusebius, and others. Manetho could hardly have been without some knowledge of the Bible history of the world's early days; as in Egypt, more than a century before his time, the Scriptures had been translated into Greek. Three centuries before Manetho wrote, Herodotus, while traveling through Egypt, also gathered from the priests such information as they could give him respecting its early history. He could not read the inscriptions on the monuments. We can judge what reliance can be placed on the information obtained from such sources by their writings. Manetho's first book commences with a list of the gods and heroes, and other superior beings, who reigned in Egypt before the first mortal kings. When Herodotus told the Egyptians of the gods and heroes from whom the kings of Greece claimed descent, a dispute arose; the Egyptians asserting that no gods had reigned in Egypt for a much longer period than the time spoken of by Herodotus. They also told him, that since the time when the mortal kings had commenced to reign to their day, the sun had twice set in the east and risen in the west. In view of such an indefinite period, and writing from memory, no wonder, that he did not make his dynasties of the kings of Egypt agree with others, by a difference of ten thousand years. The history of Herodotus does not become trustworthy, till he reaches the time when Egypt became well known to the Greeks.

[1] Ex. vii. 11, 22.

The most interesting field, therefore, outside of the Bible, from which to glean information of the early history of Egypt, is its monuments, and the inscriptions, ancient writings and hieroglyphics, which are found so abundantly in its temples and in its tombs. As in the study of geology, there are few fields where the ignorance of learning, and the credulity of infidelity, have been oftener displayed than in the attempts to decypher the Egyptian hieroglyphics: and then, by pretended discoveries, trying to overthrow the history God has given us of the creation of the world and its early days. Various contradictory and evidently erroneous interpretations of them have been made from time to time. They are still in a great degree of doubtful interpretation.* The famous Rosetta stone, dug up by Napoleon's soldiers when in Egypt and now in the British museum, with an inscription in Greek, in Egyptian hieroglyphics, and phonetic symbols, is proving a help to the decyphering of them. It is impossible that these records of former scenes and times can, when translated, make God a liar. Written by the seed of the Serpent, heathen haters of the truth, a doubtful reliance only can be placed on them; and none at all, where they clash with the word of God. It is to be hoped, however, that they

* Baron Bunsen, one of the celebrated writers on Egyptian hieroglyphics, on the faith of them carries back Egyptian history to an era which would make the Bible chronology impossible. Of Bunsen's ciphering the eminent Sir G. C. Lewis, in a work lately published, thus speaks: "Under their potent logic all identity disappears: everything is subject to become anything but itself. Successive dynasties become contemporary dynasties. One king becomes another king, or several other kings, or a fraction of another king: one name becomes another name; one number becomes another number; one place becomes another place." With similar vivacity, the author knocks down the structure that Champollion raised on the hieroglyphics. He shows that the same symbol, according to the notion of the interpreter, is meant to have perfectly opposite meanings; and that the most ingenious theories by which sense is extracted out of one set of signs, only makes the most incomprehensible nonsense when it is tried on a second set. *Episcopal Recorder.*

may have been preserved for the purpose rather of throwing additional light on that word.

According to Herodotus and Manetho, the first king of Egypt was called Menes, alluding to Mizraim, the son of Ham. A similar name is said to be inscribed on one of the palace-temples over the leader of a long procession of kings. With changing and opposing dynasties, during the fifteen hundred years from the Pharaoh of Abraham's time to the days of Herodotus, during which period Egypt was at times divided, and had two sovereigns reigning at once, one in Upper and the other in Lower Egypt; and lost sight of the Bible history for periods of five hundred years at a time; any arrangement of the early kings of Egypt in chronological order, if ever practicable, must be attended with great difficulty.

There appears to have been an invasion by some of the descendants of Cush and Nimrod from Asia before the days of Abraham, which brought Lower Egypt for a time under the rule of the shepherd kings or Hyksos, as they were called. One of these probably ruled in Egypt when Abraham was there, as he needed no interpreter, and as among the gifts given to him by the king were Egyptian slaves, among whom was Hagar, the Egyptian bondwoman. A change of rulers appears to have occurred before Joseph's days, as then an interpreter was used, and slaves were brought from Canaan to be sold in Egypt. Joseph, alluding to the national hatred of the Hyksos, said, "Every shepherd is an abomination to the Egyptians:" and also adopted the language, "Ye are spies" to his brethren, which intimated they came from a suspicious quarter.

Among the Egyptian names celebrated by tradition and heathen history is that of Sesostris. For the variety of the works attributed to him, and the uncertainty regarding his existence and the time he lived, the name of Sesostris in Egypt corresponds with that of Semiramis in Assyria. There were probably several kings of that name. To one Sesostris has been attributed the invention of the first geographical maps. In these the different parts of the known world were represented as members of a body of which Egypt was the heart. He was also said to have been one of the scribes of the sacred books, particularly that which taught the hieroglyphic art. Herodotus declares that he saw the colossal statues of Sesostris, his wife and four children in front of one of the Egyptian temples, and also, pillars in Asia Minor and elsewhere recording the fact that "Sesostris, king of kings, subdued this country by the force of his arms." His conquests are said to have extended in almost every direction.

For more than two thousand years the prophecies in the word of God concerning Egypt have been fulfilling. During all that time Egypt has been, as she is at the present day, "without a native prince," and "the basest of the kingdoms." The time is yet future, when again "Princes shall come out of Egypt;"[1] and the Lord shall say, "Blessed be Egypt, my people."[2]

[1] Ps. lxviii. 31. [2] Isaiah xix. 18–25.

CHAPTER XXXI.

OTHER DESCENDANTS OF HAM—THE CANAANITES—SIDON AND TYRE—THE PHILISTINES—AMALEKITES—AFRICANS.

THE history of the other descendants of Ham has much of the same features as that of Babylon and Egypt. There was the same forsaking of the worship of the true God—the same perpetual hatred of the Lord's people—the same early worldly prosperity—followed by the same degradation or destruction.

The Canaanites, descendants of Canaan, son of Ham, formed many nations: the Amorites, Hittites, Jebusites, Girgashites, Canaanites, Perizzites, and Hivites: all idolaters. Moses speaks of them as being "seven nations greater and mightier than the children of Israel,"[1] who at that time numbered millions. From some of these nations colonies were sent out into many of the islands of the Mediterranean and the coasts bordering upon it. Through trade and commerce they became rich. They also became abominably wicked. As judgments upon them, God first destroyed the cities of Sodom and Gomorrah by fire from heaven; and then, when the "cup of their iniquity was full,"[2] the whole people, old and young, were doomed to destruction: the children of Israel, by the express command of God, were appointed the executioners; and charged "utterly to destroy them."[3] Not at once fully obeying this divine command, the Canaanites remained "thorns in the side"[4] of Israel, as God foretold should be the case if Israel did not obey Him, five hundred

[1] Deut. vii. 1.
[2] Gen. xv. 16.
[3] Deut. vii. 2.
[4] Numb. xxxiii. 55; Judges ii. 3.

years: till at last they were completely subdued by David and Solomon.

Sidon, the most ancient maritime city of Phœnicia, took its name from the first-born son of Canaan. The region along the sea coast of the land of Canaan was called Phœnicia by the Greeks, because of the number of palm trees, (Greek, *phoinokes*) which grew there.

Another city founded by the Phœnicians was *Tyre*. The cradle of commerce, Tyre extended her trade to every port and became the first mistress of the seas. A strong city in the days of Joshua, it was afterwards the ally of Solomon, and continued for centuries, through its commerce, gathering the riches of the world. Few cities have been more renowned than ancient Tyre. We have a graphic description of its wealth and glory in the twenty-seventh chapter of Ezekiel: we have also by the same prophet its doom foretold. Twenty-five centuries have been attesting the truth of the prophecies contained in God's word concerning Tyre. Whilst she was rejoicing over the troubles of Jerusalem, the message came: "Thus saith the Lord God, Behold, I am against thee, O Tyrus, and will cause many nations to come against thee," "and they shall make a spoil of thy riches, and they shall break down thy walls and destroy thy pleasant houses; and shall lay thy stones in the midst of the water. And I will make the noise of thy songs to cease; and the sound of thy harps shall be no more heard. And I will make thee like the top of a rock; thou shalt be a place to spread nets upon; thou shalt be built no more."[1] All this has been literally fulfilled. The ruins of her marble palaces, of her triple walls and her lofty towers, may now be seen half buried by the drifting sand or beneath the waters which roll over them. Such have been the incursions of the sea that even the once fertile plain of Tyre is a sandy waste. A few crazy fishing boats have taken the place of her immense navy, and fisher-

[1] Ezek. xxvi. 3, 12, 14.

men are now using Tyre as a place for the spreading of their nets.

The Philistines were part of the posterity of Mizraim, the second son of Ham.[1] Leaving Caphtor,[2] the north-eastern part of Egypt, they settled along the shore of the Mediterranean, destroying the Avims who before had dwelt there.[3] The Philistines were powerful in Abraham's time. In the division of Canaan their territories were allotted to the tribe of Judah. They were enabled, however, for a long period to retain their independence. Their fortified cities, Ashkelon, Ashdod, Ekron, Gaza and Gath, forming five Satrapies or lordships, often appear in the Bible history. Giants continued among them till the time when Goliath was slain by David. For many centuries the Philistines were the most inveterate and troublesome enemies the Israelites had to encounter, frequently conquering them and holding them in bondage. After maintaining a place in history for nearly two thousand years, they were finally subdued by Jonathan, brother and successor of Judas Maccabeus, B. C. 148; and their extinction followed about fifty years after, by Alexander Jannæus, who burnt Gaza and incorporated the remnant of the Philistines with the Jews.

Another nation descended, according to the Arabian historians, from Ham, was the Amalekites. Balaam, when prophesying against Amalek, speaks of them as "the first of the nations."[4] Their country is spoken of in Abraham's time.[5] They were always bitter enemies of the Israelites. They greatly annoyed them on their journey from Egypt, and afterwards, at different times, joined with others in combined attacks against them. After the attack in the wilderness, the Lord said to Moses, "Write this for a memorial in a book: I will utterly put out the remembrance of Amalek from under heaven."[6] Four hundred years after this the

[1] Gen. x. 14.
[2] Amos ix. 7; Jer. xlvii. 4.
[3] Deut ii. 23.
[4] Numb. xxiv. 20.
[5] Gen. xiv. 7.
[6] Exod. xvii. 14.

Lord said unto Saul, "Go and utterly destroy the sinners the Amalekites."[1] Saul did not fully obey: and in consequence was himself rejected of God; and lost his kingdom. His excuse, that he had saved some things to sacrifice unto the Lord, did not avail him. He was told, "To obey is better than sacrifice."[2] They were finally destroyed by the Simeonites.[3] The last of the race that appears in history is Haman, who perished like his fathers in conflict with the Jews.[4] The word of the Lord concerning the Amalekites has been fulfilled.

The Ethiopians, or Cushites, were the descendants of Cush the eldest son of Ham. They first settled in a district called Chusistan, south of Babylon and west of Persia; afterwards they extended into Arabia, and thence into Abyssinia south of Egypt. The wife of Moses was an Ethiopian or Cushite of Arabia.[5]

Some think that Phut, another son of Ham, removed to India, and became the father of the famous sect of Buddha; he himself being the divine Buddha.

The descendants of Ham early took the lead in arms, in architecture, and in the priesthood of the nations that forsook God. They not only established their religious system in Assyria, India, and Africa, but extended it into Greece, and introduced the religion and the priesthood of the Druids, which once prevailed over the north of Europe and in the British Isles. As priests and warriors, the children of Ham thus became the early nobility or highest caste in all those countries.

Ham is still represented by the inhabitants of one of the largest continents on the earth. Kept distinct for thousands of years, unlike the descendants of Shem and Japhet, the mass of the children of Ham made no progress in civilization or religion; and they are at the present day the most abject

[4] 1 Sam. xv. 18. [2] 1 Sam. xv. 22. [3] 1 Chron. iv. 43.
[4] Esther vii. 10. [5] Numb. xii. 1.

and degraded of the children of Adam. They are not only taken as slaves to other nations, but they make slaves of one another; and worse still, they are the slaves of the most revolting and cruel superstitions. Within a few years the light of Christianity has again commenced dawning on the coasts of Africa: and through explorations recently made in the interior, previously almost inaccessible, the Lord appears to be opening a way for the Gospel, and through it for the elevation of the long degraded children of Ham. The time now appears to be near at hand when "Ethiopia shall stretch out her hands to God."[1]

[1] Psalms lxviii. 31.

CHAPTER XXXII.

JAPHET AND HIS DESCENDANTS.

FOUR thousand years ago a promise was made to Japhet coupled with a prediction : " God shall enlarge Japhet and he shall dwell in the tents of Shem ; and Canaan shall be his servant."[1] We have already noticed the fulfillment of the latter part of this prophecy. Japhet has long held rule over the children of Ham. The fulfillment of the first part has been steadily progressing for two thousand years. From Japhet sprang the two greatest of the ancient empires ; the Grecian and the Roman. The sons of Japhet have spread from Northern Asia over the continents of Europe and America, and are now constantly enlarging their borders. His very name Japhet means *enlargement*.

The other part of the prophecy is also being fulfilled. Japhet has been brought into the church, which was for so long a period only to be found in the tents of Shem ; and the present generation are seeing the literal fulfillment of the prophecy, in such cases as the English children of Japhet now occupying India and the great islands of the Pacific, habitations of the children of Shem.

In the many nations said to be descended from Japhet, may be noticed affinities in mind, disposition and manners ; and similarity may also be perceived in the construction of the words and idioms of their languages.

The sons of Japhet whose names are recorded, are " Gomer, Magog, Madai, Javan, Tubal, Meschech and Tiras."[2] He

[1] Gen. ix. 27.   [2] Gen. x. 2.

had, doubtless, many others, but these were probably mentioned, as being heads of nations.

From GOMER, the eldest, we are descended. He is spoken of by Josephus as the father of the Celtæ, the first inhabitants of Germany, France, Spain, Gaul and Great Britain. Three of his sons are mentioned. Of these ASHKENAZ is supposed to be the Ascanius, who, according to Greek tradition, was the ancestor of the Phrygians, and after whom the Euxine, at first the Axine, sea was called. TOGARMAH is thought to be the ancestor of the Turks, who came from the north of Armenia. Ezekiel refers to the "house of Togarmah of the north quarters:" and again, of their being traders "with horses, and horsemen and mules,"[1] for which the Turks have been famous. Of the other sons of Japhet, MAGOG is considered the father of the Scythian nations; MADAI, of the Medes; TIRAS, of the Thracians; and KITTIM, of the Macedonians; JAVAN, plainly settled in Greece; that country being called by his name simplified, Iun, in the Hebrew Scriptures. His name is also preserved in the Ionian sea and the Ionian dialect of the Greeks. The name of Elishah, one of the sons of Javan, is also connected with Greece; Hellas, little differing from the Hebrew Elisha, was the name by which that country was called by its own inhabitants. TUBAL and MESCHECH, the other sons of Japhet, are supposed to have gone north; the latter giving name to Mœsia, and both remembered in the names of Tobolsk and Muscovy.

The descendants of Japhet, like those of the other sons of Noah, while spreading over the earth, carried with them traditions of their first great ancestor; each nation making their history begin with the first king or first man in the world. One colony of the Greeks was called Argyves, from the ark or ship Argos: sometimes they were called Pelasgi, from Pelasgus, another name for Noah or Deucalion.

[1] Ezek. xxxviii. 6; xxvii. 14.

For a long period, the sciences, literature and civilization of the world were confined to the small portion of its surface lying in or near the spot where the worship and word of God were retained. As men separated themselves from that spot, they became more and more savage as the circle extended. In time the nations of the East bestowed the name of barbarians upon all strangers; the Chinese still considering all foreigners as such. For a long time the soil of Greece was cold and marshy; the people, being scattered in little tribes, were rude and barbarous. At the dawning of Attic civilization, Cecrops, an Egyptian, built a town on the site where afterwards the citadel of Athens rose in magnificence. He introduced morals and judicial regulations; and the country became an asylum for the persecuted. Festivals, compacts and laws thence extended their beneficial influence. These, with the introduction of letters into Greece, laid the foundation of an empire which overran the world, and of a literature which yet holds a foremost place in it.

For nearly twenty centuries after the prediction was uttered, the children of Japhet were little known or heard of. The word of God, however, was sure. Dwelling in the remote plains of Europe and Northern Asia, they were acquiring that vigor and strength which fitted them for enlargement. Founding the Grecian and Roman empires, for the last two thousand years they have been the dominant race of the world. Their onward progress has been greatly accelerated in later ages by the impetus which it has received from the enlightening and civilizing influences of the gospel, which, hitherto, has been almost exclusively enjoyed by the descendants of Japhet. Having already a foothold in almost every part of the world, Japhet is yet "being enlarged."

CHAPTER XXXIII.

SHEM AND HIS DESCENDANTS.

SHEM means *renown*. He has the honor of being the ancestor of the patriarchs and prophets; of the Israelites, the ancient chosen people of God; and also of our blessed Lord himself.

Bishop Newton and others think, that the words " He shall dwell in the tents of Shem" should be understood as referring, not to Japhet, but to God's dwelling in the tents of Shem; when He so blessed him by His presence with the Shekinah of the ark, and by his choosing Shem's country for his appearance in the flesh. He dwelt exclusively among some of the descendants of Shem, as His peculiar people, manifesting His presence from time to time, for two thousand years. In either sense the prophecy is true.

The division of the earth occurred in the days of Peleg, the fourth in descent from Shem. From this circumstance he was named Peleg, meaning *division*.[1] We are told that " the Most High divided to the nations their inheritance;" and that He " set the bounds of the people according to the number of the children of Israel."[2] The greater part of central Asia was settled by the descendants of Shem. Canaan was assigned by the Lord to the children of Abraham long before they had it.

Those of the children of Shem, whose names are left on record, were Elam, Ashur, Arphaxad, Lud, and Aram. We have already referred to Ashur and his descendants, the Assyrians. When we read of the Elamites and Lydians,

[1] Gen. x. 25.   [2] Deut. xxxii. 8.

we readily look back to Elam and Lud as the founders of those nations. Aram gave his name to ancient Syria. In the scriptures the Syrians and their language, when spoken of, are called Aramean.[1] The heathen writers also affirm that by that name they were formerly called. Naaman was an Aramean. Aram's name still lives in the country and people of the Armenians. Through Arphaxad ran the line of the promised seed. He was father of Eber, Abraham, and the Hebrews.

Speaking of the descendants of Shem, Mr. George Rawlinson says, "What is especially remarkable of the Semitic (Shem) family, is its concentration, and the small size of the district which it covers, compared with the space occupied by the other two. Once in the world's history, and once only, did a great movement proceed from the race and country, that of the Saracens, which was only temporary. It had not the power of any vigorous growth and enlargement, like that promised to Japhet and possessed by the descendants of Ham. But with its physical and material weakness is combined a wonderful capacity for affecting the spiritual condition of our species. Semitic races have influenced, far more than others, the history of the world's mental progress; and the principal intellectual revolutions which have taken place are traceable in the main to them." The Jewish, the Christian, and the Mohammedan religions, the latter differing from all false religions in maintaining the unity of God, all came through the Semitic race.

Shem lived five hundred and two years after the flood; and died, according to the usually received computation, B. C. 1846, aged six hundred years. Abraham must have been one hundred and fifty years old when Shem died.

[1] 2 Kings v. 20; Ezra iv. 7.

CHAPTER XXXIV.

THE CALL OF ABRAHAM—SEPARATION OF THE CHURCH—FIRST PROCLAMATION OF THE GOSPEL—THE JEWS—ISHMAELITES—ESAU.

THE lesson of God's wrath against the ungodly, and of his mercy towards them that trust in him, as taught by the flood, and by the saving of Noah and his household, was apparently fruitless. The survivors of the flood, while seeing the earth rapidly replenished with their descendants, saw those descendants almost universally turning away from God. Satan was again the god of this world, even before the death of Noah and his sons. Even those whom God had chosen, as the line through which the promised Messiah was to come, became idolatrous. Joshua told the Jews, "Your fathers dwelt on the other side of the flood, even Terah, the father of Abraham, and the father of Nahor; and they served other gods."[1] The other side of the flood meant beyond the river Euphrates, where the ancestors of Abraham lived. They had not, however, entirely forsaken the true God; for God is said to be the "God of Nahor."[2]

It was at this period, when the few who retained the knowledge and worship of Jehovah were scattered, like dying embers almost extinct, here and there over the earth, and the seed of the Serpent were rapidly filling it, that one of the most notable things in history occurred; this was, the calling of Abraham. God, to carry out his purpose and preserve his church, called Abraham to leave his father's house and his country, and separated him and his household from

[1] Josh. xxiv. 2; Gen. xxxi. 19, 30. [2] Gen. xxxi. 53.

the rest of mankind. This was a new thing in the world. God took one man from the rest of the race, gave him special promises, made covenants with him, and constituted him the "Father of the faithful" to the world.

From that time, for two thousand years, the visible Church of God was confined to the family of this man; and for fifteen centuries the history of this family is the only history of the world. During fifty generations of the children of Adam, the family of this man, or rather the descendants of a part of it, "elected according to the purpose of God,"[1] enjoyed exclusive privileges: to the Israelites alone, "pertained the adoption, and the glory, and the covenants, and the giving of the law, and the service of God, and the promises; of them came the fathers, and of them as concerning the flesh Christ came, who is over all, God blessed forever. Amen."[2] They were separated from the world by most stringent laws: and it was necessary during all that time for the rest of mankind to go up to Jerusalem to learn the way to be saved. The darkness of death overshadowed all other lands. Thanks be to God! when the fullness of time was come, when salvation was completed by the life, death, and resurrection of the Lord Jesus Christ, and the reservoir of truth was thus filled, the gates were opened; and the command was given to the Church to go forth and to proclaim the glad tidings of salvation to all nations and to preach the Gospel to every creature. "The Gospel preached unto Abraham," before the giving of the law, "In thee shall all nations be blessed," was the first proclamation "that God would justify the heathen through faith."[3]

Nothing can more conclusively show the hand of God in directing the history of the world, and in controlling the affairs of nations, than the prophecies and the facts connected with the history of Abraham and of his descendants. Two thousand years after the promise was made to him,

[1] Rom. ix. 11. [2] Rom. ix. 4. [3] Gal. iii. 8.

"In thy seed shall all the families, and all the nations of the earth be blessed,"[1] it was fulfilled in the advent of the Son of God, born of the seed of Abraham. The fearful prophecies of God concerning the descendants of Abraham, uttered before they entered the promised land, have been continually in progress of fulfillment, to the letter. The Jews have not only undergone the horrors of the siege, and the loss of their country, so graphically foretold and described in the 28th chapter of Deuteronomy; but they are, at this day, living witnesses to the truth of God's word. More than three thousand years ago, while on a conquering march, with visions of glory before them, they were warned of their future apostacy; and were told of the judgments that should fall upon them and upon their land. It was said to them, "Thou shalt become an astonishment, a proverb, and a by-word among all nations, whither the Lord shall lead thee."[2] "These curses shall be upon thee for a sign and for a wonder, and upon thy seed."[3] "The Lord shall scatter thee among all people, from the one end of the earth even unto the other, and among these nations shalt thou find no ease, neither shall the sole of thy foot have rest."[4] This has been literally the sad lot of this wonderful people for the last eighteen hundred years.

Besides these foretold judgments upon the Jews, there are also in the Word of God promises of blessings yet to be enjoyed by them. In some of these the world has an interest. While telling the Israelites of the woes that should come upon them, God added: "And yet, for all that, when they be in the land of their enemies, I will not cast them away, neither will I abhor them, to destroy them utterly, and to break my covenant with them: for I am the LORD their God."[5] We are told "Blindness in part is happened to Israel, until the fullness of the Gentiles be come in. And so

---

[1] Gen. xii. 3; xviii. 18; xxii. 18.   [2] Deut. xxviii. 37.
[3] Deut. xxviii. 45 46.   [4] Deut. xxviii. 64.   [5] Levit. xxvi. 44.

all Israel shall be saved ; as it is written, there shall come out of Sion the Deliverer, and shall turn away ungodliness from Jacob."[1] Paul tells us, "Through their fall salvation is come unto the Gentiles." And he informs us that the world is again to be indebted to the Jews ; he says : "Now if the fall of them be the riches of the world, and the diminishing of them the riches of the Gentiles ; how much their fullness ?"[2] The restoration and conversion of the Jews is thus connected with the great ingathering of all nations into the Church of Christ ; and the time of this is at hand.

The extraordinary predictions concerning the descendants of Ishmael, Abraham's oldest son, uttered by the Lord before Ishmael was born, have been wonderfully fulfilling ever since. His posterity have "multiplied exceedingly," and become "a great nation," in the Arabians ; and, while the conditions of the nations around them have been constantly changing, they are yet living, as they have for nearly four thousand years, like "wild men," shifting from place to place in the wilderness ; "their hand against every man, and every man's hand against them ;" and they are still "dwelling," an independent and free people, "in the presence of all their brethren."[3]

The predictions concerning Esau, the first-born of Isaac, have long since been accomplished. His family has become extinct, "cut off forever," so that there is none "remaining of the house of Esau."[4] Though their habitations "in the clefts of the rock" in Petra, are still the wonder of travelers ; "the things of Esau" have been "so searched out, and his hidden things sought up,"[5] that not a relic can be found in their ancient dwellings.

---

[1] Rom. xi. 25.   [2] Rom. xi. 11, 12.   [3] Gen. xvi. 10, 12 ; xvii. 20.
[4] Obad 18 ; Jer. xlix. 17 ; Ezek. xxv. 13, etc.   [5] Obad 6.

CHAPTER XXXV.

FAITH — FIRST FALSE RELIGIONS — FIRST IDOLATRY — FIRST WORSHIPPING OF IMAGES — ANCIENT MYTHOLOGY — INFIDELITY

NEXT to pride and selfishness, there is no principle of our nature more universal than faith. There is none so necessary to our peace as a faith well founded. · Man lives by faith from the cradle to the grave. Alas! how often he finds that it has been misplaced. The husbandman buries his seed with faith; the sailor has faith in his vessel, in his compass, and in his charts. What would society be, if suddenly every man should lose all faith? If each should at once distrust his neighbor : if children should lose confidence in their parents—husbands in their wives—men in their friends: if there should be no faith in ministers, or physicians, or in the protection of the laws: and above all, if every one should at once lose all hope of the mercy of God? Remove faith from the earth, and it would become at once a hell : and all men would at once become demons; fearing, hating, and endeavoring to destroy one another.

Faith is a necessity of our nature, springing from our relations to God : for in Him we live, and move, and have our being. Every man at times realizes his utter helplessness, and his need of help from some superior power: he also is conscious that he is to render an account of his thoughts and his deeds. All, excepting the children of God, dread an uncertain future. Man therefore must have a religion. When created, the faith of man was placed in God, and he had perfect peace. Satan tempted him to doubt; fear and hatred of God followed; man's faith became like a vessel adrift: and here we have the origin of all false religions. To fix the faith of man again on its proper object is the aim of all revelation. The Gospel call is, "Believe." He who believes the revelation God has made of His Son, receives the sealing of the Holy Spirit:[1] there is no more condemnation for him: and the word of God assures him of having an eternal life.[2]

In following the progress of the false religions that have been in the world, we notice several remarkable features in which they all agree with one another and differ from that which God has instituted.

There is a striking resemblance between the marvelous in the Bible and the marvelous in the religious history and systems of the ancient heathen world. Some of this resemblance is to be seen among the heathen even at the present day.

All the religions of the earth show traces of having a common origin. All false religions point to early facts common to them all: and, for the most part, all have retained the same rites and sacrifices of which we read in Scripture, as appointed and used in the service of Jehovah: all obviously derived from the original truth, though greatly corrupted and perverted. They "turned the truth of God into a lie."

Not only are the leading historical facts recorded by Moses in the first chapter of Genesis, such as the creation, the primeval happiness of man, the fall, the deluge, etc., to be found in the traditions and the religions of all the ancient heathen nations; but likewise, the shadows of nearly all the great doctrines of revealed truth. Ideas of a Supreme God —of God manifesting himself in the flesh—of an atonement —of a future state of rewards and punishment—of a heavenly deliverer to come, etc., may be traced, floating down through all ages, and in all religions, until " the Desire of all nations" came.

[1] Eph. i. 13.   [2] 1 John v. 13; Rom. v. 1; Gal. v. 22; Rom. iv. 7.

FIRST FALSE RELIGIONS. 151

In all ages the assertion has been true, that "there is none other name under heaven given among men whereby we must be saved,"[1] but that of the Lord Jesus Christ. False religions have aids: the Christian alone has a Saviour.

While having so much in common, there are several other characteristics in which the false religions have always been entirely in opposition to the true.

The religion which God has instituted is founded in *love*;[2] its "God is *love*;"[3] its motive power is "the *love* of Christ constraining;"[4] while every other religion that has ever existed, whether Paganism or a corrupted Christianity, has been founded in *fear*; and its motive power is *fear*.

Having lost the knowledge of God through the Fall, man, in his natural state, never has conceived a true idea of the nature, holiness, and perfections of God. Being impure himself, he cannot imagine a pure God. "Unto them that are defiled and unbelieving is nothing pure."[5] For the same reason, such a character as the Lord Jesus Christ never could have been conceived by man.

In all false systems of religion, salvation and peace are sought by a reliance on works, or human merits; in God's plan, we are "justified by faith without the deeds of the law;"[6] and "being justified by faith, we have peace with God through our Lord Jesus Christ."[7]

In all ages, Faith in Christ, working by love, has purified the heart and enabled its possessor to overcome the world. On the contrary, unbelief and false religions have always tended to moral and physical degradation. This result is inevitable from the difference of the gods worshipped. What force could such injunctions as, "Be ye holy, for I am holy," have, coming from such characters as Jupiter or Venus: or from infidels, such as Voltaire or Thomas Paine?

---

[1] Acts iv. 12. [2] John iii. 16. [3] 1 John iv. 7-13, 16.
[4] 2 Cor. v. 14; 1 John iv. 19. [5] Titus i. 15, 16.
[6] Rom. iii. 28. [7] Rom. v. 1.

As we have already noticed, the Deluge did not wash out the depraved nature of man. The judgments of God never do this. In the history of the Church, we see that even great deliverances, stringent laws, and the separation of the Church from the rest of the world, could not keep them from idolatry. Man must be born again. Immediately after the flood the corruption of the truth, therefore, grew naturally, and spread with the rapid increase of the population of the earth. Noah lived, after that event, three hundred and fifty years, and Shem, five hundred years; before the death of Shem, almost the whole world had become idolaters.

The corruption of religion being gradual, however, some knowledge of the true God was retained; and, also, some of the forms of worship required by him. Bishop Horseley compares the early ages of incipient idolatry, when the worship of idols was connected with the worship of the true God, to the Romanists, who pay such adoration to the virgin Mary and other saints, though still worshipping the Trinity. Amid the general idolatry which prevailed almost everywhere, some persons were found from time to time, in different lands, who still acknowledged God. In Canaan Abraham met Melchizedec, who was so great a priest of the Most High God that even Abraham gave tithes to him. In Gerar, it is said, king Abimelech feared God. In later days we read of Job and his friends, who probably lived in Arabia, and also, of the prophet Balaam, who lived in Moab. Centuries after, Nebuchadnezzar and Belshazzar, Darius and Cyrus, by decrees made public recognition of Jehovah, as the true God. The first to welcome the Redeemer into the world were the magi or wise men from the East. The revelations which God made of himself to our first parents and to the patriarchs; and the history of creation and of the first occurrences in the earth which He gave by the hand of Moses; and fragments of some of the prophecies, especially that of a great Deliverer to come, found their way, and were retained, though in a corrupted form, in almost all nations.

The only account of the religion adopted by those who forsook the worship of the true God before the flood, is that of Cain. No reference is made to idols or graven images during that period. From the first, Satan has continued to tempt mankind, as he did Jesus, by perverting sacred truths. The sacrifice, appointed by God to direct the faith and hope of men to the Saviour, was first perverted by Cain. The Lord's Supper, instituted as a commemoration,[1] not as a sacrifice, for " Christ was *once* offered to bear the sins of many,"[2] has since been perverted into an idolatrous worship by the Papists and other nominal Christians. Rejecting the sacrifice ordained and provided by God, the followers of Cain, if they offered at all, like him offered of their own works. Unitarianism was the first false religion.

Shortly after the flood idolatry appeared in different forms. In Babylon, the sun and moon, and afterwards the other heavenly bodies, were first worshipped. The influence which the heavenly bodies exert on the earth, giving light and heat, causing vegetation, affecting the winds and the tides, etc., led men first to regard them as ministers of God, and then to worship them, as the dispensers of benefits. In Babylon was the great temple of Belus, or the sun. It was afterwards connected with the worship of Nimrod under the name of Bel or Baal, *ruler*. Sanchoniathon, the Chaldean historian, gives the following account of its establishment: " In the second generation of men, during a great drought, *Genus* and *Genia* (supposed by Bishop Cumberland to be *Cain* and *Caina*) stretched forth their hands to heaven, in adoration of the sun, for they supposed him to be Beel Jamin, or the Lord of the heavens. Afterwards in the fifth generation, two pillars were consecrated to the elements of fire and wind." He also says, that after the flood, the first dei-

---

[1] Luke xxii. 19. [2] Heb. ix. 25, 28.

fied mortal was Noah, or Chryson, and that the several members of his family after their death were raised to the rank of gods, in connection with the heavenly bodies. The sect of the fire worshippers, which was very early founded, still exists in the East. Fire from heaven consuming the sacrifices accepted of God probably led to the first worship of fire as symbolical of the Deity. Idolatry soon enlarged itself into the deification and worship of every thing in nature, which had life, influence, or power; especially generative power. The sun, moon, and stars; the wind, fire, trees, vegetables; beasts of the field, fowls of the air,—all had some energies and influence. They became gods to men, as having some of the attributes of the Creator; and thus the doctrine of pantheism, which exists to this day, even in Christian lands, was introduced. They concluded, God was in all things, and all things were a part of God—God was the world, and the world was God. The learned Cudworth says, "The pagans agreed in two things; first, in breaking and crumbling the Deity into many gods; second, in deifying all things."

Becoming by idolatry more and more degraded, men at last began to worship inanimate things, and even the works of their own hands. Then we see a rational being, so called, such a fool as is so graphically described by the prophet Isaiah : "He heweth down cedars. He burneth part thereof in the fire. With part thereof he eateth flesh ; he roasteth roast and is satisfied ; yea, he warmeth himself, and saith, Aha, I am warm : and the residue thereof he maketh a god, his graven image : he falleth down unto it, and worshippeth it, and prayeth unto it, and saith, Deliver me ; for thou art my god."[1]

The degradation of the Egyptians in their idolatry made their worship an object of derision to the heathen satirists. Rhodius Anaxandrides, as translated by an old author, says :

[1] Isaiah xliv. 14–17.

> I sacrifice to God the beef, which you adore.
> I broil the Egyptian eel, which you (as God) implore.
> You fear to eat the flesh of swine, I find it sweet;
> You worship dogs, to beat them I think meet,
>   When they my store devour."

And Juvenal, as translated by the same author, says

> "The Egyptians think it sin to root up, or to bite
> Their leeks or onions, which they serve with holy rite;
> O happy nations, which of their own sowing
> Have store of Gods in every garden growing."

This degraded worship was preferable, however, to the cruel and horrid rites of some of the heathen, such as the Canaanites and their colony Carthage and Tyre in their worship of Molock and Kronos or Baal. They threw their children, chosen out of the best families, into the arms of an idol, which stood in the midst of a fire with arms stretched out sloping down, so that the children dropped into the glowing furnace below. The Persians and other nations buried people alive in sacrifice; Amestis, wife of Xerxes, buried twelve persons alive for the good of her soul. The offering of human victims has been almost everywhere common; it existed in America when discovered, and it exists in portions of the earth to this day. In Mexico from twenty to fifty thousand victims were said to have been offered yearly. In some nations, not cannibal, portions of these human sacrifices were eaten in obedience to their religion. In times of emergency, or to ensure success, many communities would offer human victims, and individuals their own children in sacrifice. In times of public calamity, hundreds of children would at once be seized and offered in sacrifice to appease the anger of their gods. In all ages men have been offering "the fruit of their bodies for the sin of their souls." In reviewing the sacrifices of the nations, and considering the cruel natures of the gods that required such sacrifices, Plutarch, himself a heathen, was compelled to exclaim, "Tell me now, if the monsters of old—the typhons and giants of old—were to expel the gods and rule the world in their stead, could they require a service more horrid than these infernal rites and ceremonies?" The heathen never conceived that " God is love."

The worship of animals was probably first introduced as emblems of particular attributes or traits esteemed by their worshippers; as the ox, *strength;* the lion, *courage;* etc. The Greeks refined upon this mode, by making deities of these traits bearing human forms ; and representing them by images or statues ; as Mars, the god of war ; Minerva, the goddess of wisdom ; Venus, of beauty, etc. They, however, further degraded their gods by deifying their own passions.

The worship of ancestors, and of deceased heroes, was early adopted. The children of Ham in Egypt, as we have noticed, worshipped him, as the founder of their nation and, according to their idea, of the human race, under the names Amoun and Chem.[1] Afterwards, many of the minor gods of the Greeks came in this way. The worship of deceased rulers commenced with Nimrod, and was continued till the times of the early Roman emperors ; many of whose coins, struck after their decease, gave them the title of gods. Even the star, to which Julius Cæsar was supposed to have ascended, was worshipped. Some courted, and even received that honor during their lifetime. When Herod once made an oration, the people shouted "It is the voice of God and not of a man."[2] The Romish Church has adopted the same species of idolatry in the adoration of the Virgin Mary, of the Saints, and of their relics and images.

Bishop Meade speaking of the tendency of man to idolatry says, " It is difficult to divest our own sacred poetry of the language of idolatry, as for instance in the beautiful hymn :

[1] The powers of the two Hebrew consonants forming the name of *Ham* are equal to our *ch* and *m*.

[2] Acts xii. 22.

> Star of the East, the horizon adorning,
> Dawn on our darkness,' etc., etc.

And in our great national song :

> Hail, Columbia, happy land!
> Hail, ye heroes, heaven-born band!'

"How few, in repeating and singing these lines, consider that they are using the language of paganism!"

Whatever remains of the truth were kept in the different false religions which have appeared on earth, in all, however, is seen the slimy track of the serpent. In many of them he is openly worshipped ; in all, his controlling influence as the god of this world is shown. The heathen not only acknowledged the existence of malignant spirits or demons ; but the evil spirit or principle has been worshipped all over the world in some form or other, with a view to avert calamities ; and wherever the devil had most power, and idolatry and wickedness most prevailed, there the symbol or sign of the serpent was most used. "In a short time," says an able writer, "the power of the devil was such, that he outstripped God himself in the number and splendor of his temples, the number of his votaries, and the pomp of his worship. And this was almost always accompanied with more or less of the symbol of the serpent."

Varro, the Roman historian, in speaking of the gods, says, "They call those gods which, if they had life and breath, and a man should meet them unexpectedly, would pass for monsters." Necessarily the character of their deities contributed much to demoralize the heathen. Their examples, and their worship, sanctioned the most infamous vices. It is impossible to describe them without shocking purity and modesty. No wonder then that their worshippers often

> "Sought to merit heaven
> By making earth a hell."

That there were men in early days trying to persuade

themselves and others that they were infidels, we may infer from the expression in the Psalms: "The fool hath said in his heart, There is no God."[1] A wicked heart has shown many a man with brains to be a fool. That infidels have always been despicable, even among the heathen, we may judge from Homer making Hector say,

> "The weakest atheist wretch all heaven defies,
> But shrinks and shudders when the thunder flies."

The French Revolution, in 1793, shows us the natural fruit of infidelity. The convention of France, after abolishing the Sabbath, dethroned the King of Heaven by a formal act; and then worshipped a naked prostitute as the goddess of reason. Speaking of France at this period, Alison in his history of Europe, goes on to say: "The services of religion were now universally abandoned; baptisms ceased; the burial service was no longer heard; the sick received no communion; the dying, no consolation. The village bells were silent; the sabbath was obliterated; infancy entered the world without a blessing, and age left it without hope. On every tenth day, a revolutionary preacher ascended the pulpit and preached atheism to the bewildered multitude. On all the public cemeteries was placed this inscription, 'Death is an eternal sleep.' At the same time, the most sacred relations of life were placed on a new footing. Marriage was declared a civil contract, binding only during the pleasure of the contracting parties. A decree of the convention also suppressed the academies, public schools, and colleges, including those of medicine and surgery. And in this general havoc, even the establishments of charity were not safe. The revenues of the hospitals and humane institutions were confiscated, and their domains seized as part of the national property." The vilest men then rose to power; and the most horrible butchery of thousands of her best citi-

[1] Psalm xiv. 1.

INFIDELITY.

zens, men, women, and children, followed; and all France soon ran with blood. Thus human reason, a traitor since the fall, shows what it will do when it is made a god.

The religions of the world have always formed a very important part of its history. When Adam altered his relations to God through the fall, the instant change which came upon his moral and physical nature, affected his whole future history; and not only his, but also that of all his posterity. Ever since, according to the character of their religions, have nations been elevated or debased. It will always be seen that " righteousness exalteth a nation ;"[1] and, " happy is that people whose God is the Lord."[2]

[1] Prov. xiv. 34.   [2] Psalms cxliv. 15.

CHAPTER XXXVI.

ANCIENT TRADITIONS—CREATION—CHAOS—SABBATH—GARDEN OF EDEN—MAN, ONE FAMILY—EARLY GOLDEN AGE—DETERIORATION OF THE RACE—THE FALL—SATAN—THE SERPENT—THE DELUGE—MOUNTAINS—CHERUBIMS—TOWER OF BABEL—EARLY GIANTS—END OF THE WORLD—AFRICAN TRADITIONS.

ALMOST all nations have retained, through tradition, some ideas of creation, of the Fall, of the Deluge, and of the other great facts connected with the early history of the world; all clearly derived from the same original source. The universality of a tradition serves to confirm the historical truth of the fact on which it was founded: the word of God, however, needs no such testimony. These traditions are worthy of an examination, as they are part of history, and have helped to form it.

Creation, Chaos.—The first heathen writings, which have come down to us perfect, are those of the poets Hesiod and Homer. They flourished about B. C. 900; a century after Solomon had electrified the earth by his wisdom. Hesiod's account of the origin of all things evidently presents scraps of distorted truth. He says, that Chaos (which answers to the

NOTE.—In preparing this and some of the following chapters free use has been made of a learned and interesting work, entitled "The Bible and the Classics," by the late Rev. William Meade. Such as desire to examine more fully into the connection between the Bible and the many gleams of primitive truth which have found their way into the religions of the heathen, and are scattered through the writings of the ancient heathen philosophers and poets, will be gratified by that work.

"without form and void" of the Bible) was the parent of Earth, of Erebus, and of Night. The Hebrew word for evening is *erev*, from which Erebus seems to have been formed. From Erebus and Night, he goes on to say, came the Sky and Day. From Earth came Heaven, Hills, Groves, etc. From Heaven and Earth came Ocean, etc. All these, which in the Bible history appear in beautiful succession, created by the word of God, the poet makes gods; and then adds fables concerning them that shock both common sense and decency. Some of the Greeks, dissatisfied with Hesiod's fables, invented fresh ones. The Athenians called themselves "sons of the earth" and "children of the clay," claiming that their forefather was the first of created beings; having a plain reference to the creation of Adam. Before Hesiod's time, Orpheus had taught that, In the beginning were chaos and a thick darkness; that light burst forth; that the sun, moon and stars came out of chaos; and that man was formed out of dust, and was endued with a rational soul by a supreme creative divinity. Thales, six centuries later, after learning wisdom in the East, taught nearly the same. The Phœnicians, according to Sanchoniathon, held, that dark air and chaos, mixed, formed the rudiments of all things; then appeared the sun, moon and stars; afterwards the fishes and the finite creation, and last of all two mortals were formed, the parents of the human race. Chaos, or water, or some fluid mass, is spoken of in the writings of many of the ancient philosophers and poets as that out of which the Great Mind made all all things. In time chaos itself was deified.

Sabbath.—We have already noticed the fact of the Sabbath having found its way among almost all nations. According to the Institute of Menu, the Hindoostanees hold that after the Supreme Power had created the universe he again retired into himself, from a state of energy to one of repose. *God rested.*

Garden of Eden.—The idea of the Garden of Eden also

appears in the writings of Hesiod. He describes the first period of human existence as a golden age. Men lived like gods, without pain, or care, or old age; the fields yielded their fruits untilled; and every day was crowned with happiness. Death comes into his account, but it was only a painless translation to another state. The Grecian fable, the story of the Garden of the Hesperides, and of the golden apples guarded by a dreadful dragon, that never slept, was probably founded on some tradition concerning the tree of life in the Garden of Eden, and of the guard placed at the entrance after man's fall. According to the fable, Hercules, the strong man of the ancients, partly human and partly divine, killed the dragon, and gathered the apples. This part of the fable may have arisen from the first promise: that the seed of the woman should bruise the head of the serpent, the old dragon, and thus the way to the tree of life should be again opened.

Man, one family.—The traditions of all nations, connected even with their religions, point in some form to Noah and his sons, as the fathers of the present race of men. Thus uniting in their testimony that all mankind are of one blood.

Early golden age—Deterioration of the race.—The ancient poets and philosophers speak of four successive ages through which the world had been passing, the golden, the silver, the brazen, and the iron. The comparative value of the metals representing their characters. Some of them speak of two such series; the first beginning at creation, the second after the deluge. That the first age of each was the purest, and that each successive period was marked by gradual deterioration, all history, both sacred and profane, attest most clearly. The experience of six thousand years confirms the word of God, as to the constantly falling state of man, and gives the lie to infidel teachers and pretended moral reformers, who teach that man can elevate himself. Instead of progressing morally or physically, all history, as well as the condition of the nations of the world at the present day, shows that man, in proportion as he is left to himself, and is without the influence of the Word and the Spirit of God, has always had a tendency to greater corruption; and is thus continually fulfilling the prophetic sentence pronounced at the fall, "Dying thou shalt die."

The Fall.—The Greek fables, relate that the first woman was made by the chief god, and gifted by all the lesser divinities (hence her name Pandora, *i. e.*, all gifts), on purpose to punish a certain man (Promotheus, a name signifying *more cunning*) for attempting to deceive the chief god about a sacrifice. Hesiod, after elegantly describing all the various beauties of this fair creation, entitles her "a lovely mischief to the soul of man." To this first woman, says the poet, the chief god (Jupiter) gave a box, desiring her to present it to her husband; and when he opened it, out came all sorts of evils and diseases, which spread themselves abroad, and altered the whole condition of the human race. In this we see the relics of the tradition of Adam tempted by Eve, and the direful consequences of sin; the end of the fable makes it appear that the notion of some promise connected with the Woman was also afloat in the world. At the bottom of Pandora's box, Hope is said to have remained, easing the labors, and alleviating the troubles and sorrows of the human family.

Satan—The Serpent.—In the Gothic theology, which was brought from the East, we have an account of a celebrated tree, which was the fountain of wisdom and knowledge, with an infernal serpent ever gnawing at its root. The god Thor, their middle divinity or mediator between God and man, is said "to have bruised the head of a great serpent." In India, two sculptured figures are yet extant in one of their oldest pagodas, one of which represents Chrishna, an incarnation of Vishnu, trampling on the crushed head of the serpent, while the other exhibits the serpent encircling the deity in its folds, and biting his heel. In regard to the form of the first appearance of Satan, Mr. Hardwic, after a most elaborate search into all ancient history and tradition, says, "There is found to be a most singular concert in east and west, north and south, in civilized and semi-barbarous countries, in the old world and the new, not only to the fact that serpents were somehow associated with the ruin of the human family, but that serpents so employed were vehicles of a malignant personal spirit, by whatever name he was described." In all nations there seems to be an instinctive horror of serpents, and a feeling, that, without pity or remorse, they are to be crushed under foot.

The Deluge.—Traditions of the Deluge have been almost universal in all ages and among all nations. Josephus speaks of the many Gentile historians who confirmed the Mosaic account of the deluge and the ark. Among others he quotes Berosus, the collector of the Chaldean antiquities; who in his account of Zizuthrus, the first Chaldean, almost repeats the story of Noah and the ark. After stating that Zizuthrus and his family had been taken up to heaven and made gods, Berosus adds, that the remains of the vessel were to be seen in his time, on one of the mountains of Armenia, and that people were wont to scrape the bitumen with which it had been coated to use as charms. The Egyptians called their most ancient vessels *baris*, a name given to the spot where the ark rested; and the model of a boat was carried about at one of their religious festivals. The Greeks delighted in the story of the sacred ship Argo, according to them the first ship ever constructed; from which our word ark is probably derived. The Greeks, through tradition and their poets, when their written history began, had accounts of seven different floods. That known as Deucalion's flood is most celebrated. The account given of that by Lucien is very similar to the Mosaic account. Deucalion alone, of the whole generation, was saved with his sons and their wives in an ark;

while embarking, all kinds of animals came and entered the ark with him, and were kept in harmony and from injuring him through the influence of the Deity. Traditions of the Deluge were found among the Druids of Europe, and among the inhabitants of America when it was first discovered. Dr. Arnold observes : " All the nations who have preserved any traditions of the remotest ages, agree in asserting that an elder generation had perished."

Mountains.—In the Bible history we find mountains often mentioned, as places where sacrifices had been offered, and special revelations from God received. On Mount Ararat, Noah, after leaving the ark, built an altar and offered sacrifice. Abraham was sent to Mount Moriah to sacrifice Isaac. The Lord appeared to Moses on Mount Horeb, and again to Israel, and delivered the law on Mount Sinai. The Lord chose Mount Zion for the site of the temple. Jesus gave the Sermon on the Mount, retired to mountains to pray, made Mount Olivet his favorite resort, and from a mountain ascended up to heaven. It is not strange, therefore, that the use of mountains found its way into idolatrous religions. In the Scriptures we find God's oft repeated denunciations against the high places in Israel, on which sacrifices were offered to the gods of the heathen. Among the heathen, Mount Olympus was the favorite seat of the Grecian gods ; Mount Parnassus was the haunt of the Muses. The Persians used the highest mountains in order to worship and sacrifice. Mount Athos in Macedonia has been a holy mountain from the earliest period to the present day. Almost all the ancient nations had their high mountains in esteem as places of public worship. And what is more remarkable, all of them make one of these high mountains the abode of the first gods, who were the fathers of the human race, and also the place where the ark of the deluge rested. To prevent a superstitious use of mountains, or of any particular locality for religious worship, the Lord Jesus made that memorable reply to the woman of Samaria, which ever since has made God's throne of grace accessible to man, from every part of the earth. She had told him "Our fathers worshipped in this mountain." His reply was, "The hour cometh when ye shall neither in this mountain, nor yet at Jerusalem, worship the Father," "God is a Spirit: and they that worship him must worship in spirit and in truth."[1]

The Cherubim.—When Adam and Eve were expelled from paradise, God placed on the eastern side of the garden certain beings, called *cherubims*, to keep the way of the tree of life.[2] Moses gives no description of the form of these beings; not even when the cherubims were to be made for the tabernacle. Ezekiel had visions of the cherubims, and gives a minute description of them.[3] He describes them as compounded of four different animals, viz., the man, the bull, the lion and the eagle: the man being the most prominent. It is remarkable that John in his vision[4] of the throne of God in heaven, speaks of seeing four beasts, or rather, four living creatures around the throne; and these also were like a man, a calf, a lion, and an eagle. So remarkable an appearance, says Mr. Faber, as that of the cherubim, could not easily be forgotten. The form of this great hieroglyphic, the first and source of all others, was doubtless familiar to Noah; and the symbol was afterwards placed in the tabernacle. The monstrous compounds which appear so frequently in ancient religions and history, were doubtless derived from the cherubims. Growing out of traditions of this strange being, according to learned men, was the celebrated dog Cerberus, with three heads—the dog, the wolf, and the lion—and who, according to the Greeks, was the keeper of hell: also, Hecate, or the infernal Diana, represented as having the heads of a horse, a dog, and a lion. The Osiris of the Egyptians, and Moloch, and Mithras were many-headed.

[1] John iv. 20.
[2] Gen. iii. 24.
[3] Ezek. i. 5–10; x. 8.
[4] Rev. iv. 6.

The Minotaur had the head of a man and the body of a bull. In the Zendavesta of the Persians two persons appear, one at the beginning of the old world, and the other at the beginning of the new, compounded of a man, a bull, and a horse. The celebrated Sphinx had the head of a woman, the wings of a bird, the claws and body of a lion. In the Hindoo system there is a being composed of a man and an eagle, which is placed in a pass leading to their high garden, called Garuda; answering to the garden of Eden; and, it is remarkable, the office of this creature is to prevent the approach of serpents.

The Tower of Babel—Early Giants.—The Tower of Babel, according to Berosus, the Chaldean historian, was erected by giants, who waged war with the gods, and who were at length dispersed, and the edifice beaten down by a great wind. In the ancient poems called the "Wars of the Titans," great giants are represented as having, in the early ages of the world, attempted to assault heaven; piling mountain on mountain, "Pelion on Ossa," and hurling burning rocks against the sky. In these we have traditions of the early giants, of the rebellion of men against God, and of the attempted building of the Tower of Babel. These fables of the Greeks, although rejected by their philosophers in later times, were received by the people; and had their influence in moulding their religious views.

End of the World.—Josephus relates a singular Jewish tradition, having a reference to the coming destruction of the world by fire. "The children of Seth," he says, "were the inventors of that peculiar sort of wisdom which is concerned with the heavenly bodies and their order; and understanding by Adam's prediction, that the world was to be destroyed at one time by fire, and at another time by water, they made two pillars, one of brick, the other of stone, on which they inscribed their discoveries, hoping that the former at least would be standing after the deluge, and transmit their knowledge to mankind." "This," adds Josephus, "remains in the land of Syria to this day." The pillar alluded to, and which Josephus professes to have seen, is supposed to have been one that was erected by one of the kings of Egypt to commemorate his victories. A belief that the world, at some future period, would be destroyed by fire was spread far and wide through the ancient world. The Sibylline verses, whatever be their origin, had contributed much to this. Plato tells us that the Egyptians, and, Cicero, that the Stoics, held such a belief. Plutarch speaks of the elements of the world, as things to be burnt up with it, and to end with time.

African Traditions.—In a communication giving an account of the theology and worship of the pagan African, Bishop Payne, speaking of their mythology, says : "You will share in the surprise I felt on the discovery of the resemblance of this system to that of the heathen in all ages, and to some of the great truths of revelation. I will give the account of this very much in the language in which I received it from an aged Grebo deyâ, or demon-man : " In the beginning, God (or Nyesoa—*nye*, man, *soa*, abiding,—very like Jehovah, the Eternal One) lived on earth among men. Then there was no sickness, no sorrow, no death. After a time, however, Nyesoa let fall from his hands *We*, witchcraft,—or that which causeth death. A woman got hold of this : soon a death followed. Men, dismayed, went to Nyesoa to ask the cause. He replied that *We* had fallen from him, and was in possession of a woman. She had caused the death. He told them, moreover, that he would now direct them to a test by which they could ascertain the guilt or innocence of the woman, and others suspected of like crime. He showed them the gidu-tree, and directed them to make an infusion of the bark and administer it to the woman. If guilty, it would cause her death ; if innocent, she would **vomit it** and escape. The woman drank the mixture and died. Before this, however, she had succeeded in conveying this mysterious *We* to her children. Thus sickness and death overspread the world. Men became so corrupt that Nyesoa told them he could no longer dwell among them; and he withdrew to heaven. Before leaving, however, he assured them he should always take an interest in their affairs, and that he would leave among them a class of men through whom they could communicate with him. This class are the deyâbo, or demon-men."

In this narrative, continues Bishop Payne, "we have the professedly divine origin of *gidu*, or 'sassa-wood,' reminding one of 'the waters of jealousy,' and used all through Central Africa as a test of witchcraft and other crimes;—the account, so nearly Scriptural, of God's dwelling with men, the introduction of evil by woman, and the deyâbo, representing almost exactly Balaam and the false prophets and oracles of all heathen countries;—the idea being, in all these cases, that the daimon of the Greks,—the *Ku* of the Greboes,—is sent by Nyesoa, or the Supreme Being; and hence the responses or directions of those acting under the influence of these spirits have a divine sanction."

The fables which appear in the first heathen writings and which helped to form their religious systems, were doubtless founded, or partly so, on traditions which were then floating among the nations, and which had come down the stream of time, constantly becoming more muddy, as men perverted or added to the original truth: some of these writings, however, appeared after the glory of the riches and wisdom of Solomon, and doubtless some ideas of his religion, had spread over the earth. It may be that the Greeks, as they obtained their letters from the Phœnicians and the Hebrews, may also have attained the foundations of some of these ideas from that source.

CHAPTER XXXVII.

DOCTRINAL TRUTHS RETAINED AMONG THE HEATHEN—ONE GOD—THE TRINITY—THE WORD OF GOD, THE CREATOR—GOD MANIFEST IN THE FLESH—THE IMMORTALITY OF THE SOUL—GHOSTS—AN ATONING SACRIFCE.

NOT only were the prominent facts of creation, and of the world's early history, as recorded by Moses, retained by all nations; but likewise, many of those great doctrines of revealed truth, upon a proper knowledge of which man's happiness depends. They also retained, in some form or other, the divinely appointed mode of approach to God through an atoning sacrifice. Let us now examine the views of some of these doctrines held by the early heathen.

One God.—The heathen, with their innumerable gods, generally acknowledged one, as supreme. Homer, one of the earliest heathen writers, speaks of Jupiter, as having the attributes of the true God, in such expressions as these,

" O thou supreme, high throned, all height above."
" Supreme of gods, unbounded and alone."
" Father of gods and men."

Before this, Orpheus had written,

" All things were made by God,"

And Hermes, the most ancient of Egyptian writers, wrote,

" The Lord of eternity is a great God."
" It belongs to the great God to see all things,
And to be seen of none."

Referring to the existence of an eternal being, the Creator of the world, Aristotle said, "There is one God, the king and father of all; and many gods, sons of gods, co-reigners with God; these things both the Greeks and barbarians alike affirm." Plutarch said, Though there were one, fifty, or an hundred worlds, they were all subject to one supreme, solitary, and independent God. He also informs us that the inhabitants of Thebais, one of the ancient divisions of Egypt, never would acknowledge any mortal god; but worshipped an unmade, eternal Deity. The Stoics held one God supreme and eternal, while the world was full of gods and demons: the latter created by the one God, and one day to be destroyed by him. Most of the ancient philosophers considered the gods as being part of the Supreme; and used the term gods and god as synonymous. The Buddha and Brahma of India were the same with Jupiter. Their votaries, who never mingle on other occasions, will meet and worship together at the dreadful feast of Juggernaut or Jagan-Nath, " *The Lord of the earth*," their great common Lord. The American Indians retained so clear a view of the one Great and Good Spirit (though they also worship the evil one), and they were also so free from the cruelties connected with the idolatries of the ancient world, that some have supposed them to be remnants of the lost ten tribes of Israel. This general acknowledgment of the Supreme God, the poet Pope, more celebrated as a poet than as a Christian, refers to in his universal prayer,

> "Father of all, in every age,
> In every clime adored
> By saint, by savage, and by sage,
> Jehovah, Jove, or Lord."

Mixed with these apparently clear views of the one Great God, these first heathen writers introduced the most ridiculous fables: which succeeding writers added to, and perverted, until the gods they worshipped, by the characters they gave them, and the actions they attributed to them, were monsters of iniquity, and more vile and licentious than the worst of men.

The Trinity.—Among the names which God has employed to reveal himself to us is that Great Name, "The Father, Son, and Holy Ghost;" three persons in one God. It is remarkable, that the doctrine of the Trinity has been retained, or has found its way in some form, in almost all the great religions of the earth.

The histories of Adam and of Noah, and of the three sons of each, which are named in the Bible, doubtless contributed to this. The fathers of the race were united by tradition, and were looked up to and worshipped as their gods throughout the whole heathen world. Homer, who systematized the pagan mythology, clearly shows this. After speaking of Saturn and Rhea, the first beings of the earth, he makes one of their sons, Neptune, say,

> "Three brother Deities from Saturn came,
> And ancient Rhea, earth's immortal dame.
> Assigned by lot—our triple rule we know."

These three were Jupiter, Neptune, and Pluto; the great gods of the ancient heathen, though called by different names. The rest were lesser gods.

The Persians had also their threefold distribution of the Deity; assigning to Oromasdes, Mithras, and Aramanes different works; calling Mithras the Mediator or middle. The Hindoos have their first great father, Brahm; an absolute unity beyond the grasp of human understanding. As the creator, he is called Brahma; as the preserver, Vishnu; and as the renovator, Siva; these three relations of the divine being constitute the trinity, *Timourti*, of the Hindoos. The Tartars worshipped a deity under three several names. The Buddhists, in China, have also a triplicating father. The Goths had their Odin, Vile and Ve, sons of Bura, the offspring of the mysterious Con—that is, born of the Ark. The Chaldeans said, "In the whole world shineth forth a Triad or Trinity, the head whereof is Monod or Unity." The Orphic system had its Phanus, Uranus, and Chronus. Pythagoras taught "The *first one* or unity is above all essences ; the *second* is *ideas*, and intelligible ; the *third* is the soul of the world, and partakes of the first two."

The ancient philosophers spoke of the three operations of the great Deity in such a way, that in after times, many of the early Christians were misled to think their systems differed but little from the Bible.

The Word of God, the Creator.—The Bible tells us, " In the beginning was the word, and the word was God ;" "all things were made by him."[1] The heathen obtained some knowledge of this. In India, Vach or *speech*, is the active power of Brahma. In Egypt, while Amanis was the hidden god, Phtha was the god by whom he produced the world,— was the manifested god. In Persia, Ormazd, the good, created the world by Honovu, the word.

God manifest in the flesh.—The Bible adds, "The word was made flesh."[2] This "great mystery," "Emmanuel,"[3] "God manifest in the flesh,"[4] has been a part of all religions : heathen as well as Christian. All the gods of the heathen were once men, or had at times assumed the human form. When the Apostle Paul, while traveling with Barnabas, had cured an impotent man, the people of Lycaonia cried out, "The gods are come down to us in the likeness of men," calling one Jupiter, and the other Mercurius, they wanted to offer sacrifices to them.[5] The transformations or incarnation of Vishnu, the second person of the Hindoo trinity, form the principal subject of their sacred books.

Not only have the early appearances of the Creator re-

[1] John i. 1, 3, 14.   [2] John i. 14.   [3] Matt. i. 23
[4] 1 Tim iii. 16.   [5] Acts xiv. 12.

tained a place in the heathen systems of mythology, but the promise of a great Deliverer to come was also preserved in some form throughout the world; gaining strength with time, until Jesus, "the desire of all nations," came. Thus, while Simeon, and Anna, and other pious Jews were looking for him, we see, from the East, wise men, having seen his star, come to worship him;[1] and from the West, we hear the heathen poet Virgil, while trying to flatter the emperor Augustus that he was the person referred to in the Cumæn verses, saying,

> " The last great age, foretold by sacred rhymes,
> Renews its finished course. Saturnian times
> Roll round again."
>
> " A golden progeny from heaven descends.
> The jarring nations he in peace shall bind,
> And with paternal virtues rule mankind."

The immortality of the soul.—Every man feels that he has a living soul; and he knows in his conscience that there is a coming judgment. Some of the memorable warnings of Him, who taught in love, and who came to save, are : " Fear Him, which after He hath killed hath power to cast into Hell; yea, I say unto you, Fear Him."[2] "For the hour is coming, in which all that are in the grave shall hear His voice, and shall come forth; they that have done good, unto the resurrection of life; and they that have done evil, unto the resurrection of damnation."[3]

A belief in the immortality of the soul, and of a state of future rewards and punishments, has come down through all ages, and through all religions. Homer, in his Iliad, makes his hero, Achilles, say,

> " 'Tis true, 'tis certain, man though dead retains
> Part of himself,—the immortal mind remains."

Apolonius, one of the philosophers, declared : " As to the

[1] Matt. ii. 2.   [2] Luke xii. 5.   [3] John v. 28.

opinion that good men should be rewarded after death, he could not reach either the author or original of it." Cicero says, "We conclude, from the consent of all mankind, that the soul is immortal." Seneca says, "The consent of all mankind, in their hopes and fears of a future state, is of no small moment to us." All legislators and philosophers, in every age and land, have made it a part of their system, and the founders of every form of religious worship have done the same. Such rare exceptions as the Sadducees of old and the few scattered infidels, who are generally looked upon with abhorrence, serving to confirm the rule.

The translation of Enoch, shortly after the death of Adam, was not forgotten. Accounts of it appear, in some form or other, in almost every system of religion adopted by the heathen.

The doctrine of the transmigration of souls, which is connected with a belief in immortality, is still held by a large portion of the earth's population. The indistinct knowledge which the heathen retained in their traditions, of the creation, of the deluge, and of the new world, gave them a notion of a succession of worlds; and led to the belief that Noah and his three sons were a re-appearance of Adam and his three sons, Cain, Abel and Seth; these being the only ones mentioned.

The belief that the spirits of the departed have some ethereal form after death, and that they sometimes manifest themselves to the eyes of men, has prevailed, in all time, throughout all nations. This is very remarkable, considering that the appearances of Samuel to Saul, and of Moses and Elias to the apostles at the transfiguration, are the only well authenticated cases upon which to ground a belief in ghosts. The learned Dr. Johnson, speaking of the universality of the belief in ghosts, said, that after a careful investigation he had never been able to find an authentic case of a ghost having been seen. The fact, that such a belief has always been universal, shows an involuntary consent of all mankind to the truth, that the soul is immortal.

Sacrifices.—We have already noticed that in the first act of worship, after the Fall, God accepted the offering of a lamb in sacrifice, and also that sacrifices have had a place in every religion since that time. Let us now examine the heathen accounts concerning the origin of the sacrifices they offered. Plato, the philosopher, says, " At first no animals were offered, but only the fruits of the earth and trees." Such may have been the thank-offerings of man before he sinned ; such were the sacrifices offered by self-righteous Cain. His descendants and followers doubtlessly imitated him, but after the flood bloody sacrifices soon became general.

That sacrifices were a divine appointment is one of the most universal traditions prevalent among men. Mr. Faber, after a thorough examination of the subject, affirms, that " Throughout the whole world he finds a notion prevalent that the gods could only be appeased by bloody sacrifices ; and its universality proves that all nations have borrowed it from the same common source. There is no heathen people which can specify a time when it was without sacrifice. All have equally had it, from a time which cannot be reached by their genuine records." One Egyptian tradition makes *Moth* or Taut, supposed to be Adam, the inventor of sacrifices. Another says, Osiris, supposed to be Noah, is the god who first instructed men in them. The Italians were said to have been taught by Janus, the first father. His double face, looking forward and backward, is supposed to refer to Noah, " the child of the old world and the orphan of the new," as knowing the past and the future. According to the Babylonians, Zizuthus, on quitting the ark, built an altar and sacrificed to the gods. The same was said of the Grecian Deucalion. The same of the British Hu, who sailed over the flood with seven companions, and was emphatically called the sacrificer. The Chinese Fohi raised seven kinds of animals for sacrifices to the Great Spirit. All these point to Adam or Noah, though called by various names.

Cæsar, the infidel of Rome, says, that the Druids of Gaul held, that unless the life of man was given for the forfeited life of man, the Deity of the immortal gods could not be appeased. The Athenians and Massilians, in their sacrifice of a man for the welfare of the state, show that they had an idea of a human redeemer. They loaded him with curses and prayed that the wrath of the gods might fall upon his devoted head, and thus be diverted from the rest of the citizens. They solemnly called upon him to be their ransom and their redemption, life for life, and body for body. After this ceremony they cast him into the sea as an offering to Neptune.

In the Indian mythology, we learn that Menu, their great father, had three sons, one of whom was slain in the act of performing sacrifice. The slaughtered brother was consecrated as a god and worshipped by the Thessalonians with bloody hands. The death of Abel was, doubtless, the origin of this tradition.

Sanchoniathon, the ancient historian of Phœnicia, speaks of the sacrifice by the god Chronus (the same as El or Ilus) of his son to his father Ouranus, and that the example was followed in the nation by the establishment of an expiatory sacrifice, which was considered as peculiarly mystical, having reference to things yet to come. The learned mythologist, Mr. Bryant, after giving a full account of this, concludes, " According to this, El, the supreme deity, whose associates were the Elohim, was in process of time to have a son, well beloved, his only begotten. He was to be offered up as a sacrifice to the father, by way of satisfaction and redemption, to atone for their sins and avert the just vengeance of God." Mr. Bryant leaves it to his readers to say whether this does not refer to an early tradition of Christ.

It is a lamentable fact that all these relics of original truth, which were retained by the heathen in their mythology, were mixed up with fabulous traditions and gross superstition, and with an idolatrous and cruel worship which constantly grew more and more vile, licentious and corrupt. The seed of the Serpent has ever perverted the truth; doing so even in the visible Church of Christ. Peter speaks of certain persons as wresting some things in the epistles of Paul and "also the other scriptures to their own destruction."[1] The Pharisees, the most professedly religious among the Jews, the then visible Church of God, put Jesus, who was "The Truth" itself, to death. Though they sat in Moses' seat, Jesus speaks of them as "children of the Devil."[2] Since that time all history shows that there has been a succession of his children, not only among the heathen, but also in high places, loudly proclaiming that they are "The Church," while they are "holding the truth in unrighteousness," and covering up with their traditions the pure Word of God, and are also ever zealous, like their father, to destroy them who preach, or who live, Christ.

[1] 2 Pet. iii. 16.   [2] John viii. 44.

CHAPTER XXXVIII.

THE ANCIENT ORACLES—THE SIBYLLINE BOOKS.

AS man ever since the Fall has shown anxiety in regard to the life to come; so also, in all ages and places, we find him troubled with doubts and fears as to his destiny in this life; and seeking to pry into futurity by means of some mysterious agency. We find seers and soothsayers, wizards and witches, astrologers and fortune-tellers, have always abounded. Whence is this? Among other things the ancient heathen were in the habit of consulting public oracles. How did these originate? Bishop Meade says, "We believe there is nothing very general in the world which does not point to something which existed among God's people, either before or after the flood." The earliest use of the word oracle in Scripture was in reference to the covering of the ark or chest in which the law of Moses was shut up, and from above which God manifested his will, and delivered responses to Moses. Dreams and visions, such as God sent to the patriarchs; and the interpretation of dreams, such as Joseph and Daniel were inspired to give to Pharaoh, Darius, and Nebuchadnezzar; were also oracles, or answers from God. The answers to the high priest by means of certain signs and appearances on the Urim and Thummim, which Moses had put in the breastplate,[1] were the oracles of God among the Jews. This was consulted on all important occasions. The Scriptures are called the "lively," or living, "oracles"[2] of God, in opposition to the false or dead oracles of the heathen. According to these oracles of

---
[1] Lev. viii. 8; Ex. xxviii. 30; Num. xxvii. 21.   [2] Acts vii. 38; Rom. iii. 2.

God, Christians are now directed to speak;[1] and forsaking all other oracles, they are, for their present and future welfare, to consult these only.[2] Thanks be to God! they are always living; always open for consultation.

The knowledge that God has, from the beginning, held constant communications with His people, has been preserved in some form by all nations. All men feel the want of such a counselor. This want of man, Satan, the god of this world, has, in many ways, endeavored to supply. The ancient heathen oracles were one of these ways; and some of them became very celebrated. That of Jupiter Dodona in Epirus; of Apollo at Delphi, in Phocis, near Mount Parnassus; and the temple of Jupiter Ammon in the deserts of Libya, were the principal ones. Homer mentions the two former only. In process of time they became so multiplied that there were not less than twenty-five oracles in the small province of Bœotia. These were consulted not only on important public questions, but likewise on the affairs of private life. According to the heathen tradition, Mount Parnassus was once tenanted by a mighty serpent, which had the power of speech and delivered oracular responses from a sacred cave. This Delphic serpent, which was called Python, was, according to the tradition, slain by Apollo. From this fabulous monster the name Pythius was communicated to the god, and Pythia, or Pythoness, to the priestess, who, after receiving the vapor of inspiration through the cleft of a rock, delivered the responses.

The oracular temples were generally located in deep forests or steep, craggy places. The tripod or chair, on which the priest or priestess was seated, was sometimes over the mouth of a cavern; the vapor issuing from it was said to have an inspiring or infuriating effect on those who were upon it. The oracles were consulted by all classes; even by philosophers and kings. Rich presents were made to

[1] 1 Pet. iv. 11.   [2] Deut. xviii. 19, 12.

propitiate them. Bribes were sometimes used to procure favorable answers. Answers were also sometimes specially obtained for the purpose of stimulating credulous soldiers or people, when certain objects were to be gained.

Eusebius says that there were not less than six hundred authors among the heathen themselves who wrote against the reality of the oracles. In the Christian Church learned men, in all ages, have taken different views of them. Some believing them to be nothing but human ingenuity and fraud, while others contended that they were inspired by the father of lies.

That they did deliver some answers as to future events, of a most remarkable character, cannot be denied. Among the many responses given it would be strange, however, if this did not sometimes happen. The responses were always in some enigmatical or ambiguous form; so shaped, that the credit of the oracle might be sustained, whatever might be the event. Oftentimes the answer was to be inferred, not from anything said, but from the flight of birds, or some appearance in the sky, or some unnatural sound; so that all was uncertainty. However, there must have been something very remarkable in their character and conduct, to enable them to maintain their reputation and influence for a thousand successive years. We are reminded of Jacob's prevailing prayer, "I will not let Thee go, except Thou bless me,"[1] by such instances as the following: while supplicating Apollo at Delphi, during the war with Xerxes, the Athenian messengers said, "We will never depart from thy sanctuary without a favorable answer, but will remain here until we die." The responses of the oracles certainly had the effect of stimulating to the most daring deeds of defensive war that heathen history has ever furnished.

Many of their responses are recorded by the ancient heathen historians. The famous answers to Crœsus, king

[1] Gen. xxxii. 26.

of Lydia, when about to engage in a war with Persia, are worthy of notice. Crœsus, according to Herodotus, being doubtful of the oracle, determined first to try its superhuman knowledge; and, therefore, sent a messenger, who, at the end of a hundred days, was to enquire what the occupation of the king at that time would be. The reply of the god was; "That he smelt the odor of a lamb boiled with a tortoise, while brass was at once above and beneath it;" and such, it was said, was actually the occupation of Crœsus at the time. Crœsus then sent to inquire of the Oracle whether he would be victorious in the proposed war; to which this ambiguous answer was returned; "That he would overthrow a great empire." Crœsus, wishing to be yet more sure, sent again; and inquired whether his power would ever be diminished. The Oracle in reply advised the monarch to consult his safety by flight, " Whenever a mule should reign over the Medes." Crœsus understood this as insuring him success; as a mule could not be king. But it turned out, that the mule was Cyrus, the Medo-Persian, who united the two kingdoms of Medea and Persia, and conquered Crœsus. Thus also Crœsus overthrew a great empire; but that empire was his own. In any event, with both answers the credit of the oracle was secure.

In examining the question, whether the ancient Oracles received superhuman assistance and inspiration from the great enemy of mankind and father of lies, Bishop Meade refers to such facts as the temptation of our first parents by Satan in the form of a serpent; of his putting it into the heart of Judas to betray our Lord, and into the heart of Ananias to lie unto the Holy Ghost. He then adds, "We need not fear to admit that this wise and artful being might be permitted by God to create some mischief among men by means of Oracles, and the superhuman answers made through them." That the devil has exerted great power through the priests of false religions, we may infer from the facts record-

THE ANCIENT ORACLES. 183

ed in Scripture concerning the rod of Moses. When it was turned into a serpent, the magicians of Egypt did the same. Simon, the sorcerer, who bewitched the people of Samaria with his sorceries, may have been enabled by Satan to do some wonderful things. "We read," says Mr. Faber, "in the Acts of the Apostles, of a young female who was possessed of a spirit of divination, according to our version, but with a spirit of Python, according to the original Greek. This spirit enabled her to utter certain oracular responses, which brought her masters much gain. When she beheld Paul and his companions, she cried, saying 'These men are the servants of the Most High God, which shew unto us the way of salvation. Paul being grieved, turned and said to the spirit, I command thee in the name of Jesus Christ come out of her. And he came out the same hour.'[1] Now, according to the plain import of this narrative, the young female was possessed by an evil spirit, which compelled her to utter responses of an oracular nature. The spirit was an intelligent and living agent. And he is denominated a spirit of Python, which is the precise name of the Delphic serpent which delivered Oracles from a sacred cave in Mount Parnassus. Putting these matters together," says Mr. Faber, "we certainly seem to collect that there was something more than mere juggling imposture in the responses of the ancient oracles." Bishop Meade adds: "From a careful examination of many of the most judicious, as well as learned writers, ancient and modern, I find such to have been their prevailing impressions, though there be some diversity of sentiment among them."

Though great difference of opinion prevailed among the ancients in regard to the reliability of the Oracles, still they continued to be held in high repute until the Christian era. They then rapidly declined; so that even that at Delphi was closed. The most learned among the heathen were at

[1] Acts xvi. 6.

a loss to account for this closing of their ancient Oracles. One of them, Porphyry, says, "Since Jesus began to be worshipped, no man has received any public help or benefit from the gods."

THE SIBYLLINE BOOKS.

A set of extraordinary books, under the name of *The Oracles of the Cumœan Sibyl*, were offered for sale, at an early period of Rome, to King Tarquinius Superbus at an immense price. It is said that there were originally nine books offered by the Sibyl: that on each refusal on the part of the king to purchase them, one of them was burnt, until six of them were thus destroyed; and then Tarquinius purchased the remaining three for the price originally demanded for the nine. These books were held in such high veneration that they were kept in a stone chest under ground in the temple of Jupiter Capitolinus, and were committed to the care of two chosen officers, who consulted the books only at the special command of the senate: and this not to learn future events, but what worship was required by the gods when they manifested their wrath by national calamities or prodigies. The officers in charge of the books were enjoined to keep their contents from the public under heavy penalties. Eighty-two years before the birth of Christ, the temple in which they were contained was burned, and they were consumed. The Roman senate thought it of so much importance to repair the loss, that they sent persons into various countries to collect the fragments of the books, which were supposed to be in existence, and the most learned men of Rome were employed to select from the returns what they judged to be most authentic.

The Sibylline prophecies were originally of Teukrian or early Trojan descent. They were in full circulation in the reign of Crœsus; and the promises of future empire which they made to Æneas escaping from the flames of Troy into Italy, were remarkably realized by Rome.

Bishop Horseley, in his treatise "On the Prophecies of the Messiah Dispersed Among the Heathen," speaks of the celebrated Sibylline books, as containing some of those ancient traditions and prophecies of a great Deliverer who was to come, and which were floating through the world during the patriarchal age, not merely in the family of Abraham, but in other lines. There was certainly a great resemblance between some things contained in these books as to the great Deliverer, and those in the Scriptures as to the Messiah. We have already noticed Virgil's quotation from them on this subject. Julius Cæsar, through his friends, wished to have it believed that he was the person alluded to in the Sibylline books, as a means of obtaining the kingly government of Rome; but Cicero, who had access to these documents, and who was opposed to Cæsar's elevation, denied that they were prophecies, alleging that they were not frenzied enough in their style to be the work of prophets; but he bears testimony to their excellence by saying, "Let us then adhere to the prudent practice of our ancestors; let us keep the Sibyl in religious privacy. These writings," he said, "are indeed rather calculated to extinguish than to propagate superstition." Bishop Horseley says, that "these prophecies, wherever they might be found, could be of no other than a divine original."

CHAPTER XXXIX.

THE ANCIENT MYSTERIES—FREEMASONS.

THERE is something connected with what is considered mysterious or supernatural which immediately attracts attention. This is especially the case, if in the imagination the mystery is connected with the spiritual world. When we consider our relations to the unseen, to God, to angels, and to demons, it is not strange that this feeling everywhere prevails, and that it has done so ever since the Fall. The moment we leave revelation everything becomes a mystery.

All the revelations made to us in the word of God; of Himself[1]—of His incarnation[2]—of the plan of salvation[3]—of the resurrection,[4] etc., are spoken of in the Scriptures as revealed "mysteries." Man never could have discovered them; never could have imagined them. And even when he hears of them, the natural man, unless born again of the Holy Ghost,[5] cannot understand them. Ministers are called "stewards of the mysteries of God."[6] Our Lord told his disciples, "It is given unto you to know the mysteries of the kingdom of heaven, but to them not given."[7]

It is not surprising, therefore, that Satan has in all ages taken advantage of man's natural ignorance of the unseen world, and of his thirst for the mysterious: and among the many means of leading his followers astray, has used pretended religious mysteries and oracles, table-movings, spirit-rappings, etc.

---

[1] 1 Cor. ii. 7; Col. ii. 2.
[2] 1 Tim. iii. 16.
[3] Eph. vi. 19; Col. i. 26, 27.
[4] 1 Cor. xv. 51.
[5] 1 Cor. ii. 10, 14: John iii. 5.
[6] 1 Cor. iv. 1.
[7] Matt. xiii. 11.

Among the ancients in different parts of the world there were secret celebrations, known as the Greater and the Lesser mysteries. All might be admitted into the latter; comparatively few into the former. The greater mysteries were those of the Cabiri, the Eleusinian, the Bacchic, the Samothracian, and the Mithraic. They were performed, with many religious ceremonies, in dark caves and grottos, or in the lower apartments of great temples, always with the light excluded so as to require lamps. The first thing done in the initiation of new members was to administer an oath; then whatever could be effected by alternate darkness and light, sweet sounds and discordant ones, lovely and dismal scenes, hymns and songs, gods and goddesses passing in review before the eyes—things, as one said, "most horrible and most ravishingly pleasant"—was adopted to frighten and delight. The existence of God and the gods, of a future state, and some facts in creation and in the early history of man, are said to have been some of the subjects represented in these mysteries. Plato says, "It was the end and drift of initiation to restore the soul to that state from which it fell." In time there was a general desire to be initiated; and a premium was charged for becoming so. Even children were initiated. In their first and purest state, the ancient mysteries are said to have been designed to inculcate a holy and virtuous life, in order to a happy immortality. As is apt to be the case with secret societies, all of the mysteries, by reason of their secrecy, became abominably corrupt: so much so, that, after being ridiculed on the public stage, they were at length required to be suppressed by public authority.

St. Augustine, speaking of the mysteries, says, "There were many truths which it was inconvenient to the State to be generally known; and many things, though false, it was expedient the people should generally believe; therefore the Greeks shut up their mysteries in the silence of their sacred enclosures." Herodotus, in his history, speaks very freely at times of the follies of the Grecian stories and worship. Of some religious rites, however, he dares not give the explanation. Speaking of the god Pan, he says, "Why they represent him in such a way I had rather not mention." Speaking of the blows the priests in Egypt inflicted on themselves at the great festival of Bubastis, he says, "But for whom they thus beat themselves, it were impious for me to divulge." The old Orphic poet wrote,

> "To these alone I speak, whom nameless rites
> Have rendered meet to listen. Close the doors
> And carefully exclude each wretch profane,
> Lest impious curiosity pollute
> Our sacred orgies."

In the Egyptian mysteries of Osiris, an ark, carried about by the priests, was a leading symbol in the ceremonies. The Phœnicians, in celebrating the mysteries of Cabiri, also used a consecrated ark. A sacred ark was likewise used in the mysteries of Bacchus; and the same symbol appeared in the mysteries of other nations. Learned writers on this subject consider the mysteries of the Cabiri as instituted in honor of Noah and his three sons; the latter being sometimes called Dioscori or Cabiri: and that all the mysteries embraced some memorials of the Deluge, and of the events immediately succeeding it. It may be that the Ark of the Covenant, carried by the Israelites into Canaan, may also have led to the adoption of that symbol among the religious rites of some of the heathen.

Another prominent symbol, used in the celebration of the mysteries, and carried about in the *baris* or ark, was the "mystic egg." In the heathen writings, and in their hieroglyphics, the mystic egg appears in connection with the ark and the deluge. It is said to have floated on the ocean during the deluge, and that out of it was born a new world. It is sometimes the world itself, and sometimes the great prolific father or mother of all things.

One cannot help being struck with the many points of resemblance between the ancient mysteries and a secret society still existing among us, the *Freemasons:* a society of very ancient date, which some of its advocates pretend to trace up to the great master-builder Solomon; and some to a still higher date, connecting it with the builders of Babel. All the most remarkable buildings of Greece, Egypt, and Asia Minor, have been ascribed to the Cabirian or Cyclopean architects; and the present Freemasons claim it as their privilege to preside over the commencement of great buildings. The learned Mr. Faber says, "This society is probably a fragment of those orgies which have prevailed all the world over, and have come to us through the Knights Templar." One of the main objects of this society is mutual support and assistance among its members: their secret signs enabling them to recognize one another. All the objects of true charity, however, can be accomplished without the dangers and evils generally connected with secret associations. The Gospel encourages no secret organizations. Our Lord says, "Every one that doeth evil hateth the light."[1] He requires of his followers an open profession: and enjoins upon his disciples to "love one another,"[2] and to "do good unto all men, especially unto them who are of the household of faith."[3]

[1] John iii. 20.   [2] John xiii. 34.   [3] Gal. vi. 10.

CHAPTER XL.

FIRST HEATHEN POETS—HOMER—HESIOD.

SEVERAL centuries after the writings of Moses, and of the book of Job, itself a poem of the highest order, had appeared, the literature of Greece commenced with the writings of her early poets. These first heathen poets introduced in their allegories, mixed with much fable, the events recorded by Moses; accounts of the creation of the world, of the first God or gods, and the early history of man before and after the deluge. Some of them were therefore called divine poets. The term *vates*, or prophets, was applied to them. The most celebrated were *Musœus, Orpheus, Linus, Amphion* and *Hermes*. They are supposed to have lived from 1,400 to 1,250 years before Christ.

Orpheus, or the author of the Orphic verses, whoever he was, the authorship being doubtful, had more scriptural views than the others. These views of truth became more and more obscured by the fictions of the later poets. The same darkening of the truth is noticeable in the writings of the successive celebrated philosophers of Greece, of Persia, and of China. Plato, one of these philosophers, acknowledges, that "the nearer the originals the truer;" and, "the higher we go up to the ages nearest creation, the more visible the traces of truth." "These things, however," he says, "were wrapt up in the fables of the poets; that he could only try to make the best use of them until some one came to explain them." Speaking of the traditions of the eastern countries, Plato said, "Their knowledge of the Deity was derived from the gods;" "the ancients, who lived nearer to the gods than we, have transmitted it unto us." He speaks of Adam's state of innocence under the fable of Saturn's golden age, but adds that " we want a fit interpreter of the fable."

The tribes, which had settled in Greece, were in comparative barbarism and ignorance, when their early poets, by their verses and instructions, contributed to their elevation. This is probably referred to when these poets are spoken of as taming wild beasts by their harps and lyres, and their verses.

Several centuries after these early poets had passed away, there appeared in Greece, at about the same time, the celebrated poets *Homer* and *Hesiod:* who, according to Herodotus, lived not more than four hundred years before his day. This, at the furthest, reaches back to 850 years before Christ; which would be nearly two centuries after Solomon had spoken " three thousand proverbs : and had written a thousand and five songs ; and, because of his wisdom, his fame was in all nations round about."[1] We might well wonder, that clearer views of the God of Solomon did not spread at the same time, did we not know the tendency of man, as instanced for a time by Solomon himself, to idolatry. The writings of Homer, and of Hesiod, are the first heathen writings in the world which have come down to us in perfect form ; the earlier ones coming in fragments only.

Homer was called the " strolling bard," because of his travels through so many countries. His Iliad gives an account of the siege of Troy, and his Odyssey, an account of the wanderings of Ulysses from Troy to Ithaca. These first heathen poems excel all other poems which have since appeared in heathen literature ; and for nearly three thousand years have excited the admiration of all learned men.

Combining the information they gathered by traveling in the neighboring countries with the ideas derived from their

[1] 1 Kings iv. 31, 32,

earlier poets, Homer and Hesiod classified the gods; adding many things unknown before: and thus formed the system of the great pagan mythology of the ancient Greeks and Romans. It is thought that Homer must have read all the books of Moses, and borrowed many passages from them. The principal facts recorded by Moses reäppear in the works of Hesiod and Homer in a corrupted form.

Speaking of Homer, Mr. Pope, his translator, says, "Though he has some very low thoughts, yet he has more noble and excellent ones than any other writer: his style bears a greater resemblance to the sacred writers than any others, and his writings a remarkable parity with Scripture." A general spirit of piety pervades his works; we find in them much of divine truth, though perverted. There is a constant acknowledgment of the gods; and man's dependance upon them is shown by the continued offering of prayers and sacrifices; particularly before engaging in battle, or entering on any great enterprise. The principle which pervades the poem is,

"Those who revere the gods, the gods will bless."

He speaks of man's dependence on some superior power thus,

"If thou hast strength, 'twas Heaven that strength bestowed,
For know, vain man, that valor is from God:
'Tis man's to fight, but Heaven to give success."

Homer's accounts of God and of the gods, their origin and their character, are confused and contradictory. At times he ascribes attributes to Jupiter which would make him equal to the eternal and self-existent God as set forth by Moses: speaking of him, as the

"Supreme of gods, unbounded and alone;"
"Ever just and true:"

and making him say,

"If I but stretch this hand,
I heave the gods, the ocean and the land."

"And what I speak is Fate."
"And Fate our word obeys."

While at other times, he speaks of Jupiter as having an earthly origin and birth ; and also, the basest of human passions. Such contradictions constantly occur, likewise, in all the heathen mythologists and philosophers ; throwing their systems of theology into confusion. The heathen could not comprehend an eternal God ; nor imagine a pure One. Homer wrote also a number of hymns to the gods. After his death, temples were built and sacrifices offered to him.

Hesiod gives us the first regular heathen history of creation, of the gods, and of the hero-gods : the cosmogony, theogony and heroölogy, which were according to the prevailing traditions of his day, or according to his own fancy. His account of the gods was afterwards denounced by Plato, Socrates and others, as derogatory to the gods and injurious to men. Hesiod professed to write under the inspiration of the Muses. His accounts of creation and of the early facts in the world's history are evidently founded on the Mosaic history. Passing by, and leaving out, God, the Creator, Hesiod makes Chaos, first ; and next, the earth ; and then by means of Love, night appears ; and day or light from darkness ; then the heavenly bodies are born from the earth ; and, last of all, from Cœlus and Terra, the heaven and the earth, Saturn, the first of the gods, is born. Many facts in the early history of mankind are also plainly referred to by him. In his description of the different ages he speaks of man's first estate of purity and happiness ; then, of a degenerate race " by angry Jove engulfed ; " and then of a third, a race of " many-languaged men." Hesiod speaks of the share woman had in bringing evils on the human race, thus : at the instigation of Jupiter, Vulcan

"Moulded from the yielding clay
A bashful virgin's image ;

> And lo! from her descend the tender sex
> Of woman: a pernicious kind;
> A bane to men;
> Ill helpmates of intolerable toils." *

We do not know what Hesiod's experience was with the fair sex; or whether he was an old bachelor; but, at all events, he was a heathen; for he goes on to say,

> "The name Pandora to the maid was given;
> For all the gods conferred a gifted grace
> To crown this mischief of the mortal race."

Then comes the account of the introduction of evil into the world through woman; who, though forbidden to do it, through curiosity, open a casket containing all the ills of life.

> "The woman's hands an ample casket bear,
> She lifts the lid, she scatters ills in air;
> Hope sole remained within, nor took her flight,
> Beneath the casket's verge concealed from sight."

A reference, doubtless, to the promised seed of the woman, the Messiah, the Hope of the world.

* Elton's translation.

CHAPTER XLI.

FIRST HEATHEN PHILOSOPHERS—THALES—PYTHAGORAS—SOCRATES—PLATO—ARISTOTLE—ZOROASTER—LAOU-TSE—CONFUCIUS.

GOD'S history of creation, by the hand of Moses, and the philosophical speculations of Job and his friends, had been nearly a thousand years in the world; and during all that time God had been confirming his written word by miracles, and by preserving a chosen people, whose religious rites kept continually commemorating the facts spoken of in that word; when a succession of men appeared in Greece and other countries, who, to this day, are celebrated as philosophers. Some of these philosophers were evidently, as their name implies, "lovers of wisdom." To acquire knowledge, they traveled through all the great civilized nations then existing; examining their religions, their traditions, historical monuments, &c. They obtained thus some ideas of the true God. Their codes of morals, their speculations in regard to the immortality of the soul, and their religious views, were greatly in advance of even the refined idolatry of the Greeks. The surrounding darkness making their light appear the more brilliant.

When we consider, that traditions of the leading events of the first ages of the world existed among all nations, and that references to some of these were preserved in their religious rites; and also, that for so long a period before their day the clear Word of God had been written, and had been, during the lives of some of the later of these philosophers, translated into the leading language of the world; and that this word had been continually read or expounded for a thousand years in the synagogues of a peculiar nation located in the centre of the then known world; a nation, whose kings, shortly before, were the most powerful on earth, and the most celebrated for wisdom; when we bear all this in mind, instead of being surprised at finding gleams of truth in the writings of these men, the wonder is, that they had not clearer views. We should be surprised at this, did we not now constantly see the "wise of this world" sitting a whole lifetime under the preaching of the gospel, without understanding even its first principles. Truly, "faith is the gift of God;"[1] and He alone can "open the heart" to "understand the Scriptures!"[2]

The eloquence, sincerity, and peculiar teachings of these philosophers drew many disciples to them. Their writings have ever since been in the hands of every scholar; and many of them are now daily used in our schools and colleges. And what is still more strange, their dim discoveries of truth, mixed as they are with great darkness, are what many of the learned men of the world at the present day are trying to build their hopes for eternity upon. Many are preferring the misty speculations, and the cold morality of heathen philosophers groping for the truth, to the clear teachings of the "light of the world," the Lord Jesus Christ.

Among the first of these philosophers appears *Thales;* who died about five hundred and forty-eight years before the Christian era, in the eighty-sixth year of his age. Four hundred years before this, the fame of the wisdom of Solomon was in all nations round about;[3] and he had drawn people from the utmost parts of the earth to hear him.[4] Thirty years before the death of Thales, B. C. 580, Nebuchadnezzar issued his proclamation "unto all people, nations, and languages that dwell in the earth," stating what

---
[1] Eph. ii. 8.
[2] Acts xvi. 14; Luke xxiv. 45.
[3] 1 Kings iv. 31.
[4] Luke xi. 31.

God had wrought towards him. He had previously decreed, that every people and nation which speak anything against the God of Shadrach, Meshach, and Abednego should be cut to pieces.[1] Greece being enshrouded in the gross darkness of a refined and licentious paganism, Thales went abroad to obtain knowledge, and became the great mathematician, astronomer, and theologian of his day. His main doctrine was, that water was the basis of all things; and that God was the mind that formed all things out of it; that God himself was unmade. He also taught that the world was full of gods or good angels who were made by God. He drew his wisdom from Egypt, where he spent some years; and he advised his disciple, Pythagoras, to travel in search of wisdom among the ancient nations.

Pythagoras spent forty years in gathering all the knowledge he could get from the Egyptians, Jews, Phœnicians, and Chaldeans. It was during this search for knowledge, that Cyrus, king of Persia, B. C. 536, issued a proclamation throughout all his kingdom, saying, "The Lord God of heaven hath given me all the kingdoms of the earth; and he hath charged me to build him an house at Jerusalem."[2] It was also while he was on his travels that Darius "wrote unto all people, nations, and languages, that dwell in the earth" with a decree, "that in every dominion of my kingdom men tremble and fear before the God of Daniel; for He is the living God."[3] And also, another similar decree, confirming the decree of Cyrus, to aid the Jews in building the house of God at Jerusalem.[4]

It is remarkable, that about the same time these first philosophers were gaining wisdom from the East, the celebrated philosophers of Persia, India, and China, commenced to teach, and to give forth those writings, which, though twenty-four centuries have passed since their day, are still moulding the religion of more than half of the population of the earth.

[1] Danl. iii. 29; iv. 1.   [2] Ezra i. 1.   [3] Danl. vi. 25.   [4] Ezra vi. 8.

In Persia, Zoroaster commenced changing the religion of that country. In India, Buddha began to new-model its religion; and in China appeared the celebrated Laou-tse and Confucius.

Our Saviour told his disciples, "Ye are the light of the world."[1] This has always been true of the Lord's people wherever they have been. Even when in captivity, or scattered by persecutions, the Word of God goes with them and prevails.[2] It was about the time when the Jews were in captivity in Babylon; and when from that place, the capital of the great empire of the world, its kings, constrained by the wonderful works of the God of Jews, were issuing decrees calling upon all nations to acknowledge the true God; it was at that time that all these philosophers first appeared. Each of these great minds, thus partially enlightened, when they returned to their own countries, began to be preachers and teachers. Each of them drew disciples, founded religious sects, and laid the foundations of an influence which has existed to the present day.

Each of the first philosophers of Greece, Persia, and China, thus drawing their knowledge of the truth from nearer the fountain head, necessarily had clearer views than were held by their disciples. We must bear in mind, that these founders of great religious sects were only partially enlightened; and that they still remained heathen. Not fully comprehending the truth, they could not transmit even the little light which they had received to their followers. The successive teachers in those sects, by adding fables, and their own fancies, continued to make the stream more muddy, until, in some cases, the original truth was almost entirely lost.

Without examining in detail all the erroneous speculations of these philosophers, in their endeavors to find, or manufacture truth; let us take a glance at their religious views.

[1] Matt. v. 14. [2] Acts viii. 4.

With all their knowledge, they could not comprehend creation. They considered matter eternal, and confounded the Creator with the thing created. Pythagoras believed that God was the soul of the world, and that the human soul was a portion of God. Socrates believed that the mind of man was part of the Great Mind. Plato held that the eternal God made the world, and that the world, proceeding eternally from him, was God. Strange to say, these same doctrines are openly taught at the present day by some learned heathen in Christian lands.

The ideas of the true God thus obtained and held by the first philosophers of Greece, though very limited, were too pure for the people to bear. On his return to Greece, Pythagoras was afraid to proclaim his whole system; and Socrates, though he complied with the religion of the Greeks, was condemned to death for rejecting the traditions giving such scandalous accounts of the gods.

We have nothing of *Pythagoras* now extant: nor is it certain that he ever wrote any philosophical composition. It is supposed that his knowledge was contained in a select number of sentences, which he explained to his disciples. There are some Pythagorean fragments, which have come to us through his followers, corrupted by their speculations and additions. His doctrine was divided into two parts; public and private: being afraid, as we have noticed, to proclaim his whole system. He was noted for loving to see and hear, rather than to talk. This, together with the want of authentic writings, involves every thing pertaining to Pythagoras in mystery. While he believed in one uncreated, supreme, universal God, whom he called Zeus, or Jupiter, he also believed in many inferior deities, such as, the sun, moon, stars, heroes, and demons. He was also the great advocate of the wide-spread doctrine of the transmigration of souls; declaring that he himself had passed through many such changes. He said that he had received the same instructions from the Druids of Gaul, the Magi of Persia, the Brahmins of India, and the priests of Egypt: showing that the religious views held in these different countries were all derived from one source. Pythagoras died B. C. 496, having outlived Thales fifty years. On account of his talents and influence he was held by the ancient Greeks and Romans in almost superstitious reverence.

Next appeared the wise and good *Socrates*, who sought to allure men from vain speculations about the universe and the gods to morals and practical religion. The morals of the Grecians, like those of the gods they worshipped, were very corrupt. His great disciple, Plato, said, "That God alone could save the young men of his day from ruin." One might suppose that he was speaking of the young men of the present time. Socrates, therefore, rejected the gods of the poets, or denied that they were guilty of the actions imputed to them. He believed in one God, supreme above all others, the Maker of the world, seeing and knowing all things. In his "Memorabilia," he says, "As the soul is known by its operations, so God is known by his works." He believed, however, also in many inferior gods; and spoke of sacrificing a cock to Esculapius, just before his death. Being accused of contempt for the household gods, and of corrupting the youth by his doctrine, he was condemned to death, and drank hemlock. How sad was that death! how dark! notwithstanding all his wisdom and goodness. How different it was from that of the true Christian! to whom "to die is gain;" and "to depart is to be with Christ."[1] Instead of saying with Paul, "I have kept the faith; henceforth there is laid up for me a crown of righteousness;"[2] hear Socrates, when dying, declaring to his mourning friends, that he was going he knew not whither; and whether it would be better, or worse with him, the gods only could tell.

Plato was born B. C. 428. His doctrines, though some-

[1] Phil. i. 21, 23.   [2] 2 Tim. iv. 7.

what corrupted, have been better preserved than most others, from having been committed to writing. He, also, had some doctrines which he did not make public or commit to writing; warned, perhaps, by the fate of Socrates. By traveling he added to the information which he had gained from Socrates. His views were so pure and lofty, that he was called the "divine Plato." With apparently clear ideas of God, as the Creator, and of His providence, he, at the same time, unites with Him, in the government of the world, a throng of gods and demons; the inferior deities being deputies of the Supreme, the "God over all," "who always was, and never was made;" "who made man and all things." He said, "The supreme God was hard to be found; and when found, not easy and safe to be declared." Plato wrote very forcibly on the immortality of the soul. Socrates, who before him had defended that doctrine, had said, that the knowledge of there being no punishments hereafter would be "good news to the wicked."

Aristotle, another of the celebrated philosophers of Greece, was born B. C. 384. He was a pupil of Plato for twenty years. Plato called him "The mind of the school." Aristotle was the tutor of Alexander the Great; chosen by his father Philip. He formed a new sect in opposition to the Academy—the school of Socrates and Plato, and taught in a grove near Athens, walking about while teaching. Like his teacher, he also believed in one God; "the first immovable Mover," as he called him: "the Mind that willed all things, and disposed them in the wisest and best manner." He acknowledged lesser gods whom he called "the divinity," and he divided the heavens into forty-seven spheres, over which the gods presided. He says, "It has been delivered to us from ancient times that the stars also were deities." He refers also to an ancient writer who considered "Love" to be the first cause. All other things, he said, "were fabulous; and used to satisfy the multitude, and for the utility of life, and to teach men obedience to civil laws." Aristotle was the greatest logician of his age; and his works on this subject are still held in high esteem.

About the same time that Greece was being benefited by the instructions of her first philosophers, *Zoroaster* was reforming the religion of the Medes and Persians. The religion of the ancient Persians (Parsees) was the worship of fire, symbolical of the Deity, to which we have already alluded. At a later time the ancient worship was changed into the worship of the stars (Sabeism), especially of the sun and of the morning star. The priests were called Magi. This religion yet survives in India among the Parsees, who profess to be still in possession of the sacred books of Zoroaster. They assert that they do not worship fire or the sun, but only use them as symbols of the Fountain of eternal light and purity. Zoroaster asserted the existence of a supreme Being, all powerful and eternal; from whom eternally proceeded, by his creative Word—*Honovu*, two principles; *Oromasdes*, the Creator of good, and *Aramanes*, the principle of darkness. Zoroaster speaks of the conflict of these powers, of the triumph of the good; of a resurrection, and of the restoration of all things. He speaks of five successive periods of creation, and of man's being formed on the sixth; of man's innocence, and happiness, until tempted by Ahriman, the liar, to eat fruit which he brought; and that man thus became subject to misery and death. In compiling the Zendavesta, the sacred book of the ancient Persians, Zoroaster, who flourished about the time of the captivity in Babylon, evidently obtained his ideas of creation and of the Fall of man from the Jews.

A recent writer, speaking of the Chinese philosopher, *Laou-tse*, says; Le-eurl, or Laou-tse, " old master," was the founder of the Taouists in China. He lived in the sixth century before the Christian era, and was cotemporary with, though older than Confucius, who once visited him seeking instruction, and who always spoke of him with respect. Laou-tse is said to have traveled west of China in search of knowledge, and thus is supposed to have come in contact with some of the captive Israelites in the Babylonian empire. Appearing at the same time with the first great philosophers of Greece and Persia, with them he caught glimpses of divine truth, and, like them, he was misrepresented by his followers, who constantly grew more and more degenerate. Laou-tse bequeathed his doctrines to posterity in " five thousand words" which constitute the *Taou tah king*—" The Rule of Reason and Virtue." The work abounds in acute apothegms, and some of its passages rise to the character of sublimity; but so incoherent are its contents, that it is impossible for any literal interpretation to form them into a system. One of the most remarkable passages to be met with in the pagan literature of any country appears in this work; showing an idea of the true God, referring apparently to his Trinity of persons, and containing an enigmatical expression which appears to veil the name of Jehovah.

> " That which is invisible is called *Ye*,
> That which is inaudible is called *He*,
> That which is impalpable is called *Wei*.
> These three are inscrutable,
> Therefore they are blended in one.
> The first is not the brighter,
> The last is not the darker.
> It is interminable, ineffable,
> And dates from a time when nothing existed.
> It is a shape without shape; a form without form,
> A confounding mystery!" [1]

The three syllables, *Ye*, *He*, and *Wei*, which appear in the first three lines, are arbitrary sounds, having no meaning in the Chinese language; combined they make *Yehewei*; which is as near as possible, in the Chinese language, to the original Hebrew pronunciation of Jehovah.

[1] Taou tah king—14th Sec. W. A. P. M.

About 550 B. C. the celebrated *Kong-fu-tzee* or *Confucius* collected the traditions of Fo and Laou-tse. Before his day the Chinese, while they believed in a Supreme God, worshipped genii and tutelary gods, and offered victims and sacrifices on high places. The Chinese have always been conspicuous for the homage they paid to their ancestors, blended with their religious rites; worshipping their spirits or manes, they made gods of them. Confucius confined himself so entirely to practical things, good laws, and maxims of morality, that not a single doctrine respecting the Deity, and the immortality of the soul, is to be traced in his writings. His style is extremely laconic. His morality is of a higher order than that of any other pagan writer. The doctrine of the forgiveness of injuries is emphatically set forth and enjoined by him. It is strange also to hear such words as these from a pagan: "Worship the Deity as though he were present." "If my mind is not engaged in worship, it is as though I worshipped not." Confucius, however, never refers to a pure and righteous God, whose moral law is broken by sin. The Chinese moralists had very imperfect ideas of a future state. Instead of a future retribution, they endeavored to support virtue by rewards and punishments administered by Divine Providence in this life. After his death, Confucius became one of the chief objects of worship by the Chinese. The whole empire was dotted over with temples to him. Sixty thousand animals were provided by government, besides numerous private ones, to be sacrificed to his manes.

Speaking of the ancient philosophers, the learned Dr. Shuckford, in his " Connection of Sacred and Profane History," says: " If we look over all the philosophers, and consider what the treasures of knowledge were, which they had amongst them, we shall find that there were many beams of true light shining amidst their dark and confused notions; but this light was never derived from any use of their reason, for they never could give any reasonable account of it. The invisible things of God had been some way or other related to them; and as long as they were contented to transmit to posterity what their ancestors had transmitted to them, so long they preserved a considerable number of truths; but whenever they attempted to give reasons for these opinions, then in a little time they bewildered themselves. Under a notion of advancing their science, they ceased to retain the truth in their knowledge, and changed the true principles of things which had been delivered to them into a false, weak, and inconsistent scheme of ill-grounded philosophy."

CHAPTER XLII.

FIRST THEATRES—FIRST ACTORS—FIRST TRAGEDIES.

THEATRICAL representations have been found in some form in almost all lands. By some they have been thought to have originated from a natural tendency to mimicry, almost universal. This is in a great measure true as regards the modern drama. But it will be found that in most countries dramatic representations originally sprang from, and were connected with, their religion; that they grew out of their religious festivals. It was so with the ancient heathen, as far back as their history reaches; it is so with the Indian in his characteristic buffalo and other dances of the present day. In early Greece, at the periodical festivals of their several deities, bands of singers and choristers, accompanied by musical instruments, sang the praises of the god. At some of these festivals, beside the singers, there were performers personating fauns and satyrs; they being, in popular belief, the regular attendants of the god. Thus these festivals became a kind of carnival. From these religious festivities started the splendid drama of the Greeks. The singers and performers at these festivals were first stimulated to rivalry by the gift of a goat as a prize for the best improvisation. Hence the word *Tragedy*, or song of a goat. About the middle of the sixth century, before Christ, *Thespis*, a native of Icaria, introduced a change by coming forward in person, with his features masked, and describing with gestures some mythological story: and then, by some remark, or by asking a question, making, from time to time, the chorus join in. On account of this, he is considered the inventor of the drama.

A second actor, with the introduction of dialogue, scenery, and dresses, was added by *Æschylus*, who was born of noble family about the year 525 before Christ, and is considered the "father of Tragedy," and the "theological poet" of Greece. He and his two celebrated brothers served their country in war, and were highly distinguished for their great bravery in several battles. Æschylus came nigh losing his life once under a charge of profanation, for introducing on the stage something connected with the mysteries. The Athenians stood ready to stone him to death, when his brother Aminias interceded for him, by dropping his robe and showing the stump of his own arm lost at the battle of Salamis. The Athenians could not withstand such an appeal and Æschylus was pardoned. He afterwards left his native city and went to Sicily, and died there in the sixty-ninth year of his age. His death, if the common account is true, was of a singular nature. While sitting motionless in meditation in a field, his head, now bald, was mistaken for a stone by an eagle, which happened to be flying over him with a tortoise in her claws. The bird dropped the tortoise to break the shell, and the poet was killed by the blow. Æschylus was a follower of Pythagoras. In his sacred tragedies, seven of which remain, the great problems which lie at the foundation of faith and practice are discussed. In this respect they find their nearest counterpart in the book of Job. The actors in his plays handle the grand themes of theology very much as they are handled by the good and evil angels in Milton's "Paradise Lost."

Sophocles was born about thirty years after Æschylus. Being of a wealthy family, he was highly educated at an early age. When only sixteen years old he gained prizes for music; and at the age of twenty-five he bore off the prize in the tragic contests from all competitors, among whom was the veteran Æschylus, who had been for thirty years the master of the Athenian stage. Twenty times did Sophocles bear off the first prize. His theology was not so strongly marked in its character, and had not so much of primeval tradition as that of Æschylus: proving what Æschylus had before held, that the more nearly tradition reached the beginning, the more truth is in it. Of the hundred tragedies written by Sophocles, seven only have come down to our day. In his old age Sophocles was appointed a priest to Alon, one of the hero-gods of Greece. He had previously served the state as a general and in other offices of trust. He died at the advanced age of ninety. A statue of him, discovered within the last twenty-five years, and now in the Vatican at Rome, represents him as the perfection of beauty and symmetry.

Part of God's plan of saving men is "by the foolishness of preaching."[1] We have seen that preaching has been in the church since the days of Enoch. In this God meets a want of our nature, not only of the word itself, but in the plan of presenting it. How ready even little children are to listen to a tale well told! This mode of presenting instruction was adopted by the first heathen poets and historians. One of these poets presented his poems with a plot, and in a dialogue form spoken by himself and others, and the theatre appeared.

"The theatre," says an old Roman writer, "was invented for the worship of the gods and the delight of men." It owes its birth and growth to heathen worship: and when introduced it was used to impart instruction in religion. The drama was first exhibited in open air by day, under the pure light of heaven. It was a public institution; and the audience might be counted by tens of thousands, comprising all classes of the people. At times there were thirty thousand spectators in the theatre at Athens. Our word *person* comes from the mask worn by the actors in these plays, who, to make themselves heard in the vast amphitheatres, had the

[1] 1 Cor. i. 21.

mouth of the mask formed trumpet-shaped. Hence they were called *per-sona* from the sound coming through. "Strange as it may sound to modern ears," says Bishop Meade, " the Greek stage came nearer than anything else to the Greek pulpit; the people hung on the lips of the lofty, grave tragedians, for instruction touching the origin, duty, and destiny of immortal beings. It was the express office of the chorus, which held the most prominent place in the ancient drama, to interpret the mysteries of Providence; to justify the ways of God to men, and to plead the cause of truth, virtue, and piety. Hence it was usually composed of aged men, whose wisdom was fitted to instruct in the true and right, or of young women, whose virgin purity would instinctively shrink from falsehood and wrong. Greek tragedy carried men back to the origin of our race, up to the providence of the gods, and on towards the retribution of another world."

In the course of a comparison of the Greek and Roman classics, in referring to the writers of the first plays, Dr. Bethune says: "It remained for one in our own language to combine the supernatural grandeur of Æschylus, the chastened sublimity of Sophocles, and the truthful tenderness of Euripides, with the pungent wit (and, alas! too often the conceits and the grossness) of the licentious friend of the young Alcibiades?"

Speaking of these first plays, Professor Tyler[1] says: "No Calvinist was ever a more strenuous asserter of the doctrine of decrees, than the chorus in these dramas; at the same time no Methodist ever offered up more frequent or more fervent prayers." One of the plays says,

"That which is fated may come to your praying."

The great doctrines of hereditary depravity, retribution, and atonement, also plainly appear in them. Like other pagan

[1] "Theology of Æschylus and Sophocles," by Professor Tyler.

writings, however, they are inconsistent, confused, and contradictory as regards the only true God. Being produced shortly after the first philosophers had begun to enlighten Greece by their purer doctrines, it may have been on account of these comparatively pure teachings, introduced into his plays, that Æschylus came so near being stoned to death.

In the writings of the ancients are found many ideas, which, being revived from time to time in a new form, we are apt to consider new. Thus Cromwell's celebrated saying, "Trust Providence, but keep your powder dry," appears in Æschylus in another form: When Thebes is defended, "The people must pray indeed, but look well to the fortification." The Scripture injunction has always been, "Watch and pray." The reproduction of old ideas caused a French wit to exclaim against the ancients as plagiarists, "Confound the fellows, they stole all our thoughts before we were born."

At an early period the theatre became, in a measure, a political arena: great questions of state were discussed in it by the help of the ancient myths. Afterwards Demosthenes, Pericles, and others, by their oratory in the great assemblies of the people, swayed them at their pleasure. It was to the theatre the Ephesians "rushed with one accord"[1] when the tumult was raised against Paul by the workmen of the shrines of Diana. Like all human inventions, even when intended for good, the theatre, instead of making the people more religious, soon became by its teachings, its surroundings, and its associations, a school of vice and crime. In all ages, and in all countries, its tendency uniformly has been to corrupt the morals of the people. The heathen condemned it; and everywhere it now constantly requires the watchful eye and the strong arm of the law to restrain its evil influence.

[1] Acts xix. 29.

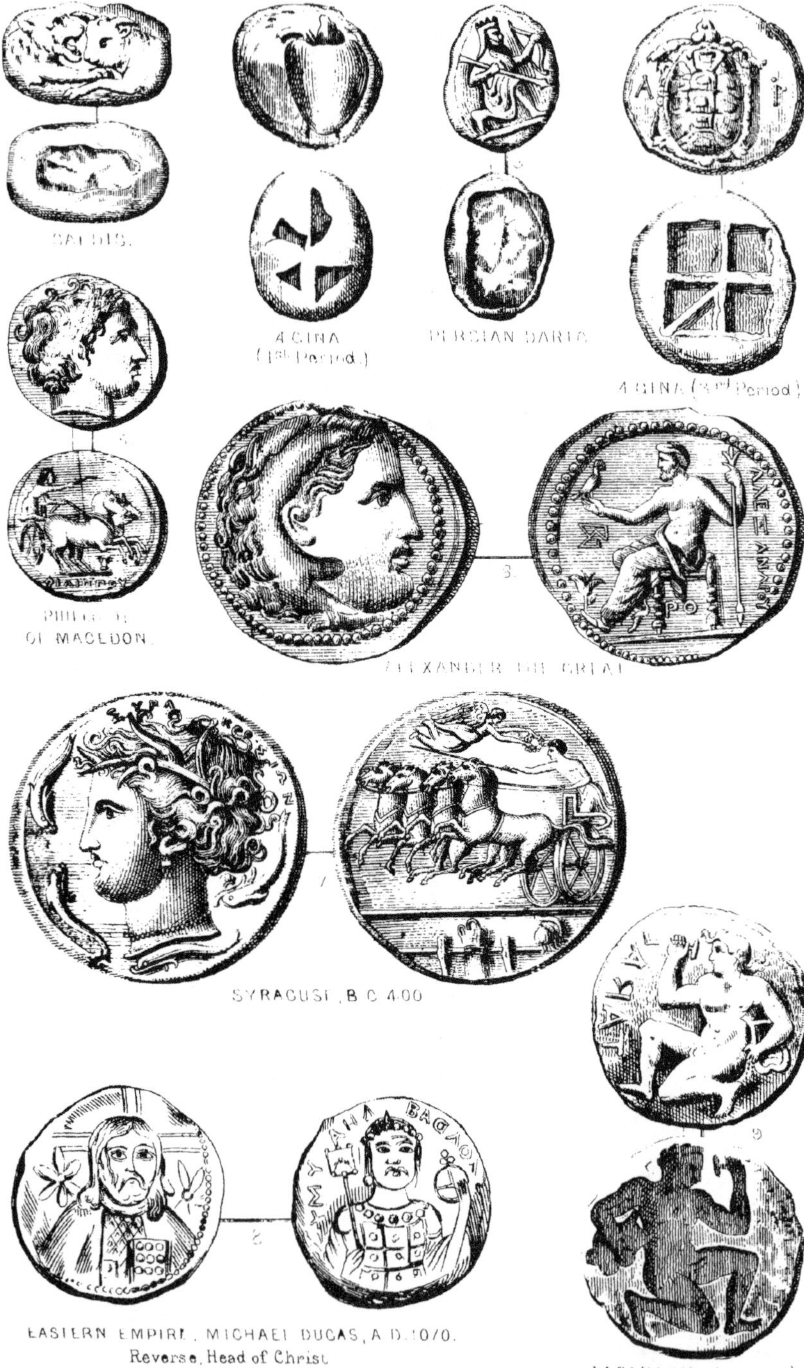

CHAPTER XLIII.

FIRST MONEY—ANCIENT COINS.[1]

THE use of the almost blasphemous expression "the almighty dollar," shows the hold which money has on the hearts of men. The Scriptures tell us "The love of money is the root of all evil."[2] Not money, but the love of it; "covetousness which is idolatry."[3]

It is not surprising, therefore, that money has held an influence in history. How small a sum sufficed to form a link in that chain, which ended in the redemption of the people of God! "What will ye give me, and I will deliver him unto you? And they covenanted with him for thirty pieces of silver. And from that time, Judas sought opportunity to betray Jesus."[4]

Let us take a glance then, at the representative of that power, which exerts such an influence in the world; namely, money; particularly ancient coins, or first money.

The study of coins has an interest much beyond the mere gathering of tokens, or of the cents of the different years, for which some persons have a mania at the present day. Ancient coinage is closely connected with ancient history; verifying it, and shedding light upon it. There is no reason why cents of the dates of 1799 and 1804 should be more valuable than those of 1798 and 1803, excepting, that they

---

[1] Those interested in coins will find "Humphrey's Coin Collector's Manual" a valuable and interesting work on the subject; also, "Ackerman's Introduction to Ancient and Modern Coins."

[2] 1 Tim. vi. 10.   [3] Col. iii. 5.   [4] Matt. xxvi. 15.

are not so plenty. But ancient coins, bringing to our view the great rulers of the earth two thousand years ago; presenting us the likenesses of Alexander the Great and his successors, of the kings of Syria, the Ptolemies of Egypt, and the Cæsars of Rome—coins commemorating the great events of their reigns, showing us the deities they worshipped, etc.—as we handle such coins, the money of their day, and look upon the image and superscription, we are at once carried back to their times. Who can look at some of the coins of Titus, struck when Jerusalem was destroyed, bearing the words JUDÆA CAPTA, and the figure of the mourning captive under a palm tree, without being deeply moved, while touch and sight bring to mind the horrors of that siege, foretold, and so vividly depicted by Moses, sixteen hundred years before;[1] and fix the fact of the destruction of that city, which will be dear in its associations as long as the world shall last.

TITUS.

CONQUEST OF JUDEA.

Coins are among the most certain evidences of history. In the latter part of the Greek series, they illustrate the chronology of the reigns. In the Roman series, they fix the dates and the succession of events. The reigns of some of the Roman Emperors might almost be written from their coins.

Deut. xxviii. 52.

FIRST MONEY—ANCIENT COINS. 213

The first account we have of the use of money was for the purchase of a grave. It is found in the touching story of the buying of a burying-place by Abraham, to bury his dead wife out of his sight.¹ Money appears then to have been in common use. Before this, we read of Abimelech's giving Abraham a thousand pieces of silver.² As cities cannot live without commerce, it is likely gold and silver were used as currency in the city founded by Cain, to whom Josephus attributes the first coining of money.

At the present day among uncivilized nations, and even in many of the thinly settled parts of the United States, trade is carried on by barter; and money, by many, is seldom, if ever, seen. Traveling traders would naturally take that which was of general use and not perishable; also what was most valuable, and, therefore, could be most conveniently carried. Hence the choice of metals; and thus, gold and silver, in the earliest ages, became a medium of exchange, and served as money wherever civilization existed.

In Abraham's time, as it is at the present day in the East, and in the adjusting of exchange between foreign nations, their value, as money, was ascertained by weight. "Abraham weighed the silver, four hundred shekels, current with the merchant."³

In the book of Job, the shekel is called *kesitah* (a lamb), the weight being probably made in that form. We see weights in the form of sheep and other animals, in the Egyptian paintings, and they have been discovered in similar forms among the Assyrian remains recently brought to light. The lamb may have been adopted to signify that that weight of silver represented the value of a lamb; other weights may have represented the value of an ox. The first Roman coinage, which we shall notice further on, appears to confirm this theory; the coins being made bearing the figure of the animal.

[1] Gen. xxiii. 4. [2] Gen. xx. 16. [3] Gen. xxiii. 16

ANCIENT METHOD OF WEIGHING MONEY.—FROM A TOMB IN EGYPT.

The first money of the Egyptians appears to have been in the form of rings. Ring-money was in circulation in the north and west of Europe until after the invasion of Cæsar: and they are frequently found of various sizes in gold, silver, and iron, both in England and Ireland.

For convenience, a standard of purity of metal and of a fixed weight was introduced, and used by independent states and cities, with the emblem of the city stamped upon the piece. These emblems often represented the deities they worshipped. On the early coins, a bunch of grapes stood for Bacchus, an ear of wheat for Ceres, etc.; afterwards, the idealized heads or figures of these deities were stamped upon them. It is not known when these were first introduced. The utility of such pieces of money became universally felt. The great value of the discovery was so evident, that its origin became invested with a mystic character, and instead of giving the honor of it to Him who has made every provision for the wants of man; Saturn,

Mercury, and other heathen divinities, have successively received the credit of this important invention. It is somewhat surprising, that Homer, who wrote more than a thousand years after Abraham's time, makes no mention of coined money; although almost everything else, connected with the affairs of common life in his days, is touched upon in his celebrated writings.

The plentifulness of many coins more than two thousand years old, and the low prices at which they can be purchased, lead many persons to doubt whether they can be genuine. But coins of Alexander the Great, of Constantine, and of many other Roman emperors, are exceedingly common, and can be purchased for a few shillings each, and some, for a few cents.[1] As they were the currency of the whole world in their respective days, vast numbers of them were coined. For safe keeping, particularly in times of war and of invasion, quantities of these coins were buried; the owners were, perhaps, killed or carried away; leaving these deposits to be dug up twenty centuries afterwards. From time to time, large quantities of ancient coins are thus brought to light, in different places where the Greek or Roman empire once extended.

According to Herodotus, the Lydians first coined money

---

[1] The following taken from the priced catalogue of coins of W. S. Lincoln and Son, London, 1861, will give some idea of the value of ancient coins. The prices vary according to the condition and size of the coin, and also, the rarity of the type: some bringing very high prices.

Persian Darics—Silver, five shillings; Gold, £2.2.0.
Greek Regal—Philip II. of Macedon; Gold, £1.15.0 to £3.3.0.
" " Alexander the Great; Gold, £1.10.0 to £2.2.0; Silver, from two shillings and sixpence to £1.1.0; Copper, one shilling and one shilling and sixpence.
Greek Autonomous—Ægina—Silver, two to seven shillings.
" " Athens—Silver, two to twelve shillings.
" " Corinth—Silver, two to five shillings.
" " various cities—Copper, from threepence upward; generally from one to two shillings each.

of gold and silver. The Arundelian marbles tell us, that Phido, the Argive, first struck silver coin in the island of Ægina. How early coins were struck in these places is unknown: the date generally assigned to them is in the eighth century before the Christian era. These coins yet exist in considerable numbers, and are easily procurable. They are stamped with the symbol of the state, and, as were the primitive coins, on one side only. (*Plate*, No. 1, Sardis, Lydia; *Plates*, Nos. 2 and 4, Ægina.)

An Ionian coin of the city of Miletus, now in the British Museum, is considered to exhibit marks of more ancient fabric than any coin hitherto discovered.

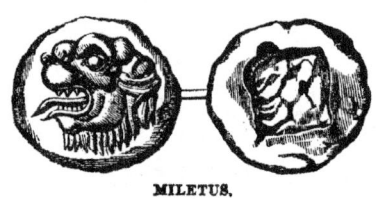

MILETUS.

The Persian Darics, mentioned by Herodotus, are coins of about the same period. They are to be had both in gold and silver. (*Plate*, No. 3.)

Greek Autonomous—50 various—preservation indifferent, one shilling and sixpence the lot.
Egypt—Ptolemy I.—Gold, £1.5.0 to £12.12.0.
" " Silver, £1.0.0; Copper, one shilling and sixpence.
Roman Family Coins, Silver Denarii—two shillings and upwards; generally about three shillings each.
Roman Imperial Coins, various Emperors—Gold, £1.1.0 to £2.2.0.
" " " " " Silver, from one shilling upwards; generally about three shillings each.
Roman Imperial Coins, various Emperors—Brass, from sixpence upwards.
" " " " " 20 various—Brass, two shillings and sixpence the lot.
Roman Imperial Coins—50 various, chiefly very poor—Brass, one shilling and sixpence the lot.
English Coins—William the Conqueror—Silver Pennies, two shillings.
" " Henry II., Edwards I. and II.—Silver Pennies, one shilling and sixpence, etc.

FIRST MONEY—ANCIENT COINS. 217

The rude indentation on the reverse of the early pieces appears to have been succeeded by a hollow square, which in later examples is divided into segments, and these again, afterwards have some object delineated within them; still later, an object appears, occupying the whole area formed by the indented square, and shortly after the full stamp on each side presents us with the finished coin.

At a very early period some of the Greek colonies adopted a mode of coinage known as the *incused*. The punch-mark forming a distinct design, sunk in the coin, corresponding with the design raised by the die. (See *Plate*, No. 9.) The incused mode was soon abandoned in favor of the more usual method.

It is remarkable, that they, who established, more than twenty-five centuries ago, the first coinage as a circulating medium, laid the foundations of the very forms, sizes, and divisions, found at the present day in all the various currencies of Europe; this is strikingly seen in that of Great Britain: the stater, drachma, and obolus, corresponding very nearly with the sovereign, shilling, and penny.

The art of coinage rapidly improved, and coins of surpassing beauty soon appeared in different states: those of Philip II., of Macedonia (*Plate* No. 5), and of his son, Alexander the Great (*Plate* No. 6), in immense quantities. The latter were struck in the various cities of Greece and Asia, the first letter of the name, or the recognized type of the city being put in the field.

The coinage of that period was far finer than it was a thousand years afterwards. The Greek and Roman Churches, holding the truth in unrighteousness, produced the dark ages in the arts, as well as in other things; showing in this also, that a perverted Christianity is more debasing than a refined paganism. (See *Plates*, Nos. 7 and 8.)

No coins are found of the kings of Israel and Judah. The

earliest known coins of the princes of Judea commenced with the shekel of Simeon, B. C. 134–135.

SHEKEL.

It is strange, also, that no coins are found of the Pharaohs, or of the celebrated kings, of ancient Egypt. The coins of the kings of Egypt commence with Ptolemy Soter, B. C. 300–285,

PTOLEMAIC COPPER COIN.

and end with Cleopatra, B. C. 50–30. Cleopatra has more credit for beauty, in history, than her likeness on her coins would warrant.

ANTHONY AND CLEOPATRA.

FIRST MONEY—ANCIENT COINS. 219

The first Roman coins, according to Pliny, were of brass; and called, from the device of domestic animals stamped upon them, Pecunia, from *pecu*, cattle; from which comes our word pecuniary. Some of these pieces stamped with an ox, some with a sow, etc., are yet extant; they are quite rare. One in the Pembroke collection, oblong square shaped like a brick, weighed nearly five pounds avoirdupois. The common piece called the Æs, *brass* or *bronze*, was first made of the weight of twelve ounces. The weight of it was afterwards reduced by the exigency of the State in times of war. The Æs, or pound, was divided into halves, quarters, ounces, etc., called semis, quadrans, uncia, etc. The specimens of the Æs now existing have on one side the two-faced head of Janus, and on the reverse the prow of a galley. This device is referred to by Macrobius, where he speaks of the Roman boys when gambling, tossing up the pieces and crying, Heads or ship.

ÆS.

The Roman mint was in the temple of Juno Moneta, and this occasioned the origin of our word "money."

The series of Roman family or consular coins before the empire, of which there are a great variety, are very interesting; as in them we first find records of historical events, or popular traditions: such as one of the coins of the Tituria family, commemorating the rape of the Sabines, and a coin of the Æmilia family, illustrating a passage in Josephus, who informs us that M. A. Scaurus having invaded Arabia, Aretas, the king of that country, purchased peace of the Romans for the price of five hundred talents.

TITURIA.
Rape of the Sabines.

ÆMILIA.
Purchase of Peace by King Aretas.

The series of Roman imperial coins furnish an unrivaled collection of authentic portraits, extending from Julius Cæsar down to Constantine the Great and his immediate successors. Their reverses are extremely various: a new coin being struck by each emperor to commemorate every conquest, and almost every important event of his reign.

TIBERIUS.

NERO.

The first coins of ancient Gaul or France, and of the ancient Britons, were apparently copied from the silver coins of

FIRST MONEY—ANCIENT COINS. 221

Philip of Macedon, which found their way over Europe. The coinage of these countries became more and more rude as copies were afterwards made from copies.

EARLY GAULISH AND BRITISH.

This fact shows that a rude execution is not always a proof of an early coinage. We have already referred to this in the comparison made between the beautiful coins of four centuries before the Christian era with the rude coinage of ten centuries later.

Some rare ancient coins bring very high prices; but sometimes such coins suddenly become very plenty. In the last century the coins of William the Conqueror of England were extremely scarce, and they continued to bring high prices till in 1833, when an immense number, amounting to about twelve thousand, were discovered in a leaden chest at Beaworth in Hampshire.

It is remarkable that notwithstanding the abundance of gold and silver in Mexico and Peru when they were discovered, the natives did not use them for currency. The circulating medium of the Aztecs was Cocoa seed. The Peruvians used for the same purpose the pod of the *Uchu* or capsicum. In Africa at the present day the common white cowrie shell is their money or representative of value. In the year 1840, nearly four hundred thousand pounds of these shells were imported into Calcutta for the African market. It is said that it takes camels' loads of these shells to purchase an article of value : making it rather inconvenient to carry a purse while shopping. In Nubia, rings of gold and silver are the currency. In Manilla, an iron ring is in common circulation. In Abyssinia, glass beads, white cotton cloth, and blocks of salt, are currency. All showing, as we have already intimated, that ornaments or necessaries brought into a country by traders may be used as money and become currency, till gold and silver, current everywhere, take their place ; and showing also, that many portions of the world are about as civilized now as the section where Homer lived three thousand years ago, where an ox could be bought for a bar of brass three feet long, and a woman who understood several useful arts was considered equal in value to four oxen.

From the earliest times the coinage of money was considere a State or royal prerogative. In all ages to the present, it was therefore considered treason to counterfeit it. The Latin word *nummus*, money, from which comes our word numismatics, relating to coins, was taken from the Greek *nomos*, law—*nomisma*, a piece of money, to express that the weight, purity and value were fixed by law.

The counterfeiting of the public money was probably as early as the first public coinage. Counterfeits of the earliest coins, apparently made in their day, have been found. They are of copper, plated or cased with silver, and some of them are considered by coin collectors, for specimens of art and as curiosities, almost as valuable as the true coins. That there were forgers in early days, we may infer from the laws of Solon, six centuries before the Christian era, by which counterfeiters were to be punished with death. Among the Romans, general pardons did not include the forger. According to the laws of Constantine the Great, counterfeiters were to be burnt alive : and the law of England to a late period was, the counterfeiter, if a man, was to be drawn and hanged ; but if a woman, she was to be burnt.¹

Thanks be to God! that which man needs most can be bought "without money and without price,"² faith, and eternal life, being the gifts of God, through Jesus Christ our Lord.³

¹ Statute 25th, Edward III.   ² Isaiah lv. 1; Rev. xxii. 17.
³ Rom. vi. 23; Eph. ii. 8.

CHAPTER XLIV.

TYPES AND SYMBOLS IN CREATION, HISTORY AND REDEMPTION.

FROM the beginning, the Creator has revealed Himself and His purposes in creation, providence, and revelation. In each of these fields we find a remarkable succession of types. Every step of the progressive work of creation has in it a type of something greater that was to come after it. Every step in the development of the plan of Redemption likewise presents a type showing more clearly Him who was to come. The great Antitype in each is the Creator and Redeemer of the world. The early history of the world is, in a great degree, made up of a succession of types. The mode of worship, which God instituted for the first four thousand years, was almost entirely typical. Through types and shadows, through things seen and temporal, we have been enabled to conceive things unseen and eternal.[1]

In creation the human appears to be the pattern form, or archetype of animal existences. In the structure of all animal forms, from fishes to man, there are striking resemblances designed to assimilate the lower, as near as circumstances would admit, to the higher. Thus, for instance, every segment, and almost every bone, present in the human hand and arm, exist also in the fin of the whale, though they do not seem to be required for the support and movement of that undivided and inflexible paddle : and one can think of no specific reason for such a peculiarity of structure, excepting

---

[1] Those wishing to enter more fully into these subjects are referred to the work on *Typical Forms and Special Ends in Creation*, by Dr. McCosh and Dr. Dickie, and to *The Typology of Scripture*, by Dr. Fairbairn. Much of this chapter has been taken from those works.

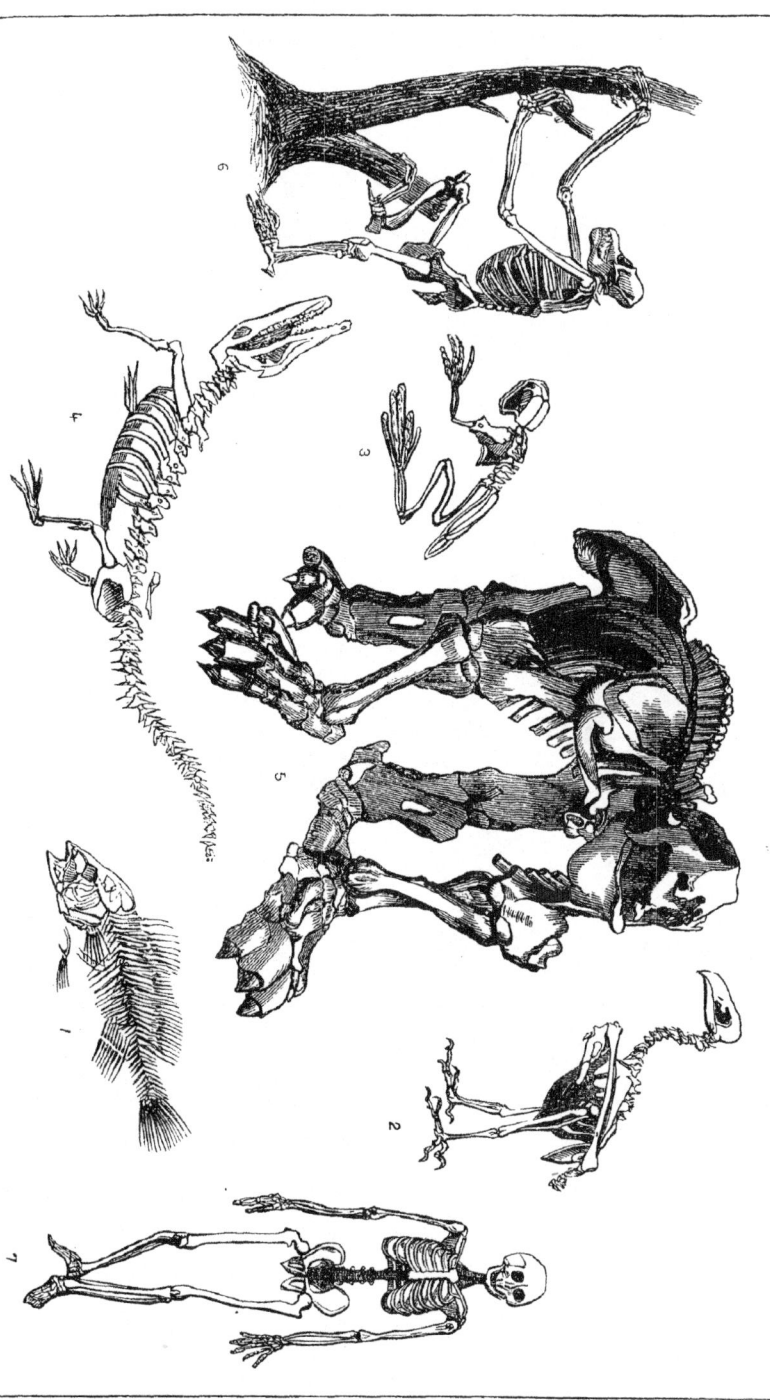

TYPES IN CREATION.

1.—Fish. 2.—Fowl. 3.—Frog. 4.—Crocodile. 5.—Megatherium (extinct animal.) 6.—Chimpanzee. 7.—Man.

the intention of having it brought into the nearest possible conformity to the archetype. Most strikingly does the similarity of the human type, coupled with its relative superiority to the others, appear in regard to the brain, which is the most peculiar and distinguishing part of the animal frame. "Nature," says Hugh Miller, in his *Footprints of the Creator*, "in constructing this curious organ in man, first lays down a grooved cord, as the carpenter lays down the keel of his vessel; and on this narrow base the perfect brain, as month after month passes by, is gradually built up, like the vessel from the keel. First it grows up into a brain closely resembling that of a fish; a few additions more convert it into a brain undistinguishable from that of a reptile; a few additions more impart to it the perfect appearance of the brain of a bird; it then developes into a brain exceedingly like that of a mammiferous quadruped; and finally, expanding atop, and spreading out its deeply corrugated lobes, till they project widely over the base, it assumes its unique character as a human brain. Radically such at the first, it passes through all the inferior forms, from that of the fish upwards, as if each man were in himself a compendium of all animated nature, and of kin to every creature that lives. Hence the remark, that man is the sum total of all animals—'the animal equivalent,' says Oken, 'to the whole animal kingdom.' In the words of Professor Owen, 'all the parts and organs of man had been sketched out in anticipation, so to speak, in the inferior animals; and the recognition of an ideal exemplar in the vertebrated animals proves, that the knowledge of such a being as man must have existed before man appeared.'"

The history of God's operations in nature furnishes a striking analogy to His plan in providence, as brought out in the history of redemption. Here, in like manner, is a grand archetypal idea in the person and kingdom of Christ, towards which, for ages, the Divine plan was continually working. Partial exhibitions of it appear from time to time in certain personages, events, and institutions, that rise prominently into view as the course of providence proceeds, but all marred with obvious faults and imperfections in respect to the great object contemplated; until, at length, the idea is seen embodied in Him to whom all the prophets gave witness—*the God-man, fore-ordained before the foundation of the world.*

Again, to quote the language of Hugh Miller, "The Creator, in the first ages of His workings, appears to have been associated with what He wrought simply as the producer or author of all things. But, even in those ages, as scene after scene, and one dynasty of the inferior animals succeeded another, there were strange typical indications which pre-Adamite students of prophecy among the spiritual existences of the universe might possibly have aspired to read—symbolical indications to the effect that the Creator was in the future to be more intimately connected with His material works than in the past, through a glorious creature made in His own image and likeness. And to this semblance and portraiture of the Deity—the first Adam—all the merely natural symbols seem to refer. But in the eternal decrees it had been forever determined that the union of the Creator with creation was not to be a mere union by proxy or semblance. And no sooner had the first Adam appeared and fallen, than a new school of prophecy began, in which type and symbol were mingled with what had now its first existence on earth—verbal enunciations; and all pointed to the second Adam, 'the Lord from heaven.' In him creation and the Creator meet in reality and not in semblance. On the very apex of the finished pyramid of being sits the adorable Monarch of all:—as the son of Mary—of David—of the first Adam, the created of God; as God and the Son of God, the eternal Creator of the universe. And these—the two Adams—form the main theme of all prophecy, natural and revealed. And that type and symbol should have been employed with reference not only to the second, but—as held by men like Agassiz and Owen—to the first Adam also, exemplifies, we are disposed to think, the unity of the style of Deity, and serves to show that it was He who created the worlds, that dictated the Scriptures."

As creation presents to us a series of types foreshadowing the coming of the Creator, so in history, in revelation, and in the mode of worship which God instituted, we likewise see a succession of types progressively revealing to us, more and more clearly, God the Saviour, the plan of redemption, and the world to come. From the beginning the people of God have been instructed in spiritual things by means of types, as models or exemplars. As " the law was our schoolmaster to bring us unto Christ, that we might be justified by faith,"[1] and will continue to serve as such; so these types, so prominent in history, composing so large a part of the ancient forms of worship, and referred to so frequently in the New Testament, were constructed to express symbolically the great truths of a spiritual religion. They yet serve to enable us the better to understand the things which are spiritual, while some of them "are written for our admonition, upon whom the ends of the world are come."[2] The explanation of the leading types of the old dispensation, showing their fulfillment in Christ, forms the subject matter of the Epistle to the Hebrews. The prophetical import of types and their connection with the antitype show that both were preördained, and that the God of revelation and the God of providence is one.

Not only are the sacrifices, and the tabernacle, with its furniture and services, affirmed to have been of a typical nature, but frequent reference is made in the Scriptures to various persons or characters, and likewise to transactions or events, as being typical. Among these persons are Adam

[1] Gal. iii. 24. [2] 1 Cor. x. 11; ix. 10.

(Rom. v. 11, 12, 19 ; 1 Cor. xv. 22), Melchizedec (Heb. vii.), Sarah and Hagar, Ishmael and Isaac, and, by implication, Abraham (Gal. iv. 22–25), Moses (Gal. iii. 19 ; Acts iii. 22–26), Jonah (Matt. xii. 40), David (Ezek. xxxvii. 24 ; Luke i. 32, etc.), Solomon (2 Sam. vii.), Zerubbabel and Joshua (Zech. iii. iv. ; Hag. ii. 23). Among the events spoken of as typical, are, the preservation of Noah and his family in the ark (1 Pet. iii. 20); the redemption from Egypt, and its passover-memorial (Luke xxii. 15, 16 ; 1 Cor. v. 7); the exodus (Matt. ii. 15) ; the passage through the Red Sea ; the giving of manna ; Moses' veiling of his face while the law was read ; the water flowing from the smitten rock ; the serpent lifted up for healing in the wilderness, and some other things that befell the Israelites there (1 Cor. x. ; John iii. 14 ; vi. 33 ; Rev. ii. 17). We look forward, in accordance with the Revelation, to another Paradise, containing the tree of life and the cherubim. The eternal Sabbath is also yet future.

Sometimes a prediction is connected with the type : as when Zechariah takes occasion from the building of the temple in Jerusalem to foretell the more glorious temple to come : " Behold the man, whose name is the Branch ; and He shall grow up out of His place, and He shall build the temple of the Lord ; even He shall build the temple of the Lord,"[1] etc. The building of the temple was itself typical of the incarnation of God in the person of Christ, and of the raising up in Him of a spiritual house that should be " an habitation of God through the Spirit." (John ii. 19 ; Matt. xvi. 18 ; Eph. ii. 20, 22.)

Speaking of these types, McCosh says, " In the natural kingdom all inferior organisms point onward and upward to man ; in the spiritual kingdom all life points onward and upward to Christ. A typical system runs through the whole Divine economy revealed in the Word. First, Adam is the

[1] Zech. vi. 12, 13.

type of man. He and his posterity are all of the same essential nature, possessing similar powers of intuition and understanding, of will and emotion, of conscience and free agency, and God acts towards them in the dispensations of grace as in the dispensations of nature, as being one. Then, from the time of the Fall, we have two different typical forms, the one after the seed of the serpent, the other after the seed of the woman. Henceforth, there is a contest between the serpent and Him who is to destroy the power of the serpent, between the flesh and the Spirit, between the world and the Church. Two manner of people are now seen struggling in the womb of time—a Cain and an Abel, an Ishmael and an Isaac, an Esau and a Jacob, an Absalom and a Solomon, the elder born after the flesh, and the younger after the Spirit."

In short, there are now, as there have ever been, but two men on our earth typical or representative; the first man, which is Adam, the second, which is Christ. "And so it is written, The first man Adam was made a living soul; the last Adam was made a quickening spirit. Howbeit, that was not first which is spiritual, but that which is natural; and afterward that which is spiritual. The first man is of the earth, earthy; the second man is the Lord from heaven."[1] Each Adam was the federal head of his seed. The seed of the first Adam sinned and died in him: the children of Christ, the second Adam, forever stand in "their head;[2] having in him a perfect righteousness. "As, by the offence of one, judgment came upon all men to condemnation: even so by the righteousness of one the free gift came upon all men unto justification of life. For, as by one man's disobedience many were made sinners, so by the obedience of one shall many be made righteous:"[3] "as in Adam all die, even so in Christ shall all be made alive."[4]

[1] 1 Cor. xv. 45–47.
[2] Col. i. 18.
[3] Rom. v. 19.
[4] 1 Cor. xv. 22.

Again to use the words of McCosh, "It had been determined, in eternity, that ' He whose delights were with the children of men,' should come to our earth in the fullness of time. He is called ' the Lamb slain from the foundation of the world ;' and as soon as man falls, there are symbols of Him. The prefigurations of Christ may be divided into three classes :—typical ordinances, personages, and events. These ordinances all impart substantially the same instruction ; all point to guilt contracted, to God offended, to a propitiation provided, and to acceptance secured through this propitiation ; the four great cardinal truths of revealed religion, as addressed to fallen man. There were sacrifices, in which the offerer, placing his hand on the head of the animal, and devoting it to destruction in his room and stead, expressed symbolically his belief in those great saving truths. There was the tabernacle, with the people worshipping outside, and the Shechinah, which had to be sprinkled with blood, in its innermost recesses, pointing to an offended God, but a God who was to be propitiated through the shedding of blood. There was the ark of the covenant, with the tables of the law inside, and the pot of manna, and the rod that budded, and, over all, the cherubim shadowing the mercy-seat—fit symbol of an arrangement by which the law is fulfilled, and provision made for a revival of life, and a supply of spiritual food by a God ready to meet with, and to commune with us on the mercy-seat. There is the scape-goat, with the sins of the people laid upon it, pointing, as clearly as the Baptist did, to "the Lamb of God, which taketh away the sins of the world." The typical persons shadowed the prophetical, priestly, and kingly offices of Christ. The typical events exhibit the same truths in a still more impressive form : such as the flood, in which many perish, but a few, that is, eight souls, are saved by an ark symbolical of the Saviour. The most instructive of these events is the deliverance from Egypt. The state of the Hebrews as bondsmen, the deliverer prepared for his work by suffering, the method of the deliverance in the midst of contests and judgments, the wonderfully instructive journey through the wilderness, with the provision made for the sustenance of the people, and the statutes delivered, are as certainly anticipations of a higher redemption to follow, as the fish's and reptile's digits are anticipations of the fingers of men. We are trained in this training of the children of Israel; and by means of the discipline through which they were put, our imagining faculty has acquired some of our clearest and liveliest, some of our most profound and comforting representations of the method of redemption."

Every Christian sees in the deliverance of the people of God from Egypt, and in their journey through the wilderness, the type of his own experience. His deliverance from the "powers of darkness" by the Almighty power of God is miraculous. While journeying towards the promised inheritance he finds himself constantly falling into sin, and as constantly delivered by his Saviour. He needs daily to apply to the "Lamb that was slain" for pardon and for righteousness. It is necessary for him daily to gather a supply of heavenly manna, to feed upon Christ the "true bread from heaven."[1] He drinks "the same spiritual drink; for they drank of that spiritual Rock that followed them; and that Rock was Christ."[2] He knows that the great High Priest, Christ Jesus, after "he had by himself purged our sins," "hath entered into the holy place, having obtained eternal redemption for us," "into heaven itself, now to appear in the presence of God for us:"[3] and he has the assurance, that when he reaches Jordan, he will find there Jesus, the High Priest; for He has passed before him with the ark of the covenant, and will be with him in the midst of the river, holding back the waters of death, until he has passed triumphantly into the heavenly Canaan.

John vi. 32, 48.   1 Cor. x. 4.   [3] Heb. i. 3; .ix. 12. 24.

God has likewise always used *symbols* to impart a knowledge of Himself and to instruct us in spiritual things. These symbols should be studied, for the noblest study of mankind is not man, but God. Paul, who was very highly educated, said, "I count all other things but loss for the excellency of the knowledge of Christ Jesus my Lord."[1] He might well say so: for the knowledge of Him is the foundation of all knowledge; it "is life eternal."[2] The burning Bush, the cloud over the Tabernacle and the mercy seat, and the Dove, were symbols in which God manifested himself. He reveals himself to our comprehension in a most lovely and loving aspect in the symbolical names which He has assumed; such, as our Father, Husband, Elder Brother, Redeemer, Comforter, Shepherd, Shield, Refuge, Dwelling-place, etc., etc. Most of the public teachings of our Saviour were by the use of symbolical allegories, or parables. God has also ordained certain symbols to be used until the end of the world as seals of covenant blessings. The great Sacraments of the Church have always been symbolical. Circumcision, and the Passover, in the old dispensation, and Baptism, and the Lord's Supper, in the new, are *symbols* of deep import; designed to instruct, and to seal covenant blessings to the people of God.

We still live under a dispensation of types and symbols. The great spiritual temple, of which "Christ is the corner stone,"[3] is still in progress of erection. As in nature each leaf bears in it the image of the entire tree, so each living stone in this temple is carved after the similitude of the whole temple. Christ is the "head of the body, the Church."[4] Every member of that body, created anew in the likeness of God, "is predestinated to be conformed to His image."[5] Here we bear his image; in heaven, "we shall be like Him, for we shall see Him, as he is."[6]

[1] Phil. iii. 8.
[2] John xvii. 3.
[3] Eph. ii. 20–22.
[4] Col. i. 18.
[5] Rom. viii. 29.
[6] 1 John iii. 2.

CHAPTER XLV.

ANALOGIES IN CREATION AND THE COURSE OF NATURE TO REVEALED RELIGION.

IN creation, and in what we call the laws of nature, there are many striking analogies to the great revelations contained in the word of God concerning *His moral government, man's responsibility, a future life, and a future eternal state of rewards and punishments.*[1]

As the manifold appearances of design in creation prove it to be the work of an intelligent mind, so particular causes of pleasure and pain distributed amongst His creatures prove that they are under His government, as subjects under a moral ruler, or as children under a parent. The immediate effects of virtue and vice show that we are under such a Ruler. The natural attendants of innocence and virtue are a sense of inward security and peace, a mind open to the gratifications of life, complacency, and joy; while vice is naturally attended with uneasiness and apprehension. The moral nature given to us also proves that we are under a moral Governor. All good men approve virtuous actions, and sometimes public honors are accorded to them, while vicious actions are punished as mischievous to society. In the domestic circle children are rewarded or punished according to their deeds. All these declarations of the Author of Nature, being so clearly for virtue and against vice in the

---

[1] The leading thoughts of this chapter are taken from the celebrated work entitled "The Analogy of Religion Natural and Revealed to the Constitution and Course of Nature," by Joseph Butler, late Lord Bishop of Durham, to which the reader is referred as the most complete work on that subject.

natural government of the world, are grounds to hope and to fear that they will be rewarded and punished in accordance with His word in higher degrees hereafter.

The general doctrine of Religion is that our present life is a state of preparation for a future one: a state implying trial, difficulties, and dangers. In the natural government of God we find ourselves in such a state of trial. He has annexed pleasure to some actions and pain to others which are in our power to do or forbear, and has given us a notice of such results beforehand. People often blame others, and even themselves, for their misconduct in their temporal concerns. Many miss that happiness which they might have attained in the present life, and many run themselves into extreme distress and misery, not through incapacity of knowing, or of doing better, but through their own fault. Every one knows the hazards which young people run upon their setting out in the world. Thus, in our natural or temporal capacity, we are in a state of difficulty and danger, analogous or like to our moral and religious trial upon which our final happiness or misery depends.

Many things in nature, besides the changes which we have already undergone and which we know that we may undergo without being destroyed, suggest to us that we shall survive death and exist in a future state. We have abundant evidence that the same creatures may exist in different degrees of life and with different capacities of action, of enjoyment, and suffering. Our changes since infancy, the change of the caterpillar to a chrysalis, and then to a butterfly, and the vast enlargement of their locomotive powers by such change, are instances of this general law of nature. The matter composing our bodies is constantly changing, and every few years is entirely different from what it was, yet we do not lose our existence or identity. We know that our living powers exist, even when through sleep or a swoon we are unable sensibly to exercise them. We see that men may lose their limbs, their organs of sense, and even the greatest part of their bodies, and yet remain the same living agents: so that we may infer, that they might lose the whole body and still exist the same.

The same may be inferred, if we consider our body as constituted of organs and instruments of perception and motion. Optical experiments show that we see with our eyes in the same sense as we see with glasses; both being instrumental in preparing objects for, and conveying them to the perceiving power. In dreams, we find we possess a latent power of perceiving sensible objects, in as strong and lively a manner, without our external organs of sense, as with them. So in regard to our power of moving or directing motion by will and choice; upon our losing a limb this active power remains unlessened: it can walk with an artificial leg. A man determines that he will look at such an object with a microscope, or if lame that he will walk to such a place with a staff a week hence. His eyes and his feet no more determine in these cases than the microscope and the staff. Thus our organs of sense and our limbs are certain instruments which the living persons ourselves make use of, and there is no probability that the alienation or dissolution of these instruments is the destruction of the perceiving and moving agent.

Our powers and capacities of reason, memory, and affection, are independent of the body; so that we have no ground to think that the dissolution of the body will be the destruction of those powers. In some diseases, persons the moment before death appear to be in the highest vigor of life. They discover apprehension, memory, reason, all entire; with the utmost force of affection; sense of a character of shame and honor; and of the highest mental enjoyments and sufferings, even to the last gasp.

Our capacity of happiness and misery makes the question of a future life of great importance, and the thought that our happiness or misery depend upon our actions here adds to its importance. We see in the present state a system of rewards and punishments. Pleasure and pain are the consequences of our actions : and we are endowed by the Author of our nature with capacities of foreseeing these consequences. All we enjoy and a great part of what we suffer *is put in our own power.* We are to provide ourselves with and make use of that sustenance which He has appointed to preserve our lives, if we do not, they are not preserved. Some by the use of certain means have ease and quiet, while others will follow those ways the fruit of which they know beforehand by instruction, example, and experience, will be disgrace and poverty, and sickness and untimely death. The pain which we feel upon doing what tends to the destruction of our bodies, say, by wounding ourselves or by too near approaches to fire, are associated by the Author of Nature to prevent our doing what thus tends to our destruction ; and show as plainly as by a voice from heaven, that, if we acted so, such pain should be inflicted upon us. Thus the whole analogy of nature agrees with the general doctrine of religion that God will reward and punish men for their actions.

Let us now examine the circumstances in the natural course of punishments at present, which are analogous to what religion teaches concerning a future and an eternal state of punishment. Punishments now often follow, or are inflicted in consequence of actions which procure present advantage, and are accompanied with much pleasure : for instance, sickness and untimely death are the consequence of intemperance, though accompanied with the highest mirth and jollity ; and these punishments are often much greater than the advantages or pleasures obtained by the actions. These punishments or miseries are often delayed a great while ; sometimes till long after the actions occasioning them are forgotten ; and after such delay, they often come suddenly, with violence and at once. The excuse of

ANALOGIES IN NATURE TO REVELATION. 237

the natural thoughtlessness of youth does not prevent the consequences of early rashness and folly; the success, happiness, or misery of the whole future life depend in a great degree upon the manner in which they pass their youth. We have seasons and opportunities for procuring advantages at certain times, which, if neglected, can never be recalled. If the husbandman lets his seed-time pass without sowing, the whole year is lost to him beyond recovery. Though men may sometimes retrieve their affairs, and recover health and character, there is a *certain degree* which, if exceeded, no reformation is of any avail; repentance is too late to relieve; poverty and sickness, remorse and anguish, infamy and death, the effects of their own doings, overwhelm them beyond possibility of remedy or escape.

These things are not accidental; but proceed from the general laws by which God governs the world in the natural course of His providence: and they are so analogous to what His word teaches us concerning the future punishment of the wicked, that both would naturally be expressed in the same words; "Because I have called, and ye refused; I have stretched out my hand, and no man regarded; but ye have set at naught all my counsel, and would none of my reproof: I also will laugh at your calamity; I will mock when your fear cometh; when your fear cometh as desolation, and your destruction cometh as a whirlwind; when distress and anguish cometh upon you. Then shall they call upon me, but I will not answer; they shall seek me early, but they shall not find me."[1]

There are many analogies in history to the teachings in the Word of God connecting the salvation of the righteous with the perdition of the wicked. The signal preservation of the Lord's people has generally been connected with the destruction of His enemies. It was thus when Noah and his household were saved, and the rest of the world were

[1] Prov. i. 24–31.

destroyed; when Lot and his family were saved, and Sodom and Gomorrah were burnt; when the Israelites were delivered and the Egyptians were drowned; when Mordecai and the Jews were preserved, while Haman and his followers were slain, etc. We are told that it will be so at the end of the world, when the saints shall be delivered and the nations gathered against them shall be destroyed by fire from heaven.[1] It will be so at the last day, when the great final separation shall take place, when the wicked "shall go away into everlasting punishment; but the righteous into life eternal."[2]

Our Saviour often made use of the analogies of nature in his parables, especially in those describing the kingdom of heaven and the great harvest at the end of the world. The parable of the man who sowed good seed in his field, into which his enemy came and sowed tares, and the explanation of it, are full of instruction: "He that soweth the good seed is the Son of man; the field is the world; the good seed are the children of the kingdom; but the tares are the children of the wicked one; the enemy that sowed them is the devil; the harvest is the end of the world; and the reapers are the angels. As, therefore, the tares are gathered and burned in the fire; so shall it be in the end of the world."[3] Paul, likewise, in his description of the resurrection, refers to an analogy in nature. He uses a short method with the skeptical inquirer who asks, "How are the dead raised up? and with what body do they come? Thou fool, that which thou sowest is not quickened except it die."[4]

---

[1] Rev. xx. 8, 9.
[2] Matt. xxv. 46.
[3] Matt. xiii. 24–30, 36–43.
[4] 1 Cor. xv. 35.

CHAPTER XLVI.

NEW MANIFESTATION OF GOD—THE GREATEST EVENT IN HISTORY—THE MOST WONDERFUL BEING—THE LORD JESUS CHRIST, THE SON OF GOD AND THE SON OF MAN—FOUNDATION OF A NEW UNIVERSAL KINGDOM.

THE most wonderful, and by far the most important event in all history, was the coming of the "Creator of all things,"[1] the eternal Son of God, into the world: his taking a human nature;[2] joining it with his divine, and then, as the Messiah or Christ, suffering and dying to redeem and save a chosen people.[3] It is the great fact of history: the key which opens history and enables us to understand it. Through it alone we learn the purposes and workings of Him who makes history: the past is explained, and the future is revealed to us. Take the life, sufferings, and death of the "Lamb of God," and their results, out of history, and it becomes to us a sealed book: as it is described by John in Revelation, "no man in heaven, nor in earth, neither under the earth, was able to open the book, neither to look thereon:" until He who is "in the midst of the throne, a Lamb as it had been slain," omnipotent and omniscient, prevailed to open the book and to loose the seals thereof.[4] In history, as well as in the way of salvation, the Lord Jesus Christ is the "Light of the world."[5]

Let us take a glance at the previous revelations of himself made by the Creator, and at the effects they had produced. During the four thousand years then past, God had been

---
[1] John i. 3, 10; Col. i. 16, 17; Heb. i. 2, 10. [2] John i. 14; Phil. ii. 6, 7.
[3] John x. 15; Titus ii. 14; Rev. v. 9. [4] Rev. v. 3, 5, 6. [5] John viii. 12.

maturing and developing the work of redemption. While doing this, He had been revealing himself in divers ways, each more and more distinct, to the children of men: and they, with each clearer manifestation of God, had shown more evidently their hatred of Him. *In creation*, " the invisible things of Him are clearly seen by the things that are made, even his eternal power and Godhead ;" but " they glorified him not as God, but changed the glory of the incorruptible God into an image made like to corruptible man, and birds, and four-footed beasts, and creeping things."[1] In His *providence*, He had made the sun to rise and had sent rain and fruitful seasons on the just and on the unjust ; but everywhere men were discontented, neither were they thankful. He made a clearer revelation of himself, showing that " God is love,"[2] when He proclaimed his *law* and his *commandments*, the whole of which are contained in the precepts, " Thou shalt love God with all your heart and your neighbor as yourself :"[3] but men universally rejected his law : no man ever kept it.[4] He at last revealed himself visibly and fully : " *God was manifest in the flesh*,"[5] in the person of the Lord Jesus Christ : and although He came expressly to save sinners, and was continually engaged in going about doing good, the cry of the whole multitude was, " Away with him, crucify him." Such is the treatment God has always received from fallen man : and such is the treatment he now receives from all men ; till they are born again of the Holy Ghost.

Although during the four thousand years which had passed since the creation, God had kept a visible church in the world ; had been continually sending in His name teachers and prophets ; had given by inspiration a written word containing the evidences of its divine origin by its wonderful revelations and by the purity of its teachings ; and had been confirming that word by miracles and by signs following,

---

[1] Rom. i. 20, 21. [2] 1 John iv. 16. [3] Mark xii. 29 ; Rom. xiii. 10.
[4] Rom. iii. 10, 20, 23. [5] 1 Tim. iii. 16.

and by prophecies foretelling events, many of which had afterwards been fulfilled; still, with the exception of Judea, the whole world had sunk into the darkness of heathenism, when Jesus Christ appeared. And even Judea itself, the then visible church of God, held the truth in such unrighteousness that when He who was "the Truth" appeared, Judea was the first to raise the cry, "Crucify him."

In accordance with the prophecies long before proclaimed in the word of God, the Assyrian, Chaldean, Median and Persian, and Grecian empires, had successively passed away, and Nineveh, that great city, had disappeared. The last of the great empires spoken of by Daniel was then controlling the world; and the time which he had foretold had come, when "the God of heaven was to set up a kingdom, which shall never be destroyed."[1] The seventy prophetical weeks (the four hundred and forty-nine days or years) of which he spoke, were accomplished, "when the Messiah the Prince was to come and be cut off but not for himself."[2] The world was prepared for the advent of Christ. There was universal peace: the Scriptures had been translated two centuries before into the leading vulgar tongue, and were read in the Jewish synagogues then scattered in the various countries: many of the promises contained in the word of God of the coming of a great Deliverer had found their way among the nations. Men were expecting a great Restorer of the race and the Jews were looking for the promised Messiah. It was at this time that the most important event in its bearings on the destinies of all mankind occurred. God fulfilled the wonderful word spoken by Isaiah: "Unto us a child is born, unto us a son is given: and the government shall be upon his shoulder: and his name shall be called Wonderful, Counsellor, the Mighty God, the Everlasting Father, the Prince of Peace. Of the increase of his government and peace there shall be no end, upon the throne of David, and

[1] Dan. ii. 44.   [2] Dan. ix. 25.

upon his kingdom, to order it and to establish it for ever."[1] The promised Seed of the woman, who was to crush the serpent's head;[2] he "in whom all the nations of the earth were to be blessed,"[3] appeared.

The Messiah was appropriately named "*Wonderful.*" He frequently spake of himself as "the Son of Man." He was a man: and what a man! the most wonderful that ever existed. When he appeared nearly all men were idolaters: and the most awful corruption of morals everywhere prevailed; even in Judea itself. Nazareth, where Jesus lived from early childhood till he was thirty years old, was so notorious for its degradation, that it had become a proverb: "Can there any good thing come out of Nazareth?"[4] There he lived until he entered upon his short ministry of three years, in a polluted atmosphere, a working carpenter: poor, unknown, untaught, inexperienced, and unbefriended. What could be expected from such a man surrounded by such influences?

Behold the man! See him come forth even from Nazareth, so pure, so holy, that he can challenge his enemies, "Which of you convinceth me of sin?"[5] And while all the rest of the best men that have ever lived have constantly felt that they were sinners, and abhorred themselves as such, this man is so pure as to be unconscious of guilt or sin: and can say, "I do always those things that please the Father:"[6] "the prince of this world cometh, and hath nothing in me."[7]

See this man! without learning, having "never learned letters."[8] Hear him uttering far sublimer truths, proclaiming more expanded ideas of the human soul and of eternity, teaching a far higher standard of morals, introducing a purer worship of God, and giving much clearer views of God himself, infinitely above all that can be gathered from

---

[1] Isaiah ix. 6, 7. [3] Gen. xii. 3; Acts iii. 25, 26. [5] John viii. 46.
[2] Gen. iii. 15. [4] John i. 46. [6] John viii. 29.
[7] John xiv. 30. [8] John vii. 15.

the teachings of the wisest and most learned men who had ever lived before him. And while they who are called the philosophers and the wise men of the world, after years of study and of travel in pursuit of knowledge, doubtingly put forth only a few confused, contradictory, uncertain, and unsatisfactory teachings, with which they confess that they themselves are not satisfied; hear this young man, uttering great truths as one having authority to command obedience to his words, saying: "Ye have heard this, and that: but I say unto you, Thus, and So."[1] Well might the officers sent to apprehend Jesus exclaim, "Never man spake like this man."[2]

See this man! a carpenter's son coming from despised Nazareth; not having where to lay his head;[3] himself required to pay tribute, and so poor that he had not the small coin required of him:[4] hear him say to Pilate, "I am a king."[5] The Jews were then restless under the Roman yoke; they were looking for the promised Messiah; their idea was, that he would occupy the throne of David as the greatest monarch on earth, and make their kingdom surpass in grandeur all the kingdoms of the world. When they had seen the miracles this man performed, they thought God must be with him, and that he was the prophet that was to come; and they were about to take him by force and make him a king.[6] See him escaping from them, turning away from earthly power and glory, and choosing poverty and the cross instead.

See this man! without education or friends: starting a novel kingdom, hitherto unheard of in the world. A universal spiritual kingdom in the hearts and consciences of men. Commencing it by proclaiming, "If any man will come after me, let him deny himself, and take up his cross,

---

[1] Matt. v. 22, 28, 34, 39, 44.
[2] John. vii. 46.
[3] Matt. viii. 20.
[4] Matt. xvii. 27.
[5] John xviii. 37; Luke xxiii. 3.
[6] John vi. 15.

and follow me."[1] A kingdom entirely contrary to the prejudices, superstitions and hopes of his own countrymen; in every way different from the religious views and the manner of life hitherto received and cherished by the whole world: entirely in opposition to the natural heart; and intended to crush Satan, who controls the natural heart of all men. No wonder that all classes of men at once demanded that Jesus should die. No wonder that, to procure his death, Satan himself entered into Judas.[2]

See this man! founding the greatest kingdom the world has ever seen; having only a few followers, from the lower walks of life, ready to forsake him and flee at the approach of danger; and beginning his kingdom by telling them, "Ye shall be hated of all men for my sake."[3] See him calmly enduring frowns, reproaches, and curses; never doubting, never hesitating, never disappointed; steadily pursuing his way, knowing and foretelling that that way led to sufferings and a cruel death. He collected no armies, no resources of power or war; invaded no territory; assumed no state; expressly said his kingdom was not of this world, therefore, his servants did not fight;[4] affected no singularity; his dress, his speech, and his mode of living continuing to the last the same as those of the common people. He went about doing good; uttered a few truths to any sort of persons, anywhere, at any time, in the simplest words; left not a line or a word of writing; and died an ignominious death. Hear him in his agony in the garden: "O my Father, if this cup may not pass away from me, except I drink it, thy will be done."[5] Hear him in his agony on the cross, praying for his murderers: "Father, forgive them; for they know not what they do."[6] Was there ever a kingdom thus started? What a king! What a man![7]

---

[1] Matt. xvi. 24.   [2] Luke xxii. 3.   [3] Matt. x. 22.
[4] John xviii. 36.   [5] Matt. xxvi. 42.   [6] Luke xxiii. 34.
[7] "The Christ of History: an argument grounded in the facts of his life

THE MOST WONDERFUL BEING IN HISTORY. 245

But, still more wonderful! this son of man was, also, the "Son of God;" *Jehovah*, the LORD. Joining the two natures, God and man, he became the Messiah, or Christ.[1] To the world, and to each one of us, this is the most interesting fact in all history. *Our eternal happiness, or our everlasting misery, depends upon our faith in this fact.* "Whosoever believeth that Jesus is the Christ is born of God,"[2] and "hath eternal life;"[3] and "he that believeth not the Son, is condemned already; shall not see life: but the wrath of God abideth on him."[4]

To this wonderful being, the Lord Jesus Christ, are ascribed the names;[5] the works;[6] and the attributes, of God.[7] He is the Creator of all worlds;[8] of all things, visible and invisible;[9] and by him all things consist.[10] Angels and men are directed to worship him;[11] and to honor him as equal with God.[12] He is omnipotent;[13] having "all power in heaven and in earth;"[14] "angels, and authorities and powers being made subject unto him."[15] He is omniscient;[16] he is omnipresent.[17] Well might he, who was "God manifest in the flesh,"[18] say to the leper: "*I will; be thou clean;*"[19] and to

---

on earth," by John Young, a very able and interesting work; proving the divinity of Jesus from some of the historical facts, which present his *manhood;* has furnished many thoughts for this chapter.

[1] Matt. xvi. 15, 16.
[2] 1 John v. 1; Matt. xvi. 17.
[3] John iii. 16, 36.
[4] John iii. 18, 36.
[5] Isaiah ix. 6; John i. 1; xx. 28; Rom. ix. 5; Acts vii. 59, 60; Heb. i. 8; 1 John v. 20.
[6] John v. 21; i. 3; Col. i. 16.
[7] Col. ii. 3, 9; Heb. xiii. 8; John viii. 58.
[8] John i. 10; Heb. i. 2.
[9] Col. i. 16.
[10] Heb. i. 3; Col. i. 17.
[11] Heb. i. 6; Luke xxiv. 52; 1 Cor. i. 2; Phil. ii. 10; Rev. v. 8, 13; vii. 9. 10.
[12] Phil. ii. 6; John v. 23; x. 30.
[13] John xiv. 14; Rev. i. 8.
[14] Matt. xxviii. 18; Heb. i. 8.
[15] 1 Pet. iii. 22; Eph. i. 21.
[16] Matt. ix. 4; John ii. 24, 25; Acts i. 24; John xvi. 30; xxi. 17; Rev. ii. 23.
[17] Matt. xviii. 20; xxviii. 20; John iii. 13; xiv. 18, 23; Acts xviii. 9; Eph. i. 23; 2 Tim. iv. 22.
[18] 1 Tim. iii. 16.
[19] Matt viii. 3.

the winds and waves; "*Peace, be still;*"[1] and to the dead: "*I say unto thee, arise;*"[2] and to the sinner: "*Thy sins be forgiven thee.*"[3]

The Lord Jesus Christ is well called the "Word;"[4] for in and through him alone we know all that we know of God and of the way of salvation: he is the only "way" to God. All the types; all the sacrifices; all the promises, in the Word of God, centre in him. Well might the heavenly host, at his advent, praise God; saying, "Glory to God in the highest, and on earth peace, good will toward men."[5] Well might the angel say, "Behold, I bring you good tidings of great joy, which shall be to all people! For unto you is born this day in the city of David a Saviour, which is Christ the Lord."[6] Well might the disciples be glad, when they saw their crucified Lord risen from the dead![7] Well might they worship him with great joy, after he was carried up into heaven while in the act of blessing them![8] Well may we rejoice! The loving Jesus has entered into heaven with his human body; has there all power; is head over all things to his Church: is "the same yesterday, and to-day, and forever;"[9] with all his human sympathies;[10] with the same loving heart, that responded to every cry of distress that was made to him; that wept with Mary and Martha at their brother's grave; and that raised the widow's son. He is as willing now, as when on earth, to receive the most degraded; and to forgive even the chief of sinners; and is "able to save to the uttermost all that come unto God by him."[11] Well may the sheep of the King of kings "rejoice always!"[12] for "He gives them eternal life; they shall never perish, neither shall any pluck them out of his hand."[13]

---

[1] Mark iv. 39.
[2] Luke vii. 14.
[3] Matt. ix. 2.
[4] John i. 1.
[5] Luke ii. 14.
[6] Luke ii. 10.
[7] John xx. 20.
[8] Luke xxiv. 51, 52.
[9] Heb. xiii. 8.
[10] Heb. iv. 15; v. 2.
[11] Heb. vii. 25.
[12] Phil. iv. 4.
[13] John x. 28.

CHAPTER XLVII.

THE NEW KINGDOM—ITS WONDERFUL PROGRESS.

THE resurrection of the Lord Jesus Christ from the dead; his repeated appearances to his disciples; "his opening their understandings that they might understand the Scriptures, how it was written in Moses, and the prophets, and the Psalms, that it behooved Christ thus to suffer, and to rise from the dead on the third day;"[1] and his ascension before their eyes into heaven; gave renewed confidence to his terror-stricken followers, who had been so sorely disappointed at his ignominious death, although he had repeatedly foretold to them that death, with all its attending circumstances. The scattered few began the assembling of themselves together in his name, in a retired room, with closed doors, for fear of the Jews. Thus did the kingdom, which was to overthrow all opposing kingdoms, commence its course.

The new kingdom thus strangely founded, was as wonderfully to make its way in the world. Opposed to the natural desires and inclinations of all men; and intended to destroy the power of Satan, the god of this world; it is not surprising, that, wherever it appeared, rulers and people at once rose up to prevent its progress. In Jerusalem persecutions immediately arose; and the humble followers of the meek and lowly One were pursued even to strange cities, and taken to prison and to death. The new kingdom, however, strange to say, was extended by persecutions; and kept extending the more, as the world rose against it. Soon the

[1] Luke xxiv. 44-46.

whole power of the Roman empire, which then controlled the world, was repeatedly put forth to blot out all traces of it from the face of the earth. But, in three short centuries, we see this kingdom, its subjects gathered chiefly from the poor of this world, its adherents everywhere persecuted, yet making no resistance; we see it obtain control of the great Roman empire, and counting even the emperor himself among its professed subjects. And since then it has been extending, until it has become acknowledged by the whole civilized world.

To the eye of sense, no task could have been more hopeless, than that undertaken by the first followers of Jesus. A few "unlearned and ignorant men,"[1] are sent forth with the command: "Go teach (or disciple) all nations."[2] They were directed to commence a crusade against "the lust of the flesh, the lust of the eye and the pride of life" common to all men, and cherished by all; a crusade to overturn the religions of the world; they were to proclaim salvation by faith alone, in One, just put to death as a malefactor. They were to call men, everywhere, to forsake the faith of their fathers, to deny themselves, and to take up a cross; to give up friends and all their worldly prospects; to meet persecutions, and most probably to suffer a cruel death. They were sent forth, warned that they would meet all this themselves. What a mission for a few friendless, uneducated men to undertake! But they had the eye of faith. They knew whom they believed. They had his promise: "Lo, I am with you alway, even to the end of the world."[3] And they at once, fearless of all danger, and certain of success, went forth to conquer the world.

The extension of this kingdom in the world has been a continual extraordinary manifestation of the presence and power of God: and its progress brings more clearly to view that Great Being, the glorious Third Person of the God-

---

[1] Acts iv. 13.   [2] Matt. xxviii. 19.   [3] Matt. xxviii. 20.

head, the Holy Ghost; who is now, though everywhere present, manifesting himself particularly on earth; personally gathering in the subjects of Christ's kingdom; and, while extending that kingdom over the whole earth, is shaping the history of individuals, of nations, and of the world.

CHAPTER XLVIII.

THE HOLY GHOST—THE UNPARDONABLE SIN.

IT is not surprising that the world, ignorant of God, should be ignorant of the Holy Ghost; but it is a sad fact, that there is a deplorable ignorance in the Church, in regard to His person, and to His work. We are too apt to think of the Spirit as a mere influence. Till we realize *the personality* of the Holy Ghost, our ideas regarding Him must be confused and unsatisfactory. May He enlighten us, as we now turn our thoughts more especially to Him.

We have already noticed the coöperation of the Holy Spirit, as one of the Godhead, in the work of creation. Before the advent of Christ, it was He who imparted instruction to the Church of God; for we are told, "all scripture is given by inspiration of God;"[1] and, "holy men of God spake as they were moved by the Holy Ghost."[2] The human body of Jesus, born of the virgin Mary, was "conceived in her by the Holy Ghost."[3] He afterwards descended upon Jesus "in a bodily shape like a dove,"[4] after his baptism. The Lord Jesus, when he was about to finish his work on earth, before leaving his disciples assured them that the "Father would send the Holy Ghost, the Comforter, to abide with them; to teach them all things; and to guide them into all truth."[5] He also directed them to baptize in the name of the Holy Ghost, as one of the glorious Trinity in Unity, in whose name the Church was to be gathered.

If the Holy Ghost had not come down personally among

---

[1] 2 Tim. iii. 16.　　[3] Matt. i. 18, 20.　　[5] John xiv. 16, 26; xv. 26;
[2] 2 Pet. i. 21.　　　[4] Luke iii. 22.　　　　　xvi. 7, 13.

men, the kingdom of Christ would have disappeared from the earth when he and his immediate followers left it; those sent forth to disciple all nations would never have made a single convert; and we, never would have heard even the echoes of the "glad tidings of great joy." There has not been a true subject brought into that kingdom since the ascension of Christ, but by the direct agency and power of the Holy Ghost.[1] John expressly declares this when he says, that they "who believe that Jesus is the Christ are born of God;"[2] "are the sons of God;"[3] and "are born not of blood (that is, not by being born of members of the Church, though of Abraham himself[4]), nor of the will of the flesh (that is, not because they have so willed it), nor of the will of man (that is, not by the power or acts of others), but of God."[5] "Verily, verily," said Jesus, "I say unto thee, except a man be born of water (that is, enter the visible Church by baptism), and of the *Spirit*, he cannot enter into the kingdom of God. Ye must be born again."[6] The subjects of this kingdom, thus begotten, not of themselves, but of the Holy Ghost, are spoken of, as having been raised from a state of previous *death* to life;[7] as having had *faith given* to them;[8] and as being *created* anew.[9] This new birth of the soul is spoken of, as the putting forth by God Almighty of "the *exceeding greatness of his power*, according to the working of his mighty power, which he wrought in Christ, when he raised him from the dead."[10]

The apostles were directed to wait in Jerusalem, until they received power, after that the Holy Ghost came upon them:[11] then, they were to be witnesses for Christ unto the uttermost parts of the earth. At the day of Pentecost, the Holy Ghost descended with "a sound from heaven as of a

---

[1] 1 Cor. xii. 3.
[2] 1 John v. 1.
[3] 1 John iii. 1.
[4] Rom. ix. 7; Luke iii. 8.
[5] John i. 12; vi. 65.
[6] John iii. 5, 6, 7.
[7] Eph. ii. 1, 5.
[8] Eph. ii. 8.
[9] Eph. ii. 10; Gal. vi. 15.
[10] Eph. i. 19.
[11] Luke xxiv. 49; Acts i. 8.

rushing mighty wind, and it filled all the house where the waiting disciples were assembled. And there appeared cloven tongues as of fire, and it set upon each of them. And they were all filled with the Holy Ghost, and began to speak with other tongues, as the Spirit gave them utterance."[1] Thus filled with the Holy Ghost, the apostles began their mission to bring the world back to God, by preaching "Jesus Christ and him crucified." No wonder, now, that the new kingdom began to spread, in spite of all opposition, throughout the earth. The same day, in Jerusalem, the very place where, a few days previously, Jesus had been crucified, under Peter's first sermon, "there were added unto them about three thousand souls."[2] And afterwards, "the Lord added to the Church daily such as should be saved:"[3] so that, in a few days, "the number of the men that believed was about five thousand."[4]

It is of great importance, that we should acknowledge the direct agency of the Holy Ghost in everything done in building up the spiritual Church of Christ. Not only is each member of that Church born of the Holy Ghost, but "the Spirit dwells in each,"[5] making the body of every believer "the temple of the Holy Ghost."[6] The Holy Ghost calls whom He will, and sends the Gospel to particular individuals: "The Spirit said unto Philip, Go near and join thyself to the chariot;" in which the Ethiopian eunuch was reading the prophecy of Isaiah; and then, after the conversion of the eunuch, "the Spirit caught away Philip, that the eunuch saw him no more."[7] Cornelius, although he was devout, prayerful and charitable, yet could not be saved excepting through faith in Christ. His prayers and his alms came up as a memorial before God; and the *Spirit* sent Peter to teach him the way to be saved. The Spirit said

---

[1] Acts ii. 1.   [2] Acts ii. 41.   [3] Acts ii. 47.
[4] Acts iv. 4.   [5] 1 Cor. iii. 16; Rom. viii. 11; 2 Cor. vi. 16.
[6] 1 Cor. vi. 19.   [7] Acts viii. 29, 39.

to Peter, "Behold three men seek thee, go with them, for I have sent them."[1] It was on account of the personal presence of the Holy Ghost, that Peter told Ananias that Satan had filled his heart to lie to the *Holy Ghost*.[2] When the apostles and elders met in convention, the Holy Ghost directed them as to the decision which they made.[3] The elders of the different churches were made overseers or bishops of the flock committed to them, by the *Holy Ghost*.[4] In extending Christ's kingdom, the Holy Ghost selects missionaries to do particular work, and sends them to such places as are fixed upon by himself. "The *Holy Ghost* said, Separate me Barnabas and Saul for the work whereunto I have called them." "So they, being sent forth by the *Holy Ghost*, departed unto Seleucia."[5] Afterwards they were "forbidden of the *Holy Ghost* to preach the word in Asia," and "they essayed to go in Bithynia: but the *Spirit* suffered them not."[6] And in addition to all this, the life and the spiritual growth of each member of the Church are through Him alone; all the wisdom, knowledge, gifts, and graces, given to the individual members of the Church, "all these worketh that one and the self-same *Spirit*, dividing to every man severally as he will."[7] Truly, the personal presence of the HOLY GHOST, and his continued wonderful working, personally gathering the children of God, and personally building up Christ's kingdom, is neither realized, nor acknowledged, as it should be.

There is also a lamentable ignorance, even in the church, of one of the principal characteristics of the Holy Ghost; and that is *love*. Being made known to us as the *Holy Spirit*, we are too apt to fix our thoughts almost exclusively on His holiness: and to overlook His infinite condescension, and His wonderful love. We speak of the love of the Father,

---

[1] Acts x. 19, 20, 43, 44.   [2] Acts v. 3.   [3] Acts xv. 4, 28.
[4] Acts xx. 28.   [5] Acts xiii. 2, 4.
[6] Acts xvi. 6, 7.   [7] 1 Cor. xii. 8, 11; Gal. v. 22.

and of the love of the Son; but how little we realize the love of the Holy Ghost! God is love. God the Holy Ghost is love. His names, "the Comforter,"[1] "the Spirit of Grace,"[2] "the Helper of our Infirmities,"[3] "the Spirit of Adoption,"[4] are names of love. The Scriptures, written by the inspiration of the Holy Ghost, show His love: every call, every promise, every word of consolation and comfort, is from the Spirit's love: overflowing love, to the lost, the guilty, the wanderer, the backslider, the rebel: love without measure and without change. See this Holy Being coming down and dwelling with fallen man. See Him with infinite love striving against coldness, contempt, and hatred. Though year after year He is resisted, grieved, vexed, quenched, He does not forsake us, nor cease his efforts. He goes to the sinner, follows him, grieving in His holiness while witnessing his sins; speaks to him, strives with him, draws him, awakens him, quickens him, opens his eyes and leads him to the blood of Jesus. Well may we exclaim: "Herein is love, not that we loved Him but that He loved us."[5] Then see this loving Holy Spirit after He has won the soul to Christ: see Him condescending to take up His abode in it: see Him encountering resistance, coldness, doubts, and unbelief; and overcoming all with love unchangeable and unquenchable. Think then what the Holy Ghost does in each one whom by faith He has made a child of God. He leads him into all truth;[6] He reveals the things of Christ;[7] He sheds the love of God abroad in his heart;[8] He mortifies corruption in him;[9] He enables him to persevere, and keeps him in the faith;[10] He helps him in his prayers, the Spirit joining with him in the prayer and making intercession for him;[11] He is in him, the

[1] John xiv. 16.
[2] Heb. x. 29.
[3] Rom. viii. 26.
[4] Rom. viii. 15; Gal. iv. 6.
[5] 1 John iv. 10.
[6] John xvi. 13.
[7] John xvi. 14.
[8] Rom. v. 5.
[9] Rom. viii. 13.
[10] 2 Tim. i. 14; 1 Pet. i. 5.
[11] Rom. viii. 26.

Spirit of adoption, to address God, Abba, Father;[1] and He fills him with joy.[2] What amazing love![*]

At the gatherings of the subjects of the kingdom, the ministers of Christ are directed to bless the people in His name.[3] A part of that great benediction, and not the least important part of it, is, "The communion of the Holy Ghost be with you all."[4] Who can estimate the blessings flowing from that communion? Children of that kingdom, part of which is "joy in the Holy Ghost;"[5] hold constant communion with the loving Spirit who dwells in you: and "grieve not the Holy Spirit of God, whereby ye are sealed unto the day of redemption."[6]

And ye who have not yet acknowledged the Lord Jesus Christ the King of kings, as your king and your Saviour, how long will ye "resist the Holy Ghost?"[7] How long will ye continue "to tread under foot the Son of God, and count the blood of the covenant an unholy thing and do despite unto the Spirit of Grace?"[8] How long will ye run the risk of being for eternity outcasts from the kingdom of God? There is *one sin which is spoken of as unpardonable.* God hath said, "My Spirit shall not always strive with man."[9] Beware of blaspheming against the Holy Ghost; of treating Him as an unclean Spirit: for so long as you speak against Him, you will never be forgiven, neither in this world, neither in the world to come.[10] Does He still work in your conscience and in your heart, urging you to believe in the Lord Jesus Christ? there is, then, yet hope: seek His guidance; and at once join that great kingdom which is overspreading the earth and filling Heaven.

[1] Rom. viii. 15. [4] 2 Cor. xiii. 14. [7] Acts vii. 51.
[2] 1 Thess. i. 6. [5] Rom. xiv. 17.   [8] Heb. x. 29.
[3] Deut. x. 8.   [6] Eph. iv. 30.   [9] Gen. vi. 3.
[10] Mark iii. 29; Matt. xii. 32; Luke xii. 10.

[*] Tract of the Kelso Series, entitled, "The Love of the Spirit."

CHAPTER XLIX.

FIRST THINGS IN THE VISIBLE CHURCH UNDER THE NEW DIS-
PENSATION—INTRODUCTION OF MEMBERS—CHILDREN AND
HOUSEHOLDS, MEMBERS—THE LORD'S SUPPER—MODE OF
BAPTISM—NEW SABBATH—FIRST FOREIGN MISSIONS—NEW
WAY TO GOD—NEW PRIESTS—CHURCHES—FIRST SAVED—
FIRST ENTRANCE INTO HEAVEN—CONCLUSION.

"GOD created all things by Jesus Christ, to the intent that now unto the principalities and powers in heavenly places might be known by the church the manifold (or greatly diversified) wisdom of God."[1] The true church of Christ being spiritual, is invisible: and the real members of that church are only those who are born again of the Holy Ghost. The church of Christ has, however, always had a visible organization on the earth. This was requisite for its preservation and edification. In it the line of the Messiah was to be preserved according to prophecy, till he came. The church was also to be in all ages "the pillar and ground of the truth."[2] Apostles, prophets, evangelists, pastors, and teachers, were given to it for the perfecting of the saints, for the work of the ministry, for the edifying of the body of Christ."[3] It required elders, who, as rulers and bishops, should keep its members pure in morals, and from being led astray by false teachers.[4] The visible church differs from the invisible in that it has always had members

---

[1] Eph. iii. 10, 21; 1 Peter i. 12.   [2] 1 Tim. iii. 15.
[3] Eph. iv. 11, 12; 1 Cor. xii. 28.
[4] 1 Cor. v. 7, 11, 13; Acts xx. 28, 30; Titus i. 5.

THE NEW DISPENSATION. 257

who were only such outwardly : "for they are not all Israel which are of Israel."[1]

We have already noticed that all the forms of worship in the visible church have, from the beginning, been ordained by the Head of the church ; every other worship being in vain.[2] The types used in the ancient forms of worship having been consummated by the death of Christ,[3] the Lord Jesus, under the gospel dispensation, introduced new forms of admission, and terms of membership into his church. These, however, correspond with the old. Under the ancient covenant, those desiring to become members of the church were to be circumcised,[4] and to take the passover :[5] and then, if they did not continue to take the passover, they were to be cut off from the church.[6] Both of these forms were done away with at the death of Christ : " Christ our passover being then sacrificed for us ;"[7] baptism[8] and the Lord's Supper,[9] were substituted by him in their place, and they are now the public forms of admission and of continued membership in the visible kingdom of Christ; therefore, only those who are baptized, and who continue to take the Lord's Supper are members of the visible church.

The most significant feature in the mode of worship in the ancient church, and the most important, was the sacrifices ; all pointing to the atonement to be made by the Lord Jesus Christ. These were all done away with when " Christ was once offered to bear the sins of many :"[10] " for by one offering he hath perfected forever them that are sanctified."[11] Just before he was offered he joined in the last passover-feast, and told his disciples that it was about to be " fulfilled in the kingdom of God."[12] He then instituted the Lord's

[1] Rom. ix. 6, 7 ; Rev. ii. 9.
[2] Mark vii. 7; Deut. xii. 32.
[3] Heb. ix. 11 ; x. 1.
[4] Gen. xvii. 10 ; Acts vii. 8.
[5] Exod. xii. 43–48.
[6] Exod. xii. 19; Numb. ix. 13.
[7] 1 Cor. v. 7.
[8] Matt. xxviii. 19; Mark xvi. 16.
[9] Luke xxii. 19; 1 Cor. xi. 23.
[10] Heb. ix. 28.
[11] Heb. x. 14.
[12] Luke xxii. 16.

Supper: the eating of the broken bread and the drinking of poured out wine, both to be partaken of by all believers, as memorials of his body broken for them, and of his blood shed for them.[1] Since his death this has been the great feast of the Christian church, and it will be continued to the end of the world, showing forth "the Lord's death till he come."[2]

From creation, the children of God's people have always been included in the covenants which God made with their parents. It was thus with the covenants made with Adam, with Noah, Abraham, Jacob, the children of Israel, David, etc.[3] In all ages, whoever joined the visible church and thus entered into an open covenant with God and his people, brought his whole household into the church with him. Under the ancient testament or covenant, his children and his slaves were to be circumcised; and then they might partake of the passover:[4] the whole household thus at once became members of the visible church; entitled to its privileges, to its care and its discipline. Under the new covenant, likewise, the believer brought his household with himself into the visible church. Thus we see Lydia was baptized and *her household;*"[5] the jailor " was baptized, he and *all his*, straightway;"[6] and also "*the household* of Stephanas."[7] The children of believers are spoken of as "holy;[8] that is, sanctified by covenant to the Lord: they are therefore to be trained "*in* the nurture and admonition of the Lord,"[9] as already in him. Children are also expressly addressed as members of the church, and special instructions are given to them as being in covenant with God.[10] The Christian parent, therefore, who does not thus

---

[1] Matt. xxvi. 27; 1 Cor. xi. 23, 25; Luke xxii. 19.
[2] 1 Cor. xi. 26.
[3] Gen. ii. 17; ix. 1; xvii. 7; 1 Chron. xvii. 13, 23, etc.
[4] Gen. xvii. 12; Exod. xii. 44, 48.
[5] Acts xvi. 15.
[6] Acts xvi. 33.
[7] 1 Cor. i. 16.
[8] 1 Cor. vii. 14.
[9] Eph. vi. 4.
[10] Eph. i. 1; vi. 1–4; Col. i. 2; iii. 20; Gen. xvii. 7, 14; Acts ii. 38, 39.

consecrate his child and his household to God by baptism, not only breaks the covenant God has made with him; but he also robs his child and his household of the benefits of the covenant, and of their privilege of church membership.

The mode of baptism by which subjects are publicly admitted into the visible kingdom of Christ on earth, is worthy of consideration. How this is to be performed is not specifically mentioned. Some persons, thinking that John the Baptist baptized by immersion, and also that the Ethiopian eunuch was baptized the same way, which may or may not be the fact, make that mode of baptism a test of church-membership: and thus not only separate themselves from the mass of the body of Christ, but also cut off their own children from the benefit of that covenant, which, as we have before noticed, God has made, from the beginning, with believers and their children. Whatever way John baptized, one thing is certain, his baptism was not Christian baptism. His was expressly a "baptism of repentance:"[1] and it was necessary that they who were baptized by him, when they became Christians, should be baptized again.[2] The thousands converted and baptized in Jerusalem immediately after the crucifixion, could not have been immersed, even had there been sufficient water; the authorities would not have allowed it. In baptism the person is not applied to the water, but the water to the person.[3] The common mode of applying water in baptism in all ages of the Christian church, has been by sprinkling. Thanks be to God! the new kingdom, which is to extend over the whole earth, does not shut out them who dwell in the polar regions, or in deserts, or where water cannot be obtained to immerse them: it does not shut out the dying, or those too sick to be immersed; and above all, it still includes the children of His people. Under the old dispensation, the blood of the sacrifice was

[1] Acts xix. 4; Matt. iii. 11.   [2] Acts xix. 3, 5.   [3] Acts x. 47.

applied by sprinkling :[1] it is the same under the new ; Peter addresses Christians as, "Elect unto obedience and sprinkling of the blood of Christ."[2] The baptism with the Holy Ghost is frequently spoken of.[3] The mode of that baptism is very clearly and expressly stated : the Holy Ghost is poured out upon them ;[4] the Holy Ghost falls upon them.[5]

The Sabbath being made for man,[6] the day was changed to accord with the new dispensation. The first Sabbath succeeded the finished work of creation ; the new Sabbath, or Lord's day, the finished work of redemption. The first Sabbath was the first day of Adam's life after his creation ; the new Sabbath was the first day of the Church's life ; she having risen in Christ, her head. On the first day of the week the disciples assembled themselves together to commemorate the Lord's Supper and to hear preaching ;[7] and on that day, again and again, Jesus met with them.[8] John "was in the Spirit on the Lord's day."[9] And the subjects of the great King are directed, "every one of them," as a part of their religious worship, on the first day of the week, to consecrate a portion of their property, according as the Lord has prospered them.[10]

Another new thing in the Church was the work of Foreign Missions. The sending forth of ambassadors for Christ "to go into all the world and preach the Gospel to every creature,"[11] and "beseech men to be reconciled to God."[12] Before this the knowledge of the way of salvation was confined to the land of Israel alone.

One of the most remarkable events of this period was the opening of all parts of the world to the special manifestations of the presence of God. Previously, He had, although

[1] Heb. ix. 21 ; Ex. xxix. 20 ; Lev. xvi. 14, 19.
[2] 1 Pet. i. 2 ; Heb. xii. 24.
[3] Acts i. 5 ; Mark i. 8.
[4] Acts ii. 3, 18 ; x. 45.
[5] Acts xi. 15, 16 ; xix. 6.
[6] Mark ii. 27.
[7] Acts xx. 7.
[8] John xx. 19, 26.
[9] Rev. i. 10.
[10] 1 Cor. xvi. 2.
[11] Mark xvi. 15.
[12] 2 Cor v. 2.0.

everywhere present, chosen one particular spot where He revealed himself, and where only He was to be approached. God came down visibly on Mount Sinai; and went into the Tabernacle; and dwelt in it during all the journeys of the children of Israel in the wilderness: He then took up his abode with the ark of the covenant within the most holy place in the Temple at Jerusalem. There only could he be approached; and there only could offerings be made to Him. According to His law, "three times in the year all the males in Israel were required to go to that place and to present themselves before the Lord God, the God of Israel."[1] Even there, the sinner could only approach God through an atoning sacrifice, the blood of which was to be presented to God by the High Priest. A new way to God was opened to all the world by the Lord Jesus Christ, at once the victim and the priest; the magnificent temple with all its gorgeous service, the sacrifice of atonement, and the high priest, which were types of Christ, were done away with:[2] and thenceforth men could have free access to God through the Lord Jesus Christ in any part of the world: having the special promises of the Lord Jesus, "where two or three are gathered together in my name, there am I in the midst of them;"[3] and, "if ye shall ask anything in my name, I will do it."[4]

The Lord Jesus having entered into heaven not only as king, but as the High Priest of his church;[5] the special order of Priests was abolished: and now every Christian is a priest.[6]

The Church, or visible kingdom of Christ, continued to assemble in all places where disciples could be gathered to hold public worship; meetings for prayer and singing, in

---

[1] Exod. xxiii. 17; xxxiv. 23, 24.
[2] Heb. vii. 11; viii. 1, 5; ix. 8, 9, 14, 23, 24; x. 19, 22.
[3] Matt. xviii. 20.   [4] John xiv. 14.   [5] Heb. ix. 24; vii. 25.
[6] 1 Peter ii. 9; Isaiah lxi. 6; Rev. i. 6; Rom. xii. 1; Rev. xx. 6.

which all Christians joined, to edify one another and to receive instruction out of the word of God.¹ These services corresponded with that of the Synagogue under the old dispensation:² and like the synagogue, each church was governed by a number of elders, who were the overseers or bishops:³ and had deacons also, whose special office was to have the charge of the poor of Christ's flock.⁴

The term "*church*," for some centuries after the Christian era, was not applied to the buildings where Christians met; but to the elect of God, or to particular congregations of believers wherever they met, even if in a private house.⁵

The mode of worship of the early Christians was exceedingly simple: but it had the characteristic of being "in Spirit and in truth." As the kingdom of Christ made progress, Christianity became fashionable: the world joined the church; cathedral service and gorgeous ceremonial forms took the place of worship and of the meeting for prayer and mutual edification; preachers preached anything but " Christ and him crucified;" and the awful crime, now so common in many churches, was introduced, of hiring opera singers, or of allowing persons not Christians to mock God with pretended worship, to lie unto the Holy Ghost, and to sing what on their part is blasphemy.

The circumstances connected with the conversion of the first one converted and saved after the crucifixion, are worthy of consideration. They show, that however important the sacraments of Baptism and the Lord's Supper are to the perpetuity and edification of the Church, believers may be saved without them. We see a vile criminal who, according to his own confession deserved death, while suffering the penalty due to his crimes and just before his death, suddenly

---

[1] Matt. xxvi. 30; Col. iii. 16; Eph. v. 19; 1 Cor. xiv. 26.
[2] Acts xiii. 15; Luke iv. 16.
[3] Titus i. 5, 7; Acts xiv. 23; xv. 4; xx. 17, 28.   [4] Acts vi. 3.
[5] Rom. xvi. 5; 1 Cor. xiv. 23; xvi. 19.

FIRST ENTRANCE INTO HEAVEN. 263

ceasing his blasphemies, acknowledging the Lord Jesus Christ and praying to Him. We also see him at once accepted, and immediately taken to heaven.[1] He was not only saved, but he was at once assured of his salvation; without going through a long previous conflict of agonizing doubts and fears before coming to Christ and receiving Him and his salvation—without being baptized—or confirmed—or taking the communion—without subsequent misgivings—and without doing any good works. He was saved simply, and instantaneously, by faith in the Lord Jesus Christ. It is also worthy of notice that while he was saved by grace, his dying companion, having the Saviour just as near, and having apparently equal advantages, was lost.

The Lord's answer to the dying thief, "Verily I say unto thee, this day shalt thou be with me in paradise,"[2] shows that believers at death go immediately to heaven. He had previously told Nicodemus that He was in heaven, even while on earth.[3] The Saviour ascended afterwards bodily into heaven.[4] Stephen while dying saw the heavens opened: and seeing Jesus there he commended his spirit into his hands.[5] Paul tells us "to be absent from the body is to be present with the Lord;"[6] and he said "he had a desire to depart and to be with Christ."[7] He also tells us that, "Them who sleep in Jesus will God bring with him" at the last great day.[8] Till that day part of the one great family of Christ are on earth, and part are in heaven.[9]

The time foretold in prophecy appears to be at hand, when we shall hear the great proclamation, "The kingdoms of this world have become the kingdoms of the Lord and of his Christ."[10] We see a shaking among the nations. The day of the Millennium, when Satan is to be bound a thousand

---

[1] Mark xv. 32; Luke xxiii. 41, 43.
[2] Luke xxiii. 43.
[3] John iii. 13.
[4] Acts i. 11.
[5] Acts. vii. 56.
[6] 2 Cor. v. 8.
[7] Phil. i. 23.
[8] 1 Thess. iv. 14.
[9] Eph. iii. 15.
[10] Rev. xi. 15.

years, is dawning. When that is ended, "the day of the Lord will come as a thief in the night; in the which the heavens shall pass away with a great noise, and the elements shall melt with fervent heat, the earth also and the works that are therein shall be burned up."

Connecting thus the end of history with its beginning, let us acknowledge Him who is directing and shaping that history in accordance with His word: we will then with joyful hope be "looking for and hasting unto the coming of the day of God;"[1] and join the people of God in saying, "Even so come quickly Lord Jesus."[2]

[1] 2 Peter iii. 10, 12. [2] Rev. xxii. 20.

Printed in Dunstable, United Kingdom